W9-BNE-296

Country *Christmas* Crochet

Edited by Laura Scott

HOUSE of
WHITE
BIRCHES
PUBLISHERS
SINCE 1947

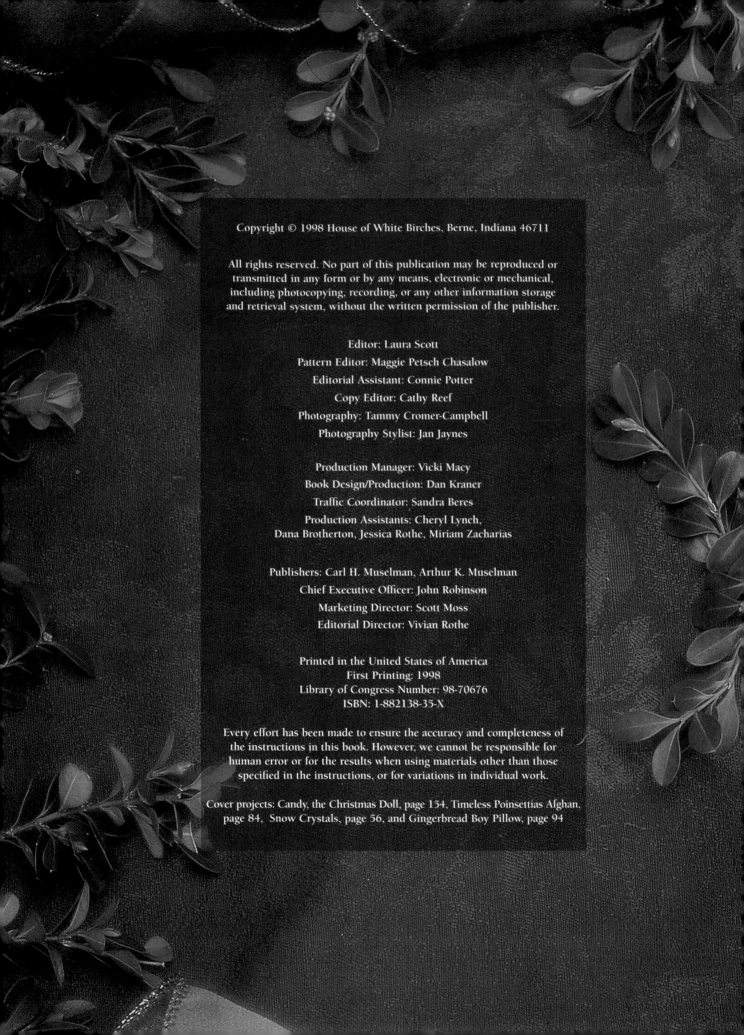

Editor: Laura Scott
Pattern Editor: Maggie Petsch Chasalow
Editorial Assistant: Connie Potter
Copy Editor: Cathy Reef
Photography: Tammy Cromer-Campbell
Photography Stylist: Jan Jaynes

Production Manager: Vicki Macy
Book Design/Production: Dan Kraner
Traffic Coordinator: Sandra Beres
Production Assistants: Cheryl Lynch,
Dana Brotherton, Jessica Rothe, Miriam Zacharias

Publishers: Carl H. Muselman, Arthur K. Muselman
Chief Executive Officer: John Robinson
Marketing Director: Scott Moss
Editorial Director: Vivian Rothe

Printed in the United States of America
First Printing: 1998
Library of Congress Number: 98-70676
ISBN: 1-882138-35-X

Every effort has been made to ensure the accuracy and completeness of
the instructions in this book. However, we cannot be responsible for
human error or for the results when using materials other than those
specified in the instructions, or for variations in individual work.

Cover projects: Candy, the Christmas Doll, page 154, Timeless Poinsettias Afghan,
page 84, Snow Crystals, page 56, and Gingerbread Boy Pillow, page 94

A Warm Christmas Welcome

Celebrate the Christmas season with all the love, joy and peace your heart can hold! And, while you're celebrating with those you love, create memories that will last you and yours a lifetime.

We who get such pleasure out of crocheting naturally want to include our favorite hobby in with the festivities and gift-giving of our favorite holiday. This collection of never-before-published crochet patterns will let you do just that.

Decorating for Christmas will take on new meaning when you crochet many of the charming accents. Colorful ornaments and garlands, festive stockings and tree skirts, and lovely doilies and centerpieces will add charm and beauty to your home.

Crocheting gifts will fill many happy hours throughout the year as you check name after name off your gift list. Handsome sweaters for the entire family, huggable dolls and toys for the little ones, and cheery kitchen helpers make gifts sure to be used and appreciated.

This collection of crocheted Christmas patterns will give you everything you need to make the holiday season complete with your personal, hand-crocheted touch.

Warm regards,

Laura Scott

Editor, *Country Christmas Crochet*

Contents

Chapter 5 • Holidays at Home

Chapter 6 • The Christmas Spirit

Chapter 7 • Bright, Shining Faces

The Holiday Hostess

Gather friends and family around and share the joy of the holiday season with those you love! With this delightful collection of Christmas pretties, you can create a cheery Christmas decor, from your cozy kitchen to the elegant dining table.

Santa Hot Mat

Design by Vicki Blizzard

This year, you can invite Santa to dinner! Crochet this delightful hot mat for holiday fun and cheer!

Experience Level: Intermediate

Size: Approximately 11½" square

Materials

❋ Worsted weight yarn: 2 oz red, 1 oz each light pink and white, and small amounts each black and dark pink

❋ Size I/9 crochet hook or size needed to obtain gauge

❋ Tapestry needle

Gauge: Rnds 1–3 of back = 3⅞" square.

To save time, take time to check gauge.

Pattern Notes

Join rnds with a sl st unless otherwise stated.

To change colors in dc, work last dc before color change in working color until last 2 lps before final yo rem on hook, drop working color to WS, yo with next color, complete dc.

Pattern Stitch

Shell: [3 dc, ch 2, 3 dc] in indicated sp or st.

Beg shell: [Ch 3, 2 dc, ch 2, 3 dc] in indicated sp or st.

Front

Rnd 1 (RS): With red, ch 4, join to form a ring, ch 3 (counts as first dc throughout), 2 dc in ring, ch 2, 3 dc in ring, changing to light pink in last dc, ch 2, [3 dc in ring, ch 2] twice, join in 3rd ch of beg ch-3, fasten off light pink and red. (12 dc)

Rnd 2: With RS facing, attach red with a sl st in last light pink ch-2 sp made, ch 3, 2 dc in same sp, ch 1, shell in next sp, ch 1, 3 dc in next sp, changing to light pink in last dc, ch 2, 3 dc in same sp, ch 1, shell in next sp, ch 1, 3 dc in same sp as beg ch-3, ch 2, join in 3rd ch of beg ch-3, fasten off light pink and red. (24 dc)

Rnd 3: With RS facing, attach red with a sl st in last light pink ch-2 sp made, ch 3, 2 dc in same sp, *ch 1, 3 dc in next ch-1 sp, ch 1, shell in next shell sp, ch 1, 3 dc in next ch-1 sp, ch 1*, 3 dc in next shell sp, changing to light pink in last dc, ch 2, 3 dc in same sp, rep from * to *, 3 dc in same sp as beg ch-3, ch 2, join in 3rd ch of beg ch-3, fasten off light pink and red. (36 dc)

Rnd 4: With RS facing, attach red with a sl st in last light pink ch-2 sp, ch 3, 2 dc in same sp, *ch 1, [3 dc in next ch-1 sp, ch 1] rep across to next shell sp, shell in next shell sp, ch 1, [3 dc in next ch-1 sp, ch 1] rep across to next ch-2 sp, 3 dc in next ch-2 sp*, changing to light pink in last dc, ch 2, 3 dc in same sp, rep from * to *, ch 2, join in 3rd ch of beg ch-3, fasten off light

pink and red. (48 dc)

Rnds 5–9: Rep Rnd 4, fasten off at end of Rnd 9. (108 dc at end of Rnd 9)

Back

Rnd 1 (RS): With red, ch 4, join to form a ring, ch 3 (counts as first dc throughout), 2 dc in ring, ch 2, [3 dc in ring, ch 2] 3 times, join in 3rd ch of beg ch-3. (12 dc)

Rnd 2: Sl st in each of next 2 dc and in ch-2 sp, beg shell in same sp, ch 1, [shell in next ch-2 sp, ch 1] rep around, join in 3rd ch of beg ch-3. (24 dc)

Rnd 3: Sl st in each of next 2 dc and in shell sp, beg shell in same sp, ch 1, *3 dc in next ch-1 sp, ch 1**, shell in next shell sp, ch 1, rep from * around, rep from * around, ending last rep at **, join in 3rd ch of beg ch-3. (36 dc)

Rnd 4: Sl st in each of next 2 dc and in shell sp, beg shell in same sp, *ch 1, [3 dc in next ch-1 sp, ch 1] rep across to next shell sp**, shell in next shell sp, rep from * around, ending last rep at **, join in 3rd ch of beg ch-3. (48 dc)

Rnds 5–9: Rep Rnd 4, fasten off at end of Rnd 9. (108 dc at end of Rnd 9)

Join Front and Back

Holding front and back with WS tog and front facing, working through both thicknesses, attach red with a sl st in last pink ch-2 sp on Rnd 9 of front, ch 3, 3 dc in same sp, *5 dc in each ch-1 sp across to next shell sp, 9 dc in shell sp, 5 dc in each ch-1 sp across to next shell sp*, 4 dc in shell sp, changing to white in last dc, 5 dc in same sp, rep from * to *, 5 dc in same sp as beg ch-3, join in 3rd ch of beg ch-3, fasten off.

Eye *(make 2)*

With black, ch 2, 8 sc in 2nd ch from hook, join in beg sc, fasten off, leaving 12" end for sewing. With white and tapestry needle, make a small highlight st near center right of eye.

Nose

With dark pink, ch 4, 11 dc in 4th ch from hook, join in 4th ch of beg ch-4, fasten off, leaving 12" end for sewing.

Mustache Half (make 2)

With white, ch 16, sc in 2nd ch from hook, sc in next ch, hdc in each of next 2 chs, dc in each of next 2 chs, 2 tr in next ch, 3 tr in next ch, 2 tr in next ch, dc in each of next 2 chs, hdc in each of next 2 chs, sc in each of last 2 chs, fasten off, leaving 12" end of loose yarn for sewing.

Eyebrow (make 2)

With white, ch 6, sc in 2nd ch from hook, [2 sc in next ch, sc in next ch] twice, fasten off, leaving 12" end for sewing.

Pompom

Rnd 1: With white, ch 4, 11 dc in 4th ch from hook, join in 4th ch of beg ch-4.

Rnd 2: Ch 1, sc in same st as joining, ch 3, [sc in next dc, ch 3] rep around, join in beg sc, fasten off, leaving 12" end for sewing.

Hat Trim

Row 1: Ch 62, dc in 4th ch from hook and in each rem ch across, ch 1, turn. (60 dc, counting last 3 chs of foundation ch as first dc)

Rnd 2: Sc in first dc, [ch 3, sc in next st] rep across to last st, ch 3, [sc, ch 3] 3 times over side of last st, working across opposite side of foundation ch, sc in first rem lp of foundation ch, [ch 3, sc in next rem lp] rep across to last st, ch 3, [sc, ch 3] 3 times over side of first dc, join in beg sc, fasten off, leaving 36" end for sewing.

Finishing

Using photo as a guide, sew pompom to top center of hat, sew hat trim to bottom edge of hat. Sew eyes, nose, mustache and eyebrows to face. ❧

Checkered Hot Mats

Design by Vicki Blizzard

Liven up your kitchen with this set of brightly colored hot mats. Red and green checks accented with cheerful motifs make these kitchen helpers extra-special!

Experience Level: Intermediate

Finished Measurement: Approximately 10½" square

Materials

❊ Red Heart Classic worsted weight yarn (3 ½ oz per skein): 2 skeins white #1 (A), 1 skein each paddy green #686 (B) and jockey red #902 (C), and small amount yellow #230 (D)

❊ Size G/6 crochet hook or size needed to obtain gauge

❊ Tapestry needle

Gauge: 18 sc and 19 sc rows = 5"

To save time, take time to check gauge.

Pattern Notes

Join rnds with a sl st unless otherwise stated.

To change color in sc, insert hook in last st before color change, yo with working color, draw up a lp, drop working color to WS, yo with next color, complete sc.

Carry color not in use loosely across back of work until needed again; do not work over color not in use.

Pattern Stitch

Picot (p): Ch 3, sl st in 3rd ch from hook.

Poinsettia Hot Mat

First Side

Row 1 (RS): With A, ch 33, sc in 2nd ch from hook, sc in each of next 3 chs, changing to B in last st, *sc in each of next 4 chs with B **, changing to A in last st, sc in each of next 4 sts with A, changing to B in last st, rep from * across, ending last rep at **, do not change to A, turn. (32 sc)

Row 2: Matching colors on working row to colors on previous row, sc in each sc across, ch 1, turn.

Rows 3 & 4: Rep Row 2, changing to B at end of Row 4.

Row 5: Working B over A and A over B, sc in each sc across, ch 1, turn.

Rows 6–8: Rep Row 2, changing to A at end of Row 8.

Rows 9–32: Work even on 32 sc in established check pattern, at end of Row 32, fasten off.

Second Side

Rows 1–32: Rep Rows 1–32 of first side.

Poinsettia

Rnd 1: With D, ch 4, join to form a ring, ch 1, 8 sc in ring, join in beg sc, fasten off.

Rnd 2: Attach C with a sl st in back lp only of any sc of last rnd, [ch 8, sc in 2nd ch from hook, hdc in next ch, dc in next ch, tr in next ch, dc in next ch, hdc in next ch, sc in last ch, sl st in back lp only of next sc on Rnd 1] rep around, fasten off, leaving 18" end for sewing.

With tapestry needle, sew poinsettia to bottom left corner of first side.

Border

Rnd 1: With WS of first and 2nd sides tog, working through both thicknesses, attach C with a sl st in upper right corner, ch 1, sc in same st, sc in each st across to next corner, 4 sc in corner st, sc evenly sp over row ends to next corner, 4 sc in corner st, sc in each rem lp across opposite side of foundation ch to next corner, 4 sc in corner st, sc evenly sp over row ends to next corner, 2 sc in same st as beg sc, ch 8 for hanging lp, sc in same st as last 2 sc, join in beg sc, fasten off.

Rnd 2: Attach A with a sl st in back lp only of last sc of last rnd, ch 3 (counts as first dc), working in back lps only, 4 dc in same st, *sk next st, sc in next st, sk next st, 5 dc in next st, rep from *around, working behind hanging lp and adjusting number of sts sk at end of rnd, if necessary, so patt rep comes out even, join in beg sc.

Holly Berry Hot Mat

First Side

Rows 1–32: Rep Rows 1–32 of first side for Poinsettia Hot Mat, substituting C for B.

Second Side

Rows 1–32: Rep Rows 1–32 of 2nd side for Poinsettia Hot Mat, substituting C for B.

Holly Leaf *(make 2)*

Row 1: With B, ch 10, sc in 2nd

ch from hook, *hdc in next ch, dc in next ch, p, dc in next ch, hdc in next ch, dc in next ch, p, dc in next ch, hdc in next ch*, 3 sc in last ch; working across opposite side of foundation ch, rep from * to *, sc in last ch, fasten off, leaving an 18" end of loose yarn for sewing.

Holly Berry (make 3)

With C, ch 4, join to form a ring, ch 1, 6 sc in ring, join in beg sc, leaving 12" length for sewing. With tapestry needle, using photo as a guide, sew holly leaves and berries to bottom left corner of first side.

Border

Rnd 1: With B, rep Rnd 1 of border for Poinsettia Hot Mat.

Rnd 2: With A, rep Rnd 2 of border for Poinsettia Hot Mat. ❧

Snowman Cookie Jars

Designs by Dot Drake

Delight the family with this set of festive cookie jars filled to the brim with all their favorite Christmas treats!

Experience Level: Intermediate

Finished Measurement: Approximately 12" tall

Mr. Snowman
Materials

※ Worsted weight yarn: 6 oz white, 2 oz each red and black, and 1 oz green

※ Size G/6 crochet hook or size needed to obtain gauge

※ Size 10 crochet cotton: small amount gold metallic

※ #3 pearl cotton: small amount red

※ 11-oz empty, clean coffee can with plastic lid

※ 2 (⅝") black shank buttons

※ 12" ¼"-wide red satin ribbon

※ 1" red pompom

※ Small amount cosmetic blusher

※ Polyester fiberfill

※ Tapestry needle

※ Craft glue

※ Sewing needle and black sewing thread

Gauge: Rnds 1–5 of body = 4" in diameter

To save time, take time to check gauge.

Mrs. Snowman
Materials

※ Worsted weight yarn: 6 oz white, 3 oz red and 1 oz green

※ Size 10 crochet cotton: small amount gold metallic

※ #3 pearl cotton: small amount red

※ Size G/6 crochet hook or size needed to obtain gauge

※ Size 7 steel crochet hook

※ 11-oz empty, clean coffee can with plastic lid

※ 2 (⅝)" black shank buttons

Materials continued on page 13

Mr. Snowman
Pattern Notes

Join rnds with a sl st unless otherwise stated.

Mr. Snowman's head is glued to top of plastic lid. To remove lid from container, reach under scarf and lift lid by edges; don't attempt to remove lid by pulling on snowman's head or it will detach.

Body

Rnd 1: With white, ch 2, 10 sc in 2nd ch from hook, join in beg sc. (10 sc)

Rnd 2: Ch 1, 2 sc in same st as joining and in each rem sc around, join in beg sc. (20 sc)

Rnd 3: Ch 1, sc in same st as joining, [2 sc in next sc, sc in next sc] rep around, ending with 2 sc in last sc, join in beg sc. (30 sc)

Rnd 4: Ch 1, sc in same st as joining, sc in next sc, [2 sc in next sc, sc in each of next 2 sc] rep around, ending with 2 sc in last sc, join in beg sc. (40 sc)

Rnd 5: Ch 1, sc in same st as joining, sc in each of next 2 sc, [2 sc in next sc, sc in each of next 3 sc] rep around, ending with 2 sc in last sc, join in beg sc. (50 sc)

Rnd 6: Ch 1, sc in same st as joining, sc in each of next 3 sc, [2 sc in next sc, sc in each of next 4 sc] rep around, ending with 2 sc in last sc, join in beg sc. (60 sc)

Rnds 7–11: Ch 1, sc in same st as joining and in each rem sc around, join in beg sc. (60 sc)

Rnd 12: Ch 1, sc in same st as joining, sc in each of next 4 sc, [2 sc in next sc, sc in each of next 5 sc] rep around, ending with 2 sc in last sc, join in beg sc. (70 sc)

Rnds 13–24: Rep Rnd 7. (70 sc)

Glue bits of polyester fiberfill evenly around outside of coffee can, place can inside snowman's body and continue stuffing until

Materials

Continued from page 12

❋ 1 yd ¼"-wide white satin ribbon

❋ 1 yd ¾"-wide red satin ribbon

❋ 1" in diameter red pompom

❋ Small amount cosmetic blusher

❋ Polyester fiberfill

❋ Tapestry needle

❋ Craft glue

❋ Sewing needle and black sewing thread

Gauge: Rnds 1–5 of body = 4" in diameter with larger hook and worsted weight yarn.

To save time, take time to check gauge.

body is nicely rounded.

Rnd 25: Ch 1, beg in same st as joining, [sc dec, sc in each of next 3 sc] rep around, join in beg sc dec. (56 sts)

Rnd 26: Ch 1, beg in same st as joining, [sc dec, sc in each of next 2 sts] rep around, join in beg sc dec, fasten off. (42 sts)

Head

Rnds 1–5: Beg at top of head, with white, rep Rnds 1–5 of body. (50 sc)

Rnds 6–13: Ch 1, beg in same st as joining, sc in each sc around, join in beg sc. (50 sc)

Rnd 14: Ch 1, beg in same st as joining, [sc dec, sc in each of next 3 sc] rep around, join in beg sc dec. (40 sts)

Rnd 15: Ch 1, beg in same st as joining, [sc dec, sc in each of next 2 sts] rep around, join in beg sc dec. (30 sts)

Stuff head with polyester fiberfill.

Rnd 16: Ch 1, beg in same st as joining, [sc dec, sc in next st] rep around, join in beg sc dec. (20 sts)

Finish stuffing head.

Rnd 17: Ch 1, beg in same st as joining, [sc dec] rep around, join in beg sc dec, fasten off, leaving 8" length for sewing.

Weave 8" length through tops of sts of last rnd with tapestry needle; pull to close; fasten off.

First Arm

Row 1: With white, ch 32, sc in 2nd ch from hook and in each rem ch across, ch 1, turn. (31 sc)

Rows 2–4: Sc in each sc across, ch 1, turn; do not fasten off at end of Row 4.

Row 5: Fold arm in half so ends of rows come tog; working through both thicknesses, sc in each of first 13 sts across last row, ch 3, sl st in last sc made for thumb, sc in each of next 2 sts, sc evenly sp across folded end of arm, sc across rem lps of foundation ch to open end of arm, fasten off, leaving a 10" length for sewing.

Stuff arm lightly. With tapestry needle, sew to side of body over Rnds 19–22.

Second Arm

Rows 1–4: Rep Rows 1–4 of first arm.

Row 5: Fold arm in half as for first arm; working through both thicknesses, sc in each sc across last row, sc evenly sp across folded end of arm, sc in each of

first 2 rem lps of foundation ch, work thumb as for first arm, sc across rem sts of foundation ch to open end of arm, fasten off, leaving a 10" length for sewing.

Stuff and sew to snowman's body as for first arm.

Hat

Rnds 1–5: With black, rep Rnds 1–5 of body. (50 sc)

Rnds 6–11: Ch 1, sc in same st as joining and in each sc around, join in beg sc; at end of Rnd 11, fasten off. (50 sc)

Rnd 12: Attach red with a sl st in same st as joining, ch 1, sc in same st as joining and in each rem st around, join in beg sc. (50 sc)

Rnd 13: Rep Rnd 6, fasten off.

Rnd 14: With black, rep Rnd 12. (50 sc)

Rnd 15: Ch 1, sc in same st as joining, [2 sc in next sc, sc in next sc] rep around, ending with 2 sc in last sc, join in beg sc. (75 sc)

Rnd 16: Rep Rnd 6; fasten off.

Leaves

With green, *ch 7, 2 sc in 2nd ch from hook, hdc in next ch, dc in each of next 2 chs, hdc in next ch, 3 sc in last ch; working in rem lps across opposite side, hdc in next ch, dc in each of next 2 chs, hdc in next ch, sc in last ch, join in beg sc, rep from * once, fasten off.

Berries

With red, *ch 4, 4 dc in 4th ch from hook, remove hook from lp, insert hook in top of beg ch-4, pick up dropped lp and draw through st on hook, rep from * once, fasten off.

Glue leaves to hat over red band; glue berries at center of leaves.

Wreath

Rnd 1: With green, ch 24, join to form a ring, ch 1, 2 sc in same

st as joining, [sc in next ch, 2 sc in next ch] rep around, ending with sc in last ch, join in beg sc. (36 sc)

Rnd 2: Ch 1, beg in same st as joining, sc in each sc around, join in front lp only of beg sc.

Rnd 3: Ch 1, working in front lps only this rnd, sc in same st as joining, ch 3, [sc in next sc, ch 3] rep around, join in beg sc. (36 ch-3 lps)

Rnd 4: Sl st in next rem lp of Rnd 2, ch 1, sc in same st and in each rem st around, join in beg sc. (36 sc)

Rnd 5: Working in both lps, rep Rnd 3, fasten off.

Make bow with red ribbon; glue to wreath on Rnd 2. With gold metallic crochet cotton and tapestry needle, work French knots evenly sp over Rnds 1 and 2 of wreath on each side of bow, staggering placement between Rnds 1 and 2.

Scarf

Row 1: With red, ch 8, sc in 2nd ch from hook and in each rem ch across, ch 1, turn. (7 sc)

Row 2: Sc in each sc across, ch 1, turn. (7 sc)

Rep Row 2 until scarf measures approximately 20" long, fasten off.

Knot 1 (3)" strand of red in each st across short end of scarf for fringe.

Trim ends evenly.

Finishing

Using photo as guide, glue pompom to face for nose. With sewing needle and black thread, sew buttons on for eyes. Work mouth with red pearl cotton and tapestry needle. Stuff hat lightly with polyester fiberfill and glue in place on top of head. Glue bottom of head to top of plastic lid. Using photo as a guide, glue top edge of scarf around bottom of snowman's head and to edge of lid, overlapping ends so fringed end is on top. Apply small amount of blusher to cheeks. Place wreath over 1 arm.

Mrs. Snowman

Pattern Notes

Join rnds with a sl st unless otherwise stated.

Mrs. Snowman's head is glued to top of plastic lid. To remove lid from container, reach under collar and lift lid by edges; do not attempt to remove lid by pulling on head or it will detach.

Body

Rnds 1–26: With larger hook, rep Rnds 1–26 for Mr. Snowman's body.

Head

Rnds 1–17: With larger hook, rep Rnds 1–17 for Mr. Snowman's head.

First Arm

Rows 1–5: With larger hook, rep Rows 1–5 of first arm for Mr. Snowman.

Stuff and complete as for Mr. Snowman.

Second Arm

Rows 1–5: With larger hook, rep Rows 1–5 of 2nd arm for Mr. Snowman.

Stuff and complete as for Mr. Snowman.

Hat

Rnd 1: With larger hook and worsted weight red, ch 6, join to form a ring, ch 1, 12 sc in ring, join in beg sc. (12 sc)

Rnd 2: Ch 1, sc in same st as joining, [ch 3, sc in next sc] rep around, ending with ch 1, hdc in beg sc to form last ch-3 sp. (12 ch-3 sps)

Rnd 3: Ch 1, sc in last sp formed, *ch 3, sc in same sp **, [ch 3, sc in next sp] twice, rep from * around to last sp,

ending last rep at **, ch 3, sc in last sp, ch 1, hdc in beg sc to form last sp. (18 ch-3 sps)

Rnd 4: Ch 1, sc in last sp formed, [ch 3, sc in next sp] rep around, ending with ch 1, hdc in beg sc to form last sp. (18 ch-3 sps)

Rnd 5: Rep Rnd 3. (27 ch-3 sps)

Rnd 6–11: Rep Rnd 4. (27 ch-3 sps)

Rnd 12: Ch 4 (counts as first dc, ch-1), *dc in same sp **, [ch 1, dc in next sp] twice, ch 1, rep from * around, ending last rep at **, ch 1, join in 3rd ch of beg ch-4. (41 ch-1 sps)

Rnd 13: Sl st in first ch-1 sp, ch 1, sc in same sp, ch 3, [sc in next sp, ch 3] rep around, join in beg sc.

Rnd 14: Sl st in next sp, ch 1, sc in same sp, [ch 3, dc in same sp, sc in next sp] rep around, ending with ch 3, dc in same sp, join in beg sc, fasten off.

Weave white ribbon through ch-1 sps of Rnd 12. Tie in bow; trim ends to desired length.

Curlicues

With larger hook and green, *ch 7, 2 sc in 2nd ch from hook and in each rem ch across, rep from * once, fasten off.

Glue curlicues to front of hat just above bow.

Collar

Row 1: With larger hook and white, [ch 3, hdc in 3rd ch from hook] 22 times, do not turn.

Row 2: Ch 3 (counts as first dc), working over ends of sts across, dc over side of last hdc made, [2 dc over side of next hdc] rep across, turn. (44 dc)

Row 3: [Ch 3, sc in each of next 2 dc] rep across, ending with ch 3, sc in last dc, turn. (22 ch-3 sps)

Row 4: [Ch 3, 2 sc in next ch-3 sp] rep across, ending with ch 3, sc in last ch-3 sp, turn. (22 ch-3 sps)

Row 5: Ch 3, sc in first sp, [ch 3, sc in same sp, ch 3, sc in next sp] rep across, turn. (43 ch-3 sps)

Rows 6 & 7: Ch 3, sc in first sp, [ch 3, sc in next sp] rep across, turn; at end of Row 7, fasten off. (43 ch-3 sps)

Weave red ribbon over 2 dc and under 2 dc across sts of Row 2.

Earrings (make 2)

With gold metallic and smaller hook, ch 3, sl st in 3rd ch from hook for p, ch 7, drop lp from hook, insert hook in first ch of ch-7, pick up dropped lp and draw through st on hook, [5 sc, ch 2, sl st in last sc made, 5 sc] in ch-7 lp, join at base of first p, fasten off. Set aside.

Purse

Rnd 1: With green and larger hook, ch 4, 11 dc in 4th ch from hook, join in 4th ch of beg ch-4. (12 dc, counting last 3 chs of beg ch-4 as first dc)

Rnd 2: Ch 1, sc in same st as joining, [ch 3, sc in next dc] rep around, ending with ch 1, hdc in beg sc to form last ch-3 sp. (12 ch-3 sps)

Rnds 3–6: Ch 1, sc in last sp made, [ch 3, sc in next sp] rep around, ending with ch 1, hdc in beg sc to form last ch-3 sp. (12 ch-3 sps)

Rnd 7: Sl st in last sp formed, ch 3, dc in same sp, ch 1, [2 dc in next sp, ch 1] rep around, join in 3rd ch of beg ch-3. (12 ch-1 sps)

Rnd 8: Ch 1, sc in same st as joining, ch 2, [sc in next dc, ch 2] rep around, join in beg sc, fasten off.

Drawstring (make 2)

With green and larger hook, ch 30, fasten off. Weave 1 drawstring through ch-1 sps on Rnd 7 of purse. Beg at opposite side of purse, weave rem drawstring through ch-1 sps of same rnd.

Flower

Rnd 1: With red pearl cotton

Continued on page 25

Pattern Note

Join rnds with a sl st unless otherwise stated.

Pattern Stitches

Beg shell: [Ch 4, tr, ch 4, 2 tr] in indicated sp.

Shell: [2 tr, ch 4, 2 tr] in indicated sp.

Jar Cover

Rnd 1 (RS): With green, ch 6, join to form a ring, ch 3 (counts as first dc throughout), work 23 dc in ring, join in 3rd ch of beg ch-3. (24 dc)

Rnds 2 & 3: Ch 3, dc in same st as joining, dc in next dc, [2 dc in next dc, dc in next dc] rep around, join in 3rd ch of beg ch-3. (54 dc at end of Rnd 3)

Rnd 4: Ch 5 (counts as first dc, ch 2), [dc in next dc, ch 2] rep around, join in 3rd ch of beg ch-5, fasten off. (54 ch-2 sps)

Rnd 5: With RS facing, attach red with a sl st in any ch-2 sp, ch 1, [sc, hdc, 5 dc, hdc, sc] in same sp (petal made), [petal in next ch-2 sp] 5 times, *remove hook from lp, insert hook from RS to WS between 2nd and 3rd petals, pick up dropped lp and draw through work to RS ** (4-petal rose made), [petal in next ch-2 sp] 6 times, rep from * around, ending last rep at **, join in beg sc, fasten off. (9 4-petal roses with 2 petals between adjacent roses)

Rnd 6: With RS facing, attach green with a sl st between 2 joined petals at bottom center of any rose, ch 5 (counts as first dc, ch 2), dc in same sp, [dc, ch 2, dc] between next 2 petals before next rose, *[dc, ch 2, dc] between 2 joined petals at bottom center of next rose, [dc, ch 2, dc] between next 2 petals before next rose, rep from * around, join in 3rd

Continued on page 19

Winter Roses Jar Topper

Design by Loa Ann Thaxton

When attending holiday parties, delight each hostess with a decorative jar filled with her favorite treats and adorned with this pretty crocheted cover.

Experience Level: Intermediate

Finished Measurement: 7" in diameter

Materials

❋ Size 10 crochet cotton: small amounts red, white and green

❋ Size 4 steel crochet hook or size needed to obtain gauge

Gauge: Rnds 1–3 = 2½" in diameter

To save time, take time to check gauge.

Angelic Napkin Holder

Design by Sandy Abbate

This darling angel napkin holder will add a touch of heaven to your Christmas morning brunch!

Experience Level: Intermediate

Finished Measurements: Approximately 4" tall x 3¾" wide

Materials

❋ Worsted weight yarn: small amounts white, yellow and pink

❋ Size E/4 crochet hook or size needed to obtain gauge

❋ 3½" length 1¼"-wide dark green satin ribbon

❋ Gold pipe cleaner

❋ Black and red marking pens

❋ Small amount cosmetic blusher

❋ Safety pin or other small row/rnd marker

Gauge: Rnds 1–3 of head = 1½" in diameter

To save time, take time to check gauge.

Pattern Note

Join rnds with a sl st unless otherwise stated.

Head

Rnd 1 (RS): With pink, ch 2, 6 sc in 2nd ch from hook, do not join this or rem rnds unless otherwise stated; mark first st of each rnd with safety pin or other small marker. (6 sc)

Rnd 2: 2 sc in each st around. (12 sc)

Rnd 3: [Sc in next st, 2 sc in next st] rep around, join in beg sc, fasten off. (18 sc)

Wings & Body

Row 1: With RS facing, attach white with a sl st in any sc of Rnd 3 of head, ch 3 (counts as first dc), 4 dc in same st, [sk next st, 5 dc in next st] twice, turn. (15 dc)

Row 2: Ch 4 (counts as first dc, ch-1), dc in next dc, [ch 1, dc in next dc] 3 times, 2 dc in next dc, dc in each of next 3 dc, 2 dc in next dc, [dc in next dc, ch 1] 4 times, dc in 3rd ch of turning ch-3, ch 1, turn. (17 dc)

Row 3: Sc in first dc, [ch 3, sc in next ch-1 sp, ch 3, sc in next dc] 4 times for first wing, dc in each of next 7 dc for body, sc in next dc, [ch 3, sc in next ch-1 sp, ch 3, sc in next dc] 3 times, ch 3, sc in 4th ch of turning ch-4, ch 3, sc in next ch of turning ch-4 for 2nd wing, fasten off, turn.

Row 4: With WS facing, attach white with a sl st in first of 7 dc of body on last row, ch 3, 2 dc in same st, dc in each of next 5 dc, 3 dc in last dc, ch 1, turn. (11 dc)

Row 5: Sc in first dc, [ch 3, sc in next dc] rep across, fasten off.

Hair

With yellow, leaving a 2" length, ch 10 for first braid; with RS facing, sc in next unworked sc

Continued on page 25

Elegant Snowflakes

Design by Laura Gebhardt

Add a touch of pure white elegance to your Christmas dinner by crocheting a place mat and napkin ring set for each guest.

Experience Level: Intermediate

Finished Measurements

Place Mat: Approximately 11¼" x 16" including border

Napkin Ring: 2¾" deep

Materials

❋ Size 10 crochet cotton: Approximately 130 yds makes 1 place mat and 1 napkin ring

❋ Size 7 steel crochet hook or size needed to obtain gauge

Gauge: In filet mesh, 19 sps and 18 rows = 4"

To save time, take time to check gauge.

Pattern Notes

Join rnds with a sl st unless otherwise stated.

When working from charts (shown on page 20), read all odd-numbered (RS) rows from right to left; read all even-numbered (WS) rows from left to right.

Pattern Stitches

Block (bl): Dc in each of next 2 sts.

Sp: Ch 1, sk next dc or next ch-1 sp, dc in next st.

Beg sp: Ch 4 (counts as first dc, ch-1), sk next st, dc in next dc.

Bl over bl: Dc in each of next 2 dc.

Bl over sp: Dc in next ch-1 sp, dc in next dc.

Sp over bl: Ch 1, sk next dc, dc in next dc.

Sp over sp: Ch 1, sk next ch-1 sp, dc in next dc.

Beg V-st: [Ch 4, dc] in indicated st or sp.

V-st: [Dc, ch 1, dc] in indicated st or sp.

P: Ch 3, sl st in last sc made.

Place Mat

Body

Row 1 (RS): Ch 146, dc in 6th ch from hook, [ch 1, sk next ch, dc in next ch] rep across, turn. (71 sps)

Row 2: Beg sp, [sp over sp] 3 times, *bl over sp, [sp over sp] 5 times, bl over sp **, [sp over sp] 7 times, rep from * across, ending last rep at **, [sp over sp] 4 times, turn.

Rows 3–45: Follow Chart A (page 20); don't fasten off at end of Row 45; don't turn at end of Row 45.

Border

Rnd 1: Working over row ends across side, beg V-st in last st of last row, ch 5, V-st over end of next-to-last row, *[ch 5, sk next row, V-st over end of next row]

21 times, ch 5, V-st in first ch-1 sp of next row, ch-5, V-st in next ch-1 sp, [ch 5, sk next ch-1 sp, v-st in next sp] 34 times, ch 5 *, V-st in last sp of row, ch-5, V-st over end of next row, rep from * to *, join in 3rd ch of beg ch-4.

Rnd 2: Sl st in first V-st sp, ch 1, sc in same sp, *ch 3, [sc, p] in next ch-5 sp, ch 3 **, sc in next V-st sp, rep from * around,

ending last rep at **, join in beg sc, fasten off.

Napkin Ring

Body

Row 1: Ch 56, dc in 6th ch from hook, [ch 1, sk next ch, dc in next ch] rep across, turn. (26 sps)

Rows 2–6: Follow Chart B (page 20); fasten off at end of Row 6, leaving short length for sewing.

With tapestry needle, sew row ends tog to form ring.

Border

Rnd 1: With RS facing, attach thread with a sl st in first ch-1 sp after seam on either edge, beg V-st in same sp, ch 5, [sk next sp, V-st in next sp, ch 5] rep around, join in 3rd ch of beg ch-4.

Rnd 2: Rep Rnd 2 of border for place mat. ❧

Winter Roses Jar Topper

Continued from page 16

Continued from page 16

ch of beg ch-5, fasten off. (18 ch-2 sps)

Rnd 7: With RS facing, attach white with a sl st in any ch-2 sp, ch 6 (counts as first dc, ch 3), dc in same sp, [dc, ch 3, dc] in each rem ch-2 sp around, join in 3rd ch of beg ch-6.

Rnds 8 & 9: Sl st to center of next sp, ch 8 (counts as first tr, ch 4), tr in same sp, [tr, ch 4, tr] in each rem sp around, join in 4th ch of beg ch-8.

Rnd 10: Sl st in next sp, beg shell in same sp, [shell in next sp] rep around, join in 4th ch of beg ch-4.

Rnd 11: Sl st in next tr and in each of next 2 chs of first shell sp, ch 1, sc in same sp, *ch 3, 2 tr between same shell and next shell, ch 3 **, sc in next shell sp, rep from * around, ending last rep at **, join in beg sc.

Rnd 12: Sl st in each of first 2 chs of next ch-3 sp, ch 1, sc in same sp, *ch 3, sc in each of next 2 tr **, [ch 3, sc in next ch-3 sp] twice, rep from * around, ending last rep at **, ch 3, sc in next ch-3 sp, ch 3, join in beg sc, fasten off.

Tie

With green, ch 150 or desired length, fasten off. Knot ends. Weave through sps of Rnd 7. ❧

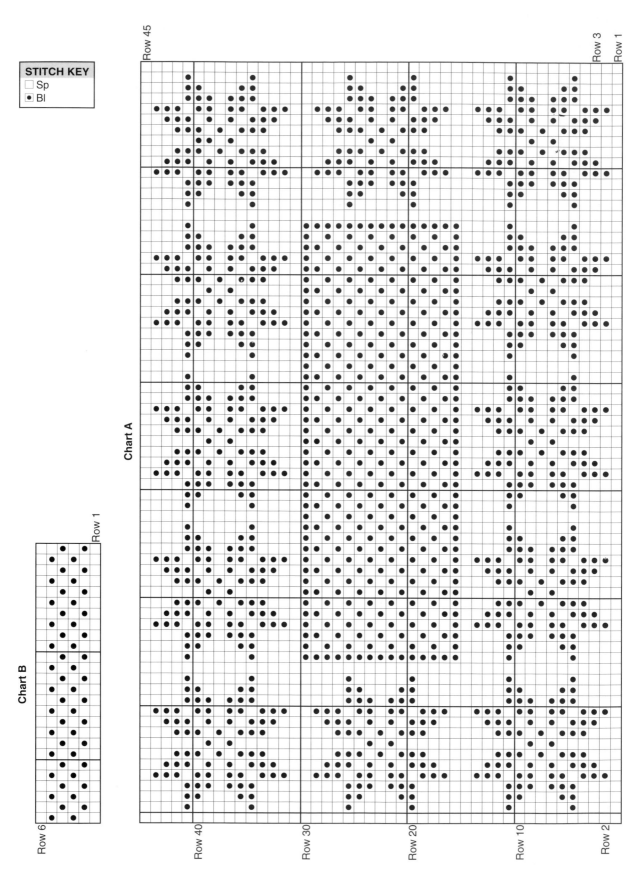

STITCH KEY
☐ Sp
⦿ Bl

Chart A

Chart B

Row 45

Row 3

Row 1

Row 1

Row 6

Row 40

Row 30

Row 20

Row 10

Row 2

Noel Magnet

Design by Zelda Workman

Dress up your refrigerator with this jumbo-size magnet! Its large size makes it strong enough to keep your long Christmas shopping list firmly in place.

Experience Level: Intermediate

Finished Measurements: 3½" x 5½"

Materials

❊ J. & P. Coats Pearl Luster Sheen acrylic sport weight yarn (100 yds per ball): 1 ball white #0001P (MC)

❊ J. & P. Coats Metallic Knit-Cro-Sheen size 10 crochet cotton (100 yds per ball): 1 ball red/green #0126 (CC)

❊ Size F/5 afghan hook or size needed to obtain gauge

❊ Size 5 steel crochet hook

❊ ⅔ yd ¼" wide white satin ribbon

❊ 2"-wide white satin bow

❊ Craft glue

❊ Tapestry needle

❊ 150 (3mm) pearl beads

❊ 2⅜" x 4¼" piece self-adhesive magnetic sheeting

Gauge: With MC and afghan hook in afghan st, 11 sts and 11 rows = 2"

To save time, take time to check gauge.

Pattern Note

Join rnds with a sl st unless otherwise stated.

Pattern Stitches

Afghan Stitch

Row 1: Retaining all lps on hook, draw up lp in 2nd ch from hook and in each rem ch across (first half of row); *yo, draw through 1 lp on hook, [yo, draw through 2 lps on hook] rep across until 1 lp rems (2nd half of row; lp that rems counts as first st of next row) *.

Row 2: Retaining all lps on hook, sk first vertical bar, [insert hook under next vertical bar, yo, draw up a lp] rep across, ending with insert hook under last vertical bar and 1 strand directly behind it, yo, draw up a lp for last st (first half of row); rep Row 1 from * to * for 2nd half of row.

Rep Row 2 for afghan st.

Beaded sc (bsc): Insert hook in indicated st, yo, draw up a lp, slide bead up to hook, complete sc.

Magnet

With MC and afghan hook, ch 23.

Rows 1–11: Work in afghan st on 23 sts; at end of Row 11, do not fasten off.

Row 12: Sk first vertical bar, [insert hook under next vertical bar, yo, draw through vertical bar and lp on hook] rep across, ending with insert hook under last vertical bar and 1 strand directly behind it, yo, draw through vertical bar and lp on hook, fasten off.

Continued on page 31

Chart A

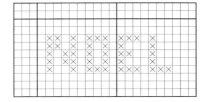

Victorian Christmas Tablecloth

Design by Nancy Hearne

The Victorian era reminds us of all things beautiful, elegant and fine. Add a touch of Victoriana to your holiday with this keepsake tablecloth worked in delicate holiday colors.

Experience Level: Advanced

Finished Measurement: Approximately 58" in diameter

Materials

❋ DMC Cebelia crochet cotton size 10 (50 grams per ball): 12 balls ecru #712, 5 balls pink #223 and 3 balls green #524

❋ Size 7 steel crochet hook or size needed to obtain gauge

❋ 8 bobbins

Gauge: 19 sps = 5"; 17 rows = 4"

To save time, take time to check gauge.

Pattern Notes

Wind 4 bobbins of ecru and 2 bobbins each of green and pink.

To change color in dc, work dc with first color until last 2 lps before final yo rem on hook, drop first color to WS, yo with next color and complete dc.

To carry color not in use across sp to its next working area, wrap color not in use around working color while working each ch st of sp. Do not carry CCs across more than 3 sps; attach new bobbin.

Carry MC across WS of work when not in use, working over it with color in use.

To inc 1 bl at beg of row, ch 5, dc in 4th ch from hook and in next ch, dc in next dc.

To inc 2 bls at beg of row, ch 8, dc in 4th ch from hook and in each of next 4 chs, dc in next dc.

To inc bl(s) at end of row, work foundation dc in same st as last dc of row, then [foundation dc in base of foundation dc just made] twice for first bl inc; work [foundation dc in base of foundation dc just made] 3 times for each additional bl inc.

To dec bl(s) at beg of row, sl st across bl(s) to be dec to point where first bl will beg, ch 3 for first dc.

To dec bl(s) at end of row, leave bl(s) to be dec unworked.

To join sections at end of openwork areas, work last foundation dc of 2-bl inc at center of joining row as follows: Yo, insert hook in base of

Continued on page 24

Chart A

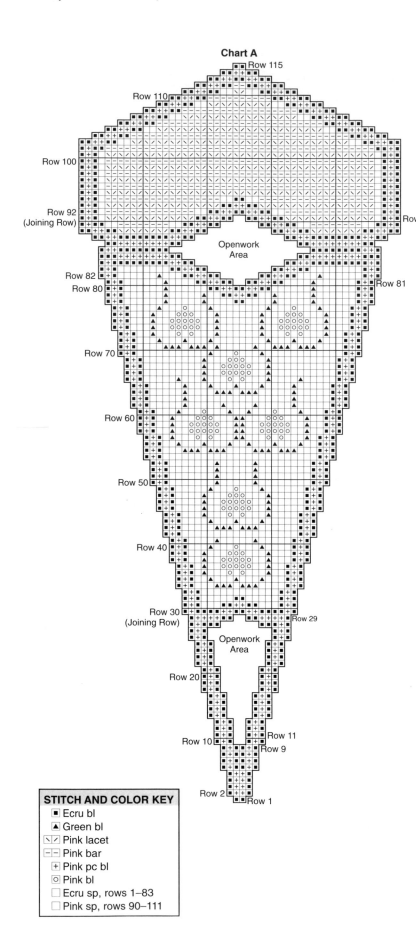

Row 115
Row 110
Row 100
Row 92
(Joining Row)
Row 91
Openwork Area
Row 82
Row 80
Row 81
Row 70
Row 60
Row 50
Row 40
Row 30
(Joining Row)
Row 29
Openwork Area
Row 20
Row 11
Row 10
Row 9
Row 2
Row 1

STITCH AND COLOR KEY
■ Ecru bl
▲ Green bl
╲╱ Pink lacet
─ Pink bar
＋ Pink pc bl
⊙ Pink bl
☐ Ecru sp, rows 1–83
☐ Pink sp, rows 90–111

foundation dc just made, yo, draw through base, insert hook in top of first st on last row of next section, yo, draw through st on hook and 1 lp on hook, yo, complete dc, continue across last row of 2nd section following chart.

Pattern Stitches

Foundation dc: Yo, insert hook in indicated st, yo, draw up a lp, yo, draw through 1 lp on hook (base made), yo, complete dc.

Block (bl): Dc in each of next 3 sts.

Sp: Ch 2, sk next 2 dc or next ch-2 sp, dc in next st.

Popcorn (pc): 5 dc in indicated st or sp, remove hook from lp, insert hook from RS to WS in top of first dc, pick up dropped lp, draw through st on hook to form pc, ch 1 to close.

Pc bl: Pc in indicated st or sp, dc in next indicated st.

Bar: Ch 5, sk 5 sts, dc in next dc.

Lacet: Ch 3, sk 2 sts, sc in next st, ch 3, sk 2 sts, dc in next dc.

Beg bl: Ch 3 (counts as first dc), dc in each of next 3 sts.

Bl over a bl: Dc in each of next 3 dc.

Bl over a sp: 2 dc in ch-2 sp, dc in next dc.

Bl over a pc bl: 2 dc in top of pc, dc in next dc.

2 bls over a bar: Dc in each of next 5 chs, dc in next dc.

Sp over a bl: Ch 2, sk 2 dc, dc in next dc.

Sp over a sp: Ch 2, dc in next dc.

Sp over a bar: Ch 2, sk 2 chs, dc in next st.

Pc bl over a bl: Sk next dc, pc in next dc, dc in next dc.

Pc bl over a pc bl: Pc in top of pc, dc in next dc.

Bar over a lacet: Ch 5, dc in next dc.

Lacet over 2 bls: Ch 3, sk 2 dc, sc in next dc, ch 3, sk 2 dc, dc in next dc.

Lacet over 2 sps: Ch 3, sk ch-2 sp, sc in next dc, ch 3, sk ch-2 sp, dc in next dc.

Lacet over a bar: Ch 3, sk 2 chs, sc in next ch, ch 3, sk 2 chs, dc in next dc.

Panel (*make 11*)

Row 1 (RS): With ecru, ch 9, dc in 4th ch from hook and in each rem ch across, turn. (7 dc, counting last 3 chs of foundation ch as first dc; 2 bls)

Row 2: Inc bl at beg of row, [pc bl over bl] twice, inc bl at end of row, turn.

Rows 3–9: Work from Chart A, read odd-numbered (RS) rows from right to left and all even-numbered (WS) rows from left to right.

First Section

Row 10: Inc bl at beg of row, pc bl over bl, bl over pc bl, leave rem sts unworked, turn.

Rows 11–29: Work from chart; at end of Row 29, ch 3, fasten off.

Second Section

Row 10: With WS facing, sk next 5 unworked dc of Row 9, attach ecru with a sl st in top of next dc, ch 3 (counts as first dc), bl over pc bl, pc bl over bl, inc bl at end of row, turn.

Rows 11–29: Work from chart; at end of Row 29, fasten off.

Row 30 (joining row): With WS facing, attach ecru with a sl st in first ch at end of Row 29 of first section, ch 3 (counts as first dc), dc in each of next 2 chs, dc in next dc; following chart, continue across, joining first section to 2nd section (see Pattern Notes).

Rows 31–115: Work from chart; at end of Row 115, fasten off.

Finishing

Beg with Row 2, join panels with ecru by sewing tips of every 4th row tog, weaving thread under sts on WS across intervening rows, ending at Row 82. 🍃

Snowman Cookie Jars

Continued from page 15

and smaller hook, [ch 5, sl st in 5th ch from hook] 5 times, do not join.

Rnd 2: [Sc, 5 dc, sc] in first ch-5 lp and in each rem ch-5 lp around, join in beg sc, fasten off.

Make large French knot at center of flower with gold metallic crochet cotton and tapestry needle.

Sew flower to top of any dc on Rnd 7 of purse.

Finishing

Using photo as a guide, glue pompom to face for nose. With sewing needle and double strand black sewing thread, sew buttons on for eyes. Pull end of thread out at top of eye after button has been sewn on and trim to approximately ⅜" long to form eyelashes.

Work mouth with red pearl cotton. Glue hat to head and bottom of head to top of plastic lid. Glue top edge of collar around bottom of Mrs. Snowman's head and to edge of lid; tie ribbon into bow. Sew 1 earring on each side of head. Place purse over 1 wrist. Apply small amount of blusher to each cheek. 🍃

Napkin Holder

Continued from page 17

on Rnd 3 of head after wing, sc in each of next 12 unworked sc of Rnd 3, ch 10 for 2nd braid, fasten off.

Trim ends of braids to ½"; untwist strands. Put braids behind wings and pull to front through sps between end and center 5-dc groups on Row 1 of wings and body.

Finishing

With black marking pen, make 2 dots for eyes; with red pen, make 1 dot for mouth. Apply blusher to cheeks. Form halo with gold pipe cleaner, leaving a 1" length at end; tack end to center back of Row 1 of wings and body.

Tie 1 (6") length of ribbon in double knot at end of each braid; trim off excess as close to knot as possible. Tie 14" length of ribbon in a bow around center dc of center 5-dc group on Row 1 of wings and body; trim ends to desired length. Insert ends of rem piece of ribbon from front to back in sp between last sc for wing and first dc for body on each side of Row 3 for wings and body. Fold napkin into fan shape and fold in half. Place angel over napkin with head at top of fold and tie ribbon into bow around napkin. 🍃

Christmas Bells Edgings

Designs by Karen E. Ferrer

Delight your overnight guests with a set of hand towels edged with filet crochet bells and bows.

Bells in a Row *(pictured at top)*

Experience Level: Intermediate

Finished Measurements: 16½" long x 2" wide at widest point

Materials

❋ Size 20 crochet cotton: 60 yds white

❋ Size 12 steel crochet hook or size needed to obtain gauge

❋ 16"-wide hand towel

❋ 20" ⅛"-wide green satin ribbon

❋ Sewing needle and white sewing thread

Gauge: In filet mesh, 13 sps = 3"; 11 rows = 2"

To save time, take time to check gauge.

Bell & Bow Towel *(pictured at bottom)*

Experience Level: Intermediate

Finished Measurements: 16½" long x 3" wide at widest point

Materials

❋ Size 20 crochet cotton: 50 yds white

❋ Size 12 steel crochet hook or size needed to obtain gauge

❋ 16"-wide hand towel

❋ 20" ⅛"-wide green satin ribbon

❋ Sewing needle and white sewing thread

Gauge: In filet mesh, 13 sps = 3"; 11 rows = 2"

To save time, take time to check gauge.

Bells in a Row

Pattern Notes

When working from chart, read all odd-numbered (RS) rows from right to left; read all even-numbered (WS) rows from left to right.

To dec bl(s) at beg of row, sl st across number of bls to be dec.

To dec bls at end of row, leave number of bls to be dec unworked.

Pattern Stitches

Block (bl): Dc in each of next 3 sts.

Beg bl: Ch 3, dc in each of next 3 sts.

Sp: Ch 2, sk next 2 dc or next ch-2 sp, dc in next dc.

Bl over bl: Dc in each of next 3 dc.

Bl over sp: 2 dc in next ch-2 sp, dc in next dc.

Sp over bl: Ch 2, sk 2 dc, dc in next dc.

Sp over sp: Ch 2, dc in next dc.

Edging

Row 1 (RS): Ch 216, dc in 4th ch from hook and in each rem ch across, turn. (214 dc; 71 bls)

Row 2: Beg bl, bl over bl, [sp over bl] 12 times, *[bl over bl] 3 times, [sp over bl] 5 times *, rep from * to * 5 times, [sp over bl] 7 times, [bl over bl] twice, turn.

Rows 3–10: Follow Chart A (page 28).

First Scallop

Row 11: Beg bl, [bl over sp] 9 times, [sp over sp] 3 times, bl over sp, turn.

Row 12: Sl st in each of first 4 dc, beg bl, [bl over sp] twice, fasten off.

Next Five Scallops

Row 11: With RS facing, sk next 8 unworked dc of Row 10, attach thread with a sl st in next dc, beg bl, [sp over sp] 3 times, bl over sp, turn.

Row 12: Rep Row 12 of first scallop.

Last Scallop

Row 11: With RS facing, sk next 8 unworked dc of Row 10, attach thread with a sl st in next dc, beg bl, [sp over sp] 3 times, [bl over sp] nine times, bl over bl turn.

Row 12: Sl st in each of first 31 dc, beg bl, [bl over sp] twice, fasten off.

Finishing

Weave ribbon through ch-2 sps of Row 2, weaving under 10-dc groups between bells; trim ends.

With sewing needle and white thread, sew edging to towel, folding row ends to back of towel approximately ¼" on each edge.

Bell & Bow Towel Edging

Pattern Notes

When working from chart, read all odd-numbered (RS) rows from right to left; read all even-numbered (WS) rows from left to right.

To dec bl(s) at beg of row, sl st across number of bls to be dec unless otherwise stated.

To dec bls at end of row, leave number of bls to be dec unworked.

Pattern Stitches

Block (bl): Dc in each of next 3 sts.

Beg bl: Ch 3, dc in each of next 3 sts.

Sp: Ch 2, sk next 2 dc or next ch-2 sp, dc in next dc.

Bl over bl: Dc in each of next 3 dc.

Bl over sp: 2 dc in next ch-2 sp, dc in next dc.

Sp over bl: Ch 2, sk 2 dc, dc in next dc.

Sp over sp: Ch 2, dc in next dc.

Edging

Row 1 (RS): Ch 216, dc in 4th ch from hook and in each rem ch across, turn. (214 dc; 71 bls)

Row 2: Beg bl, [sp over bl] 69 times, bl over bl, turn.

Rows 3–9: Follow Chart B*; fasten off at end of Row 9.

Row 10: With WS facing, sk first 63 dc of last row, attach thread with a sl st in next dc, beg bl, continue across row following chart, leave last 21 bls of last row unworked, turn.

Rows 11–17: Follow chart, dec bls at beg and ends of rows as indicated; at end of Row 17, fasten off.

Finishing

Weave ribbon through ch-2 sps of Row 2; trim ends.

With sewing needle and white thread, sew edging to towel, folding row ends to back of towel approximately ¼" on each edge. 🎀

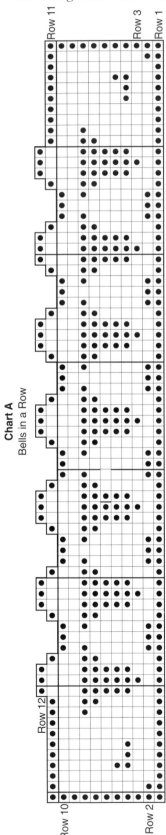

Chart A
Bells in a Row

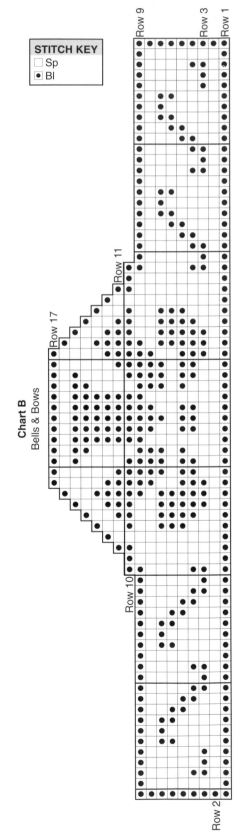

Chart B
Bells & Bows

STITCH KEY
☐ Sp
⊡ Bl

Christmas Coasters

Design by Nazanin S. Fard

With just a few quick stitches, you can crochet a pretty holiday coaster. They're elegant enough for your Christmas dinner and festive enough to use throughout the holiday season!

Experience Level: Intermediate

Finished Measurement: 4¼" in diameter

Materials

❋ DMC Baroque crochet cotton (400 yd per skein): 1 skein each white #1 (MC), Christmas red #666 (CCA) and Christmas green #699 (CCB)

❋ Size 7 steel crochet hook or size needed to obtain gauge

❋ Fabric stiffener

Gauge: Rnds 1 and 2 = 1½" in diameter

To save time, take time to check gauge.

Pattern Note

Join rnds with a sl st unless otherwise stated.

Pattern Stitches

Tr cl: Holding back on hook last lp of each st, tr in each of next 5 indicated sts, yo, draw through all 6 lps on hook.

Beg tr cl: Ch 4 holding back on hook last lp of each st, tr in each of next 4 indicated sts, yo, draw through all 5 lps on hook.

P: Ch 3, sl st in last sc made.

Coaster

Note: Make 2 with CCA border and 2 with CCB border.

Rnd 1: With MC, ch 10, join to form a ring, ch 3 (counts as first dc throughout), 23 dc in ring, join in 3rd ch of beg ch-3. (24 dc)

Rnd 2: Ch 6 (counts as first dc, ch-3), [sk next dc, dc in next dc, ch 3] rep around, join in 3rd ch of beg ch-6. (12 ch-3 sps)

Rnd 3: Ch 3, *[dc, ch 3, dc] in next sp**, dc in next dc, rep from * around, ending last rep at **, join in 3rd ch of beg ch-3.

Rnd 4: Ch 3, dc in next dc, *[dc, ch 1, dc] in next sp **, dc in each of next 3 dc, rep from * around, ending last rep at **, dc in last dc, join in 3rd ch of beg ch-3.

Rnd 5: Sl st in each of next 2 dc, in next sp and in next dc, beg tr cl over next 4 dc, ch 9, [tr cl over next 5 dc, ch 9] rep around, join in top of beg tr cl, fasten off.

Border

Rnd 1: Attach CCA or CCB with a sl st in any ch-9 sp, ch 1, beg in same sp, [7 sc, p, sc, p, sc, p, 6 sc] in each ch-9 sp around, join in beg sc, fasten off.

Finishing

Apply fabric stiffener to each coaster; stretch to size. Let dry. ❧

Cheery Cherry Table Set

Designs by Sandy Abbate

You'll enjoy using this festive table set for breakfast, lunch and dinner throughout the holiday season!

Experience Level: Intermediate

Finished Measurements

Place Mat: 14" x 19" including border

Coaster: 4½" in diameter

Materials

❋ Red Heart Sport acrylic sport weight yarn (2½ oz per skein): 2 skeins paddy green #687 (MC), 1 skein cherry red #912 (CC)

❋ Size D/3 crochet hook or size needed to obtain gauge

❋ 1½ yds ³⁄₁₆"-wide red satin ribbon

❋ Tapestry needle

❋ Small amount polyester fiberfill

Gauge: In dc, 20 sts and 11 rows = 4"

To save time, take time to check gauge.

Pattern Note

Join rnds with a sl st unless otherwise stated.

Place Mat

Row 1 (RS): With MC, ch 93, dc in 4th ch from hook and in each rem ch across, turn. (91 dc)

Row 2: Ch 3 (counts as first dc throughout), dc in each of next 2 sts, [ch 3, sk 2 sts, sc in next st, ch 3, sk 2 sts, dc in each of next 11 sts] 5 times, ch 3, sk 2 sts, sc in next st, ch 3, sk 2 sts, dc in each of last 3 sts, turn.

Row 3: Ch 3, dc in each of next 2 sts, *2 dc in next ch-3 sp, ch 1, 2 dc in next ch-3 sp **, dc in each of next 11 sts, rep from * across, ending last rep at **, dc in each of last 3 sts, turn.

Row 4: Ch 3, dc in each of next 4 sts, *dc in next ch-1 sp, dc in each of next 5 sts **, ch 3, sk 2 sts, sc in next st, ch 3, sk 2 sts, dc in each of next 5 sts, rep from * across, ending last rep at **, turn.

Row 5: Ch 3, dc in each of next 10 sts, *2 dc in next ch-3 sp, ch 1, 2 dc in next ch-3 sp, dc in each of next 11 sts, rep from * across, turn.

Row 6: Ch 3, dc in each of next 2 sts, *ch 3, sk 2 sts, sc in next st, ch 3, sk 2 sts **, dc in each of next 5 sts, dc in ch-1 sp, dc in each of next 5 sts, rep from * across, ending last rep at **, dc in each of last 3 sts, turn.

Rows 7–35: Rep Rows 3–6 alternately, ending with Row 3.

Row 36: Dc in each dc and ch-1 sp across, fasten off. (91 dc)

Border

With RS facing, attach CC with a sl st in top of first st at upper right corner, ch 1, [sc, ch 3, sc] in same st, *ch 3, [sk next st, sc in next st, ch 3] rep across to next corner, ending with sk next to last st of row, [sc, ch 3, sc] in corner st; working over ends of rows, ch 3, sc over end st of same row, [ch 3, sc over end st of next row] rep across to next corner*, ending with ch 3, [sc, ch 3, sc] in first rem lp of foundation ch, rep from * to *, ch 3, join in beg sc, fasten off.

Napkin Holder

Leaf (make 2)

Row 1: With MC, ch 10, hdc in 4th ch from hook, [ch 1, sk next ch, dc in next ch] twice, ch 1, sk next ch, [hdc, 3 sc] in last ch, do not turn.

Rnd 2: Working along opposite side of foundation ch, *3 hdc in next sp, 3 dc in next sp, 3 hdc in next sp *, 5 sc in ch-3 lp, rep from * to *, join in next hdc.

Rnd 3: Ch 1, beg in same st, sc in each st around, working 3 sc in center sc of 5-sc group at tip of leaf, join in beg sc, fasten off.

Stem

With MC, ch 44, fasten off.

Cherry (make 2)

Rnd 1: Attach CC with a sl st in last ch at either end of stem, ch 1, work 6 sc in same ch, do not join this or rem rnds unless otherwise stated; mark first st of each rnd with safety pin or other small marker.

Rnd 2: 2 sc in each sc around. (12 sc)

Rnd 3: [Sc in next st, 2 sc in next st] rep around. (18 sc)

Rnds 4–6: Sc in each sc around. (18 sc)

Rnd 7: [Sc in next sc, sc dec] rep around. (12 sts)

Stuff cherry lightly.

Rnd 8: [Sc dec] around, fasten off, leaving a 12" length of yarn.

With tapestry needle, weave 12"

length through sts of last rnd. Pull to tighten; tie securely; fasten off.

Make 2nd cherry on opposite end of stem.

Make knot in stem slightly off-center so 1 end of stem is longer than other; tack 1 leaf on each side of knot. Using photo as a guide, tack tip ends of leaves to left side of place mat, approximately halfway down. Cut 4 (11") lengths of ribbon; tie in bows at each of 4 corners of place mat; trim ends to desired length.

Coaster

Rnd 1 (RS): With MC, ch 4, join to form a ring, ch 3, work 11 dc in ring, join in 3rd ch of beg ch-3. (12 dc)

Rnd 2: Ch 3, dc in same st as joining, 2 dc in each rem st around, join in 3rd ch of beg ch-3. (24 dc)

Rnd 3: Ch 3, 2 dc in same st as joining, [ch 3, sk next st, sc in next st, ch 3, sk next st, 3 dc in next st] 5 times, ch 3, sk next st, sc in next st, ch 3, sk next st, join in 3rd ch of beg ch-3.

Rnd 4: Ch 3, *2 dc in next st, dc in next st, 2 dc in next ch-3 sp, ch 1, 2 dc in next ch-3 sp **, dc in next st, rep from * around, ending last rep at **, join in 3rd ch of beg ch-3.

Rnd 5: Ch 3, dc in each rem dc and 2 dc in each ch-1 sp around, join in 3rd ch of beg ch-3, fasten off. (60 dc)

Border

With RS facing, attach CC with a sl st in any dc of last rnd, ch 1, sc in same st, ch 3, [sk next st, sc in next st, ch 3] rep around, join in beg sc, fasten off.

With rem length of ribbon, tie a bow around any dc of Rnd 5, trim ends to desired length. ❧

Noel Magnet

Continued from page 21

With CC and tapestry needle, cross-stitch design on center following Chart A (page 21).

Border

String pearl beads onto CC.

Rnd 1: With WS facing, using crochet hook, attach CC with a sl st in upper right corner, ch 1, [bsc, ch 1] 3 times in same st, *[bsc, ch 1] in each of next 21 sts across to next corner, [bsc, ch 1] 3 times in corner st, work [bsc, ch 1] 10 times evenly sp over row ends across to next corner *, [bsc, ch 1] 3 times in corner st, rep from * to *, join in beg bsc.

Rnd 2: Ch 4 (counts as first dc, ch-1), [dc in next bsc, ch 1] rep around, join in 3rd ch of beg ch-4.

Rnd 3: Ch 1, bsc in same st as joining, ch 3, [bsc in next dc, ch 3] rep around, join in top of beg bsc, fasten off.

Finishing

Weave ribbon through ch-1 sps on Rnd 2 of border; fasten ends at back with glue. Glue bow to center bottom of border. Place self-adhesive magnetic sheeting on back of piece, leaving border free. ❧

Trimming the Tree

Whether you decorate your tree with Victorian treasures, country accents, contemporary ornaments or simply anything crocheted, you're sure to find a number of lovely ornaments to add to your collection in this enchanting chapter!

Angelic Grace

Design by Jo Ann Maxwell

With her exquisite crochet pattern and lovely finishing, this beautiful ornament will highlight your crocheting talent while adding grace and beauty to your tree!

Experience Level: Intermediate

Finished Measurements: 7¾" wide x 5" high

Materials

❋ Size 10 crochet cotton: 75 yds cream

❋ Size 5 steel crochet hook or size needed to obtain gauge

❋ 1½" plastic foam ball

❋ 5 (¾") pink satin roses with leaves

❋ Curly blond doll hair

❋ 6" length strung pearls

❋ 2 (⅛") black beads

❋ Small amount cosmetic blusher

❋ 2 ¼"-wide gold ribbon bow

❋ Dried baby's breath

❋ Commercial fabric stiffener

❋ 9" length gold craft cord for hanger

❋ Craft glue

❋ Small amount plastic wrap

Gauge: 7 dc = 1"

To save time, take time to check gauge.

Pattern Note

Join rnds with a sl st unless otherwise stated.

Pattern Stitches

Love knot (lk): Draw up lp on hook to approximately ⅜" high, yo, draw through lp on hook, insert hook between lp and long single strand alongside, yo, draw up a lp, yo, draw through 2 lps on hook.

Shell: [2 dc, ch 2, 2 dc] in indicated st or sp.

Head

Rnd 1: Beg at top of head, ch 6, join to form a ring, ch 3 (counts as first dc throughout), 31 dc in ring, join in 3rd ch of beg ch-3. (32 dc)

Rnds 2–11: Ch 2 (counts as first hdc throughout), hdc in each rem st around, join in 2nd ch of beg ch-2; at end of Rnd 11, insert plastic foam ball. (32 hdc)

Rnd 12: Ch 1, sc in same st as joining, sk next st, [sc in next st, sk next st] rep around, join in beg sc. (16 sc)

Bodice

Rnd 13: Ch 3, 2 dc in same st as joining, 3 dc in each rem st around, join in 3rd ch of beg ch-3. (48 dc)

Rnd 14: Ch 3, dc in same st as joining, [dc in each of next 2 sts, 2 dc in next st] rep around, ending with dc in each of last 2 sts, join in 3rd ch of beg ch-3. (64 dc)

Rnds 15 & 16: Ch 3, dc in each rem st around, join in 3rd ch of beg ch-3. (64 dc)

Rnd 17: Ch 4 (counts as first dc, ch-1), [lk, dc, ch 1, lk] in same st as joining, [dc, ch 1, lk] twice in each rem dc around, join in 3rd ch of beg ch-4, fasten off.

Wing (make 2)

Row 1: Ch 4, join to form a ring, ch 3, dc in ring, [ch 2, 2 dc in ring] 3 times, turn.

Row 2: Ch 3, shell in first ch-2 sp, ch 3, 7 dc in next ch-2 sp, ch 3, shell in last ch-2 sp, turn.

Row 3: Ch 3, shell in first shell sp, ch 3, sc in next ch-3 sp, dc in next dc, [ch 1, dc in next dc] 6 times, sc in next ch-3 sp, ch 3, shell in last shell sp, turn.

Row 4: Ch 3, shell in first shell sp, ch 3, sk next ch-3 sp, [sc in next dc, ch 3] 7 times, shell in last shell sp, turn.

Row 5: Ch 3, shell in first shell sp, ch 3, sk next ch-3 sp, [sc in next ch-3 sp, ch 3] 6 times, shell in last shell sp, turn.

Row 6: Ch 3, shell in first shell sp, ch 3, sk next ch-3 sp, [sc in next ch-3 sp, ch 3] 5 times, shell in last shell sp, turn.

Row 7: Ch 3, shell in first shell sp, ch 3, sk next ch-3 sp, [sc in next ch-3 sp, ch 3] 4 times, shell in last shell sp, turn.

Row 8: Ch 3, shell in first shell sp, ch 3, sk next ch-3 sp, [sc in next ch-3 sp, ch 3] 3 times, shell in last shell sp, turn.

Row 9: Ch 3, shell in first shell sp, ch 3, sk next ch-3 sp, [sc in next ch-3 sp, ch 3] twice, shell in last shell sp, turn.

Row 10: Ch 3, shell in first shell sp, ch 3, sk next ch-3 sp, sc in next ch-3 sp, ch 3, shell in last shell sp, turn.

Row 11: Ch 3, [shell in next shell sp] twice, turn.

Row 12: Sl st in each of first 2 dc and in first shell sp, ch 1, sc in same sp, ch 3, sc in next shell sp, fasten off.

Finishing

Cinch angel tightly at neck with small length crochet cotton.

Apply commercial fabric stiffener to head and bodice. Shape bodice and lk ruffle; stuff bodice with plastic wrap to hold shape; let dry. Apply fabric stiffener to wings; pin and shape; let dry. Glue wings to back of bodice. Using photo as a guide, glue hair to angel's head. Cut string pearls to fit around top of head and glue over hair at top of head to form halo. Glue 1 rose and small sprig baby's breath to top left of head above halo. Glue rem 4 roses evenly sp across front bodice above lk ruffle, gluing bow under 2nd rose from right edge of bodice. Glue small sprigs of baby's breath next to each rose. Glue black beads on angel's face for eyes. Apply small amount of blusher to each cheek. Glue ends of gold cord to top back of angel's head to form hanging loop. ⚜

Dapper Snowman

Design by Vicki Blizzard

Watch your little one's eyes light up when he sees this cheerful ornament. For holiday fun, you can crochet the body and let a child glue on the features and clothing!

Experience Level: Beginner

Size: Approximately 5" tall

Materials

❋ Crochet cotton size 10: small amount white

❋ Pearl cotton size 3: small amount black

❋ 6-strand embroidery floss: small amount orange

❋ Size D/4 crochet hook or size needed to obtain gauge

❋ 2 ceramic mitten buttons

❋ 2 (6mm) round black cabochons

❋ 9 (5mm) round black cabochons

❋ 15" length gold cord for hanger

❋ 12" length ¼" wide green satin ribbon

❋ 12" length ⅝" wide red pindot grosgrain ribbon

❋ 1 red heart rhinestone

❋ Pink powder blush

❋ Polyester fiberfill stuffing

❋ 3" compressed plastic foam ball

❋ Tapestry needle

❋ Hot glue gun

Gauge: Rnds 1–3 of hat = ⅞" in diameter with size 3 pearl cotton

To save time, take time to check gauge.

Pattern Note

Join rnds with a sl st unless otherwise stated.

Body

Note: Do not join this or rem rnds unless otherwise stated; mark first st of each rnd with safety pin or other small marker.

Rnd 1 (RS): Beg at top of head and working with 2 strands white held tog throughout, ch 4, join to form a ring, ch 1, 6 sc in ring. (6 sc)

Rnd 2: 2 sc in each sc around. (12 sc)

Rnd 3: [Sc in next st, 2 sc in next st] rep around. (18 sc)

Rnd 4: [Sc in each of next 2 sts, 2 sc in next st] rep around. (24 sc)

Rnd 5: [Sc in each of next 3 sts, 2 sc in next st] rep around. (30 sc)

Rnds 6–11: Sc in each sc around. (30 sc)

Rnd 12: [Sc in each of next 3 sts, sc dec] rep around. (24 sts)

Rnd 13: [Sc in each of next 2 sts, sc dec] rep around. (18 sts)

Rnd 14: [Sc in next st, sc dec] rep around. (12 sts)

Rnds 15 & 16: Sc in each sc around. (12 sts)

Stuff head firmly with polyester fiberfill.

Rnds 17–19: Rep Rnds 3–5. (30 sc at end of Rnd 19)

Rnd 20: [Sc in each of next 4 sts, 2 sc in next st] rep around. (36 sc)

Rnd 21: [Sc in each of next 5 sts, 2 sc in next st] rep around. (42 sc)

Rnd 22: [Sc in each of next 6 sts, 2 sc in next st] rep around. (48 sc)

Rnds 23–34: Sc in each sc around; at end of Rnd 34, insert compressed plastic foam ball and work around ball from this point on.

Rnd 35: [Sc in each of next 6 sts, sc dec] rep around. (42 sts)

Rnd 36: [Sc in each of next 5 sts, sc dec] rep around. (36 sts)

Rnd 37: [Sc in each of next 4 sts, sc dec] rep around. (30 sts)

Rnds 38–40: Rep Rnds 12–14. (12 sts at end of Rnd 40)

Rnd 41: [Sc dec] rep around, join in beg sc dec, fasten off, leaving 12" end.

Weave end through sts of last rnd and pull tightly to close opening. Knot securely.

Hat

Rnd 1: With black, ch 2, 6 sc in 2nd ch from hook, join in beg sc. (6 sc)

Rnd 2: Ch 1, 2 sc in same st as joining and in each rem sc

Rnd 5: Ch 1, working in back lps only this rnd, sc in same st as joining and in each rem sc around, join in beg sc. (24 sc)

Rnds 6–10: Ch 1, sc in same st as joining and in each rem sc around, join in beg sc; at end of Rnd 10, join in front lp only of beg sc. (24 sc)

Rnd 11: Working in front lps only this rnd, ch 3 (counts as first dc), dc in same st as joining, 2 dc in each rem st around, join in 3rd ch of beg ch-3, fasten off, leaving 12" end for sewing. (48 dc)

Nose

Rnd 1: With orange, ch 2, 3 sc in 2nd ch from hook, do not join this or rem rnds; mark first st of each rnd with safety pin or other small marker.

Rnds 2–4: Sc in each sc around; join in beg sc at end of Rnd 4, fasten off, leaving 12" end for sewing.

Finishing

With tapestry needle, sew nose to center of face. Apply pink powder blush in area of cheeks. Using photo as guide, glue 5 (5mm) cabochons to face for mouth and 4 (5mm) cabochons to front chest for buttons.

Wrap red pindot ribbon around neck for scarf, glue in place; cut ¼" fringe in both ends. Glue mitten buttons to sides of body. Glue heart rhinestone to chest.

Attach gold cord to top of head for hanger. With crochet hook, reach down through center of hat and pull hanger through. Push hat down hanger to head and sew in place.

Cut an 8" length of green ribbon and tie in a small bow, trim ends. Glue remaining ribbon around hat above brim, glue ends in place. Glue bow to ribbon, slightly off to one side. ❧

around, join in beg sc. (12 sc)

Rnd 3: Ch 1, sc in same st as joining, 2 sc in next sc, [sc in next sc, 2 sc in next sc] rep around, join in beg sc. (18 sc)

Rnd 4: Ch 1, sc in same st as joining and in next sc, 2 sc in next sc, [sc in each of next 2 sc, 2 sc in next sc] rep around, join in back lp only of beg sc. (24 sc)

Angels & Bells Swag

Design by Ruth G. Shepherd

These darling angels are thrilled to herald the coming of another Christmas! Make them part of your holiday festivities!

Experience Level: Intermediate

Finished Measurements: Approximately 1 yd long x 6" deep at widest point

Materials

❋ Worsted weight yarn: small amounts each white, pink, red, gold and green

❋ Size G/6 crochet hook or size needed to obtain gauge

❋ 8 (8mm) jingle bells

❋ 5 (15mm) jingle bells

❋ 2 yds gold cord

❋ Small amount polyester fiberfill

❋ Sewing needle and white sewing thread

Gauge: Angel's head front = 1¾" in diameter

To save time, take time to check gauge.

Pattern Note

Join rnds with a sl st unless otherwise stated.

Angel *(make 4)*

Head Front

Rnd 1 (RS): With pink, ch 3, join to form a ring, ch 1, 7 sc in ring, join in beg sc. (7 sc)

Rnd 2: Ch 1, beg in same st as joining, 2 sc in each st around, join in beg sc. (14 sc)

Rnd 3: Ch 1, sc in same st as joining and in each rem sc around, join in beg sc, fasten off. (14 sc)

Head Back

Rnds 1–3: Rep Rnds 1–3 of head front.

Hair

With gold, ch 5, 3 sc in 2nd ch from hook, 3 sc in each rem ch across; holding head front and head back WS tog and working through both thicknesses at once, sl st in any sc of last rnd, [ch 1, sl st in next sc] 9 times, leave rem sts of head unworked, ch 5, 3 sc in 2nd ch from hook and in

each rem ch across, fasten off. Stuff head with small amount polyester fiberfill; sew rem opening shut.

Skirt Front

Row 1: With red, beg at top of skirt, ch 6, sc in 2nd ch from hook, sc in each rem ch across, ch 1, turn. (5 sc)

Rows 2–4: Sc across, working 2 sc in first and last sc of row, ch 1, turn. (11 sc at end of Row 4)

Row 5: Sc in each sc across, fasten off. (11 sc)

Skirt Back

Rows 1–5: Rep Rows 1–5 of skirt front.

Sew side edges of skirt front and back tog. Sew head to top of skirt.

Legs

With pink, ch 21, sl st in 2nd ch from hook and in each rem ch across, fasten off. Sew 1 (8mm) jingle bell at each end of legs for feet.

Stuff skirt with small amount polyester fiberfill, fold legs in half and place center inside bottom of skirt. Sew bottom edges of skirt tog over fold in legs.

Wings

First wing

Row 1 (RS): With white, ch 1 (center ch), ch 5 more (counts as first tr, ch 1), tr in center ch, [ch 1, tr in center ch,] 3 times, turn.

Row 2: [Ch 3, sc in next ch-1 sp] 3 times, ch 3, sc in 4th ch of next ch-5, turn.

Row 3: [Ch 4, sc in next ch-3 sp] rep across, fasten off.

Second wing

Row 1: With RS facing, attach white with a sl st on opposite side of center ch, ch 5, tr in center ch, [ch 1, tr] 3 times in center ch, turn.

Rows 2 & 3: Rep Rows 2 and 3 of first wing.

Sew wings to back of angel.

Wrap 5" length of gold cord around angel's neck and tie in bow at front.

Bell *(make 5)*

Rnd 1: With white, ch 4, join to form a ring, ch 3 (counts as first dc), 9 dc in ring, join in 3rd ch of beg ch-3. (10 dc)

Rnd 2: Ch 4 (counts as first dc, ch 1), [dc in next dc, ch 1] rep around, join in 3rd ch of beg ch-4.

Rnd 3: [Ch 3, sl st in next dc] rep around, ending with sl st in same st as beg ch-3, fasten off.

Clapper/Hanger

With white, [ch 9, sl st in 9th ch from hook] twice, fasten off.

Sew 1 (15mm) jingle bell to 5th ch of either ch-9 lp, pull rem lp through top of bell from WS to RS for hanger; tack in place. Tie 5" length of gold cord into bow on top of bell at base of hanger.

Finishing

With green, ch 10, sl st in 10th ch from hook, *ch 15, sl st in hanger of any bell **, ch 20, sl st at top center of angel's head back, ch 5, sl st in 15th ch of last ch-20, rep from * across, ending last rep at **, ch 25, sl sl in 10th ch from hook, fasten off. ✿

Baby Bear

Design by Sandy Abbate

Make Christmas morning extra-special by delighting the youngest member of your family with this huggable baby teddy bear in his or her stocking!

Experience Level: Beginner

Finished Measurement: 5½" tall

Materials

❊ Red Heart Baby Sport sport weight yarn (1.75 oz per skein): 1 skein red #905

❊ Sport weight yarn: small amount black

❊ Size D/3 crochet hook or size needed to obtain gauge

❊ 20" length ¼"-wide green satin ribbon

❊ 2 (¼") red satin roses with leaves

❊ Polyester fiberfill

❊ Tapestry needle

❊ Craft glue

Gauge: Rnds 1 and 2 of head = ¾" in diameter

To save time, take time to check gauge.

Pattern Note
Join rnds with a sl st unless otherwise stated.

Head
Rnd 1: With red, ch 2, 6 sc in 2nd ch from hook, do not join this or rem rnds unless otherwise stated; mark first st of each rnd with safety pin or other small marker. (6 sc)

Rnd 2: 2 sc in each st around. (12 sc)

Rnd 3: [Sc in next st, 2 sc in next st] rep around. (18 sc)

Rnd 4: [Sc in each of next 2 sts, 2 sc in next st] rep around. (24 sc)

Rnds 5 & 6: Sc in each st around.

Rnd 7: 2 sc in each of next 4 sts for muzzle, sc in each rem sc around. (28 sc)

Rnds 8 & 9: Rep Rnds 5 and 6. (28 sc)

Rnd 10: [Sc dec] 4 times, sc in each rem sc around. (24 sc)

Rnd 11: [Sc in each of next 2 sts, sc dec] rep around. (18 sts)

Rnd 12: [Sc in next st, sc dec] rep around. (12 sts)

Body
Rnds 13 & 14: Rep Rnds 3 and 4. (24 sc at end of Rnd 14)

Rnd 15: [Sc in each of next 3 sts, 2 sc in next st] rep around. (30 sc)

Rnds 16–22: Rep Rnd 5.

Rnd 23: [Sc in each of next 3 sts, sc dec] rep around. (24 sts)

Rnds 24 & 25: Rep Rnds 11 and 12. (12 sts at end of Rnd 25)

Stuff head and body.

Rnd 26: [Sc dec] 6 times, fasten off, leaving 12" length for sewing. With tapestry needle, weave 12"

length through sts of last rnd, pull tightly to close, fasten off.

Ear *(make 2)*
Row 1: With red, beg at top of ear, ch 5, sc in 2nd ch from hook and in each of next 3 chs, ch 1, turn. (4 sc)

Row 2: 2 sc in first st, sc in each of next 2 sc, 2 sc in last st, ch 1, turn. (6 sc)

Row 3: Sc in each sc across, ch 1, turn.

Rnd 4: Sc dec, sc in each of next 2 sts, sc dec; working over ends of rows, sc over end st of each of last 3 rows, sc in each of next 4 rem lps of foundation ch, sc over end st of each of next 3 rows, join in beg sc dec, fasten off, leaving an 8" length for sewing.

Sew ear to side of head over Rnds 4–8. With black and tapestry needle, using photo as a guide, embroider eyes, nose and mouth over muzzle.

Arm *(make 2)*
Rnds 1 & 2: Beg at bottom of arm, rep Rnds 1 and 2 of head. (12 sc)

Rnds 3–12: Rep Rnd 5 of head. (12 sc)

Rnd 13: Rep Rnd 12 of head. (8 sts)

Stuff arm lightly.

Rnd 14: [Sc in next sc, sc dec] twice, sc in each of last 2 sts, fasten off, leaving 12" length for sewing.

Stuff arms lightly. With tapestry needle, weave 12" length through sts of last rnd, pull tightly to close, fasten off. Sew arm to side of body over Rnds 15 and 16.

Leg *(make 2)*
Rnds 1–3: Beg at bottom of leg, rep Rnds 1–3 of head. (18 sc)

Rnds 4–6: Rep Rnd 5 of head. (18 sc)

Rnd 7: [Sc dec] 4 times for front

ankle, sc in each rem st around. (14 sts)

Rnds 8–14: Rep Rnd 5 of head. (14 sc)

Rnd 15: [Sc in next st, sc dec] 4 times, sc in each of last 2 sts. (10 sts)

Stuff leg lightly.

Rnd 16: [Sc in next st, sc dec] 3 times, sc in last st, fasten off, leaving a 12" length for sewing. (7 sts)

Complete as for arm, sewing over Rnds 22 and 23 of body.

Finishing

Wrap 12" length of ribbon around bear's neck and tie in bow at front. Pull rem length of ribbon through st at top of bear's left ear and tie into bow; trim ends. Glue 1 rose to center of each bow.

To hang bear, slip bottom of a wire ornament hanger through st at top of teddy bear's head. ❧

Oinker Claus Ornament

Design by Vicki Blizzard

If you have friends who collect pigs, then this whimsical ornament will make the perfect gift they'll be sure to appreciate and hang on their tree year after year.

Experience Level: Intermediate

Size: Approximately 6" high and 5" wide

Materials

❋ Worsted weight yarn: 1 oz each dark pink, red and white and small amount of black

❋ Size G/6 crochet hook or size needed to obtain gauge

❋ 8" length ¼"-wide green satin ribbon

❋ 15" length gold cord for hanger

❋ 2 (9mm) round black cabochons

❋ 1 ruby heart rhinestone

❋ Polyester fiberfill stuffing

❋ 3" compressed plastic foam ball

❋ Hot glue gun

❋ Tapestry needle

Gauge: Rnds 1 and 2 of snout = 1⅛" in diameter

To save time, take time to check gauge.

Pattern Note

Join rnds with a sl st unless otherwise stated.

Head

Note: Do not join rnds unless otherwise stated; mark first st of each rnd with safety pin or other small marker.

Rnd 1 (RS): Beg at top of head with dark pink, ch 2, 8 sc in 2nd ch from hook. (8 sc)

Rnd 2: 2 sc in each sc around. (16 sc)

Rnd 3: [Sc in next st, 2 sc in next st] rep around. (24 sc)

Rnd 4: [Sc in each of next 2 sts, 2 sc in next st] rep around. (32 sc)

Rnds 5–13: Sc in each sc around. Insert compressed plastic foam ball at end of Rnd 13 and work around it from this point on.

Rnd 14: [Sc in each of next 2 sts, sc dec] rep around. (24 sts)

Rnd 15: [Sc in next sc, sc dec] rep around. (16 sts)

Rnd 16: [Sc dec] rep around, join in beg sc dec, fasten off, leaving 12" end. (8 sts)

Weave end through last rnd, pull to close opening, knot securely.

Snout

Rnd 1: With dark pink, ch 2, 6 sc in 2nd ch from hook, join in beg sc. (6 sc)

Rnd 2: Ch 1, beg in same st as joining, 2 sc in each sc around, join in back lp only of beg sc. (12 sc)

Rnd 3: Working in back lps only this rnd, ch 1, sc in same st as joining and in each sc around, join in beg sc.

Rnds 4–6: Ch 1, sc in same st as joining and in each rem sc around, join in beg sc.

Row 7: Ch 5 for mouth, sc in 2nd ch from hook, hdc in next ch, dc in next ch, tr in next ch, sk 3 sc on Rnd 6, sl st in next sc, fasten off, leaving 12" end for sewing.

Ear *(make 2)*

Row 1: With dark pink, leaving a 12" end for sewing, ch 4, 4 dc in 4th ch from hook, turn. (5 dc, counting last 3 chs of beg ch-4 as first dc)

Row 2: Ch 2, sk first st, [dc dec] twice, turn.

Row 3: Ch 2, sk first st, dc dec, fasten off.

Hat

Rnd 1 (RS): With red, ch 4, 5 dc in 4th ch from hook, join in 4th ch of beg ch-4. (6 dc counting last 3 chs of beg ch-4 as first dc)

Rnd 2: Ch 3, dc in same st as joining, 2 dc in each rem dc around, join in 3rd ch of beg ch-3. (12 dc)

Rnd 3: Ch 3, 2 dc in next st, [dc in next st, 2 dc in next st] rep around, join in 3rd ch of beg ch-3. (18 dc)

Rnd 4: Ch 3, dc in next st, 2 dc in next st, [dc in each of next 2 sts, 2 dc in next st] rep around, join in 3rd ch of beg ch-3. (24 dc)

Rnd 5: Ch 3, dc in each of next 2 sts, 2 dc in next st, [dc in each of next 3 sts, 2 dc in next st] rep

Beard

Row 1: With white, leaving 24" end for sewing, ch 23, sc in 2nd ch from hook and in each rem ch across, turn. (22 sc)

Row 2: Sl st in first st, sc in each of next 2 sts, hdc in each of next 2 sts, dc in each of next 12 sts, hdc in each of next 2 sts, sc in each of next 2 sts, sl st in last st, turn. (22 sts)

Row 3: Sl st in each of first 3 sts, sc in each of next 2 sts, hdc in each of next 2 sts, dc in each of next 2 sts, 2 dc in each of next 4 sts, dc in each of next 2 sts, hdc in each of next 2 sts, sc in each of next 2 sts, sl st in each of last 3 sts, ch 1, turn. (26 sts)

Row 4: Sc in first st, [ch 4, sc in next st] rep across, fasten off.

Finishing

Using photo as a guide, with black, embroider 2 eyelashes on face and make 2 small straight stitches at center of snout for nostrils. Stuff snout lightly with fiberfill and sew to center of face with mouth at bottom. Glue cabochons to face next to eyelashes.

Sew beard to bottom of face.

Place hat on top of head, fold white brim to outside, sew hat to head with red end. Wrap a piece of white yarn 35 times around fingers of 1 hand. Slide lps off fingers and tie in center with a 12" piece of white. Cut open ends of lps. Fray ends of yarn and trim to make a pompom. Attach pompom to tip of hat. Fold tip of hat over and tack in place. Tie a bow with length of green ribbon; trim ends. Glue bow to hat brim. Glue heart rhinestone on top of bow.

Sew ears to hat, slightly under hat brim. Fold ears slightly over.

Attach gold cord to top of hat for hanger. ❧

around, join in 3rd ch of beg ch-3. (30 dc)

Rnd 6: Ch 3, dc in each of next 3 sts, 2 dc in next st, [dc in each of next 4 sts, 2 dc in next st] rep around, join in 3rd ch of beg ch-3. (36 dc)

Rnds 7–10: Ch 3, dc in each rem dc around, join in 3rd ch of beg ch-3, fasten off at end of Rnd 10,

leaving 24" end for sewing.

Rnd 11: With WS facing, attach white with sl st in last st of Rnd 10, ch 1, sc in same st and in each rem sc around, join in beg sc. (36 sc)

Rnds 12 & 13: Ch 1, sc in same st as joining and in each rem st around, join with a sl st in beg sc; at end of Rnd 13, fasten off.

Keepsakes Ornaments

Designs by Jo Ann Maxwell

Do you enjoy giving extra-special crocheted gifts for Christmas? If so, then consider giving your dearest friends this three-piece set of exquisite ornaments!

Experience Level: Intermediate

Finished Measurements: Fits 2¾"-diameter ornament

Pink Perfection
Materials

❋ Size 30 crochet cotton: 35 yds ecru

❋ Size 10 steel crochet hook or size needed to obtain gauge

❋ 2¾"-diameter pink satin ornament

❋ 2 feathers

❋ Several small sprigs dried baby's breath

❋ 7" ⅜"-wide pink satin ribbon

❋ 14" 1¼"-wide pink ribbon

❋ 2 (¾") pink satin roses with leaves

❋ 10 (½") white satin rosebuds with leaves

❋ 24" ⅛"-wide gold braid

❋ 6" gold thread

❋ ½" teardrop-pearl

❋ 2 ½" pink silk tassel

❋ Sewing needle and pink sewing thread

❋ Craft glue

Gauge: 10 sc = 1"

To save time, take time to check gauge.

Pink Perfection
Pattern Note

Join rnds with a sl st unless otherwise stated.

Pattern Stitches

Shell: [2 dc, ch 2, 2 dc] in indicated st or sp.

Beg shell: [Ch 3, dc, ch 2, 2 dc] in indicated st or sp.

P: Ch 3, sl st in last sc made.

V-st: [Dc, ch 2, dc] in indicated st or sp.

Ornament Cover

Rnd 1: Ch 5, join to form a ring, ch 1, 20 sc in ring, join in beg sc. (20 sc)

Rnd 2: Ch 4 (counts as first dc, ch 1), [dc in next sc, ch 1] rep around, join in 3rd ch of beg ch-4.

Rnd 3: Beg shell in same st as joining, *ch 1, sc in next dc, ch 1 **, shell in next dc, rep from * around, ending last rep at **, join in 3rd ch of beg ch-3. (10 shells)

Rnd 4: Sl st in next dc and in shell sp, ch 1, sc in same sp, ch 7, [sc in next shell sp, ch 7] rep around, join in beg sc.

Rnd 5: Ch 1, [sc, p] in same st as joining, *ch 3, V-st in next ch-7 sp, ch 3 **, [sc, p] in next sc, rep from * around, ending last rep at **, join in beg sc.

Rnd 6: Sl st in each of next 3 chs, in next dc and in V-st sp, ch 1, sc in same sp, ch 9, [sc in next V-st sp, ch 9] rep around, join in beg sc.

Rnd 7: *Sc in first ch of next ch-9 sp, [2 sc in next ch, sc in next ch] 4 times, sk next sc, rep from

* around, join in beg sc.

Rnd 8: Sl st in each of next 3 sc, *ch 3, sk 2 sc, shell in next sc, ch 3, sk 2 sc, sl st in each of next 7 sc, ch 4, sk 2 sc, sl st in next sc, ch 6, sk 1 sc, sl st in next sc, ch 4, sk 2 sc **, sl st in each of next 7 sc, rep from * around, ending last rep at **, sl st in each of next 3 sc, join in joining st of last rnd, fasten off.

Rnd 9: Attach thread with a sl st in any shell sp, ch 1, [sc, p] in same sp, *ch 9, [sc, p] in next ch-6 lp, ch 9 **, [sc, p] in next shell sp, rep from * around, ending last rep at **, join in beg sc.

Rnd 10: Sl st in each of next 5 chs, ch 13 (counts as first tr, ch -9), [tr in 5th ch of next ch-9 sp, ch 9] rep around, join in 4th ch of beg ch-13.

Slip ornament inside cover.

Rnd 11: Sl st in each of next 5

chs, ch 1, [sc, p] in same ch, ch 9, [{sc, p} in next ch-9 sp, ch 9] rep around, join in beg sc.

Rnd 12: Sl st in each of next 5 chs, ch 7 (counts as first tr, ch-3), [tr in next ch-9 sp, ch 3] rep around, join in 4th ch of beg ch-7.

Rnd 13: Sl st into first ch-3 sp, ch 1, sc in same sp, sc in each rem ch-3 sp around, join in beg sc, fasten off.

Finishing

Glue ends of ⅜"-wide ribbon to top of ornament to form hanging lp. Cut 1¼"-wide ribbon into 2 (7") lengths. Fold ends on 1 length to center; sew across center with sewing needle and pink thread. Pull thread to gather and form bow. Rep for rem length. Glue 1 bow to top of ornament on each side of hanging lp. Cut gold braid into 2 (12") lengths. Using photo as a guide, make 3 or 4

lps with gold braid, and glue to top of ornament on each side of bow. Glue 1 feather between ends of bows on each side. Glue 1 pink rose, 3 white rosebuds and dried baby's breath on each side. Make lp approximately 1" long with gold thread, string pearl onto lp and glue to top of ornament on either side. Glue tassel to bottom center of ornament; glue rem 4 white rosebuds around top of tassel.

Blue Enchantment

Pattern Note

Join rnds with a sl st unless otherwise stated.

Pattern Stitches

Trtr: Yo 4 times, insert hook in indicated st or sp, yo, draw up a lp, [yo, draw through 2 lps on hook] 5 times.

Scallop: Dc in indicated sp, [ch 1, dc] 4 times in same sp.

Blue Enchantment

Materials

- ❋ Size 30 crochet cotton: 35 yds ecru
- ❋ Size 10 steel crochet hook or size needed to obtain gauge
- ❋ 2¾"-diameter blue satin ornament
- ❋ 14" 1¼"-wide blue ribbon
- ❋ 2 feathers
- ❋ 7" ⅜"-wide blue satin ribbon
- ❋ 4 (1") pink satin roses with leaves
- ❋ 6 (½") white satin rosebuds with leaves
- ❋ Several small sprigs dried baby's breath
- ❋ 2 ½" blue silk tassel
- ❋ 1" pink teardrop crystal bead
- ❋ 24" ⅛"-wide gold braid
- ❋ 6" gold thread
- ❋ Sewing needle and blue sewing thread
- ❋ Craft glue

Gauge: 11 dc = 1"

To save time, take time to check gauge.

Ornament Cover

Rnd 1: Ch 5, join to form a ring, ch 3 (counts as first dc), 23 dc in ring, join in 3rd ch of beg ch-3. (24 dc)

Rnd 2: Ch 1, sc in same st as joining, ch 3, [sc in next dc, ch 3] rep around, join in beg sc. (24 ch-3 sps)

Rnd 3: Sl st in first ch-3 sp, ch 5 (counts as first dc, ch 2), [dc in next sp, ch 2] rep around, join in 3rd ch of beg ch-5.

Rnd 4: Sl st in first ch-2 sp, ch 1, sc in same sp, ch 3, [sc in next sp, ch 3] rep around, join in beg sc.

Rnd 5: Sl st in first ch-3 sp, ch 6 (counts as first dc, ch-3), [dc in next sp, ch 3] rep around, join in 3rd ch of beg ch-6.

Rnd 6: Sl st in first ch-3 sp, ch 1, sc in same sp, *scallop in next sp **, sc in next sp, rep from * around, ending last rep at **,

join in beg sc. (12 scallops)

Rnd 7: [Sl st in next dc, sl st in next sp] twice, sl st in next dc, ch 1, sc in same dc, ch 7, [sc in center dc of next scallop, ch 7] rep around, join in beg sc. (12 ch-7 sps)

Rnd 8: Sl st in each of next 3 chs, ch 7 (counts as first trtr, ch 1), sk 1 ch, trtr in next ch, *ch 5, trtr in 3rd ch of next ch-7 sp, ch 1, sk 1 ch, trtr in next ch, rep from * around, ending with ch 5, join in 6th ch of beg ch-7.

Rnd 9: Ch 3 (counts as first dc), dc in each ch and in each trtr around, join in 3rd ch of beg ch-3. (96 dc)

Rnd 10: Ch 1, sc in same st as joining, ch 3, [sk 3 dc, sc in next dc, ch 3] rep around, join in beg sc. (24 ch-3 sps)

Rnd 11: Rep Rnd 6.

Slip ornament inside cover.

Rnd 12: Rep Rnd 7.

Rnd 13: Sl st in each of next 4 chs, ch 1, sc in same ch, ch 3, [sc in next ch-7 sp, ch 3] rep around, join in beg sc.

Rnd 14: Sl st in ch-3 sp, ch 1, sc in same sp, sc in each rem sp around, join in beg sc, fasten off.

Finishing

Glue ends of ⅜"-wide ribbon to top of ornament to form hanging lp. Cut 1¼"-wide ribbon into 2 (7") lengths. Fold ends on 1 length to center; sew across center with sewing needle and blue thread. Pull thread to gather and form bow. Rep for rem length. Glue 1 bow to top of ornament on each side of hanging lp. Using photo as a guide, make 3 or 4 lps with gold braid, and glue to top of ornament on each side of bow. Glue 1 feather between ends of bows on each side. Glue 1 pink rose, 2 white rosebuds and sprigs of dried baby's breath on each side. Make lp approximately 1" long with gold thread, string crystal bead onto lp and glue to top of ornament on either side. Glue silk tassel to bottom center of ornament; alternating 1 pink rose and 1 white rosebud, glue rem 2 pink roses and 2 white rosebuds around top of tassel.

Golden Ball

Pattern Note

Join rnds with a sl st unless otherwise stated.

Pattern Stitches

Trtr: Yo 4 times, insert hook in indicated st, yo, draw up a lp, [yo, draw through 2 lps on hook] 5 times.

Shell: [2 dc, ch 2, 2 dc] in indicated st or sp.

Beg shell: [Ch 3, dc, ch 2, 2 dc] in indicated st or sp.

Continued on page 55

Little Angels

Blond Angel Design by Vida Sunderman

Cherub Ornament Design by Colleen Sullivan

Grace your tree with a little touch of heaven with either of these two darling angel ornaments! See photo on page 48.

Blond Angel

Experience Level: Intermediate

Finished Measurement: Approximately 4" tall

Materials

❋ Size 20 crochet cotton: small amount white

❋ Size 7 steel crochet hook or size needed to obtain gauge

❋ Small amount pale yellow 6-strand embroidery floss

❋ 10" ⅛"-wide white satin ribbon

❋ 5" length fused pearls

❋ Commercial fabric stiffener

❋ Cone-shaped plastic foam mold

❋ Small piece plastic wrap

❋ Cotton ball

❋ 12" floral wire

❋ Craft glue

Gauge: Halo = 1" in diameter

To save time, take time to check gauge.

Blond Angel

Pattern Note

Join rnds with a sl st unless otherwise stated.

Pattern Stitches

Beg ch-1 V-st: [Ch 4, dc] in indicated st or sp.

Ch-1 V-st: [Dc, ch 1, dc] in indicated st or sp.

Beg ch-2 V-st: [Ch 5, dc] in indicated st or sp.

Ch-2 V-st: [Dc, ch 2, dc] in indicated st or sp.

Beg shell: [Ch 3, dc, ch 2, 2 dc] in indicated st or sp.

Shell: [2 dc, ch 2, 2 dc] in indicated st or sp.

P: Ch 3, sl st in 3rd ch from hook.

Beg p shell: [Ch 3, 2 dc, p, 3 dc] in indicated st or sp.

P shell: [3 dc, p, 3 dc] in indicated st or sp.

Beg cl: Ch 3; holding back on hook last lp of each st, 3 dc in same st or sp, yo, draw through all 4 lps on hook.

Cl: Holding back on hook last lp of each st, work 4 dc in indicated st or sp, yo, draw through all 5 lps on hook.

Head

Rnd 1: Ch 2, 8 sc in 2nd ch from hook, do not join this or rem rnds of head unless otherwise stated; mark first st of each rnd with safety pin or other small marker.

Rnds 2 & 3: [Sc in next st, 2 sc in next st] rep around. (18 sc at end of Rnd 3)

Rnds 4–6: Sc in each sc around. (18 sc)

Rnd 7: [Sc in next sc, sc dec] rep around. (12 sts)

Rnd 8: [Sc in each of next 4 sts, sc dec] twice. (10 sts)

Rnd 9: Rep Rnd 4; join in beg sc. Stuff head with cotton ball.

Body

Rnd 10: Ch 1, sc in same st as joining, ch 1, [sc in next sc, ch 1] rep around, join in beg sc. (10 ch-1 sps)

Rnd 11: Sl st in first ch-1 sp, beg ch-1 V-st in same sp, ch 1, [ch-1 V-st in next sp, ch 1] rep around, join in 3rd ch of beg ch-4. (10 ch-1 V-sts)

Rnd 12: Sl st in first ch-1 V-st sp, beg ch-2 V-st in same sp, [ch 1, ch-2 V-st in next ch-1 sp, ch 1, ch-2 V-st in next V-st sp] twice, ch 1, sk next ch-1 sp, [ch-2 V-st in next V-st sp, ch 1] twice, sk next ch-1 sp, [ch-2 V-st in next V-st sp, ch 1, ch-2 V-st in next ch-1 sp, ch 1] twice, ch-2 V-st in next V-st sp, ch 1, sk next ch-1 sp, [ch-2 V-st in next V-st sp, ch 1] twice, join in 3rd ch of beg ch-5. (14 ch-2 V-sts)

First Wing

Rnd 1: Sl st in first V-st sp, beg shell in same sp, [ch 1, shell in next V-st sp] 4 times, ch 1, join in 3rd ch of beg ch-3.

Rnd 2: Sl st in next dc and in shell sp, beg p shell in same sp, sc in next ch-1 sp, [p shell in next shell sp, sc in next ch-1 sp] 3 times, [3 dc, p, 2 dc, ch 3, sl

Cherub Ornament

Experience Level: Intermediate

Finished Measurement: 3" x 5½"

Materials

❊ Size 10 crochet cotton: 65 yds white

❊ Size 7 steel crochet hook or size needed to obtain gauge

❊ Small amount polyester fiberfill

❊ Sewing needle and red and blue sewing thread

❊ Cosmetic blusher

❊ 1½"-diameter sisal wreath

❊ 20" ⅛"-wide pink satin ribbon

❊ Small amount dried baby's breath

❊ 12" silver metallic thread for hanger

❊ 2 pearl-topped straight pins

❊ 7 (¼") pink satin roses

❊ Craft glue

❊ Commercial fabric stiffener

❊ Tapestry needle

Gauge: In sc, 7 sts and 7 rows = 1"

To save time, take time to check gauge.

st] in next shell sp, sl st in each of next 2 dc of same shell, [ch 1, ch-2 V-st in next unworked V-st sp on Rnd 12 of body] twice.

Second Wing

Rnd 1: [Ch 1, shell in next V-st sp] 5 times, ch 1, join in top of first dc of first of last 5 shells made.

Rnd 2: Rep Rnd 2 of first wing, ending with ch 1, join in first dc of next shell on Rnd 1 of first wing.

Skirt

Rnd 1: Sl st in ch-1 sp at base of first wing, beg cl in same sp, *[ch 4, sc in next ch-1 sp, ch 4, cl in next V-st sp] twice, ch 4, sc in next ch-1 sp, ch 4 *, cl in next sp at base of 2nd wing, rep from * to *, join in top of beg cl. (6 cls)

Rnd 2: Sl st in each of next 2 chs of first ch-4 sp, ch 1, sc in same sp, [ch 4, sc in next ch-4 sp] rep around, ending with ch 2, hdc in beg sc to form last ch-4 sp. (12 ch-4 sps)

Rnd 3: Ch 1, sc in sp just formed, *ch 4, cl in next sp **, ch 4, sc in next sp, rep from * around, ending last rep at **, ch 2, hdc in beg sc to form last ch-4 sp. (6 cls)

Rnd 4: Ch 1, sc in sp just formed, [ch 4, sc in next ch-4 sp] rep around, ending with ch 2, hdc in beg sc to form last lp. (12 ch-4 sps)

Rnds 5–10: Rep Rnds 3 and 4 alternately 3 times.

Rnd 11: Ch 1, sc in sp just formed, *8 dc in next ch-4 sp, sc in next ch-4 sp, rep from * around, ending with 8 dc in last ch-4 sp, join in beg sc, fasten off.

Halo

Ch 15, join to form a ring, ch 1, [3 sc in ring, p] 9 times, join in beg sc,

Hair

Wrap 3-strand length of yellow

embroidery floss around floral wire, tape ends down, saturate in water and let dry thoroughly. Cut short lengths of curls and glue to top, sides and back of angel's head.

Finishing

Apply commercial fabric stiffener to halo and to angel. Place small piece of plastic wrap over plastic foam cone; place angel on cone to dry. Glue halo to top of angel's head. Wrap ribbon around angel's neck, lay length of fused pearls over ribbon and tie ribbon in bow over pearls at front neck.

Trim ends of bow to length.

Cherub Ornament

Pattern Note

Join rnds with a sl st unless otherwise stated.

Pattern Stitch

Knot st: Draw up lp on hook to approximately ¼" high, yo, draw through lp, insert hook between lp and long single strand alongside, yo, draw up a lp, complete sc.

Face

Rnd 1 (RS): Ch 2, 8 sc in 2nd ch from hook, do not join this or rem rnds unless otherwise stated; mark first st of each rnd with safety pin or other small marker.

Rnd 2: 2 sc in each st around. (16 sc)

Rnd 3: [Sc in next st, 2 sc in next st] rep around. (24 sc)

Rnd 4: [Sc in each of next 2 sts, 2 sc in next st] rep around. (32 sc)

Rnd 5: Sc in back lp only of each of next 15 sts for hairline, sc in both lps of each of next 17 sts for lower face, join in beg sc, fasten off.

Back of Head

Rnd 1: Rep Rnd 1 of face.

Rnds 2–4: Working in back lps only for all rnds, rep Rnds 2–4 of face.

Rnd 5: Working in back lps only, sc in each st around, join in beg sc, fasten off.

With WS tog, sew face and back of head tog through back lps only of Rnd 5, stuffing lightly with small amount of polyester fiberfill before closing. With double strands of sewing thread, using photo as a guide, embroider eyes and mouth on center of face.

Hair

Attach thread with a sl st in rem lp of first of 15 sts of hairline on Rnd 4 of face, *ch 2 (counts as first hdc), [knot st, hdc in next rem lp] 14 times, fasten off *. Working in 15 rem lps of Rnd 5 on back of head directly behind 15 rem lps just worked on face, attach thread with a sl st in first rem lp, rep from * to *. Continuing in pattern, work hair in rem lps of Rnds 3 and 1 on back of head.

Upper Bodice

Row 1: With RS of face facing, attach thread with a sl st in first rem lp of 17 sts of lower face on Rnd 5 of face, ch 3 (counts as first dc), dc in same st, 2 dc in each of next 16 sts, ch 1, turn. (34 dc)

First Wing

Row 1: Sc in each of first 8 dc, ch 1, turn.

Row 2: Sc in each sc across, ch 1, turn.

Row 3: Sc in each sc across to last st, leave last st unworked, ch 1, turn.

Rows 4–11: Reps Rows 2 and 3 alternately. (3 sc at end of Row 11)

Row 12: Sk first sc, sc in each of next 2 sc, fasten off.

Second Wing

Row 1: With RS of face facing, attach thread with a sl st in first st on Row 1 of upper bodice at opposite end, ch 1, sc in same st and in each of next 7 sts, ch 1, turn.

Rows 2–12: Rep Rows 2–12 of first wing.

Lower Bodice

With RS of face facing, attach thread with a sl st in first unworked dc on Row 1 of upper bodice between wings, ch 3 (counts as first dc), dc in each of next 17 sts across, fasten off. (18 dc)

Edging

With RS of face facing, attach thread with a sl st in sc at upper right corner of 2nd wing, ch 3, 2 dc in same st, sl st in next st, *[3 dc over end st of next row, sl st over end st of next row] rep across wing *, 3 dc in first st of lower bodice, [sk next st, sl st in next st, sk next st, 3 dc in next st] rep across lower bodice, sl st over end st of next row of first wing, rep from * to *, ending with 3 dc in last sc on last row of first wing, fasten off.

Finishing

Apply fabric stiffener to bodice and wings only; allow to dry.

Glue 6 roses evenly sp around wreath. Wrap 12" length of ribbon around wreath between roses; glue ends in place. Glue baby's breath around wreath.

Knot ends of metallic thread to form lp. Pull knotted end of lp through center top of back of head between rnds of hair; pull other end of lp through lp just made; pull to tighten. Slide wreath down over hanger and secure to top of head with two pearl-topped pins. Make bow with rem piece of ribbon; trim ends to desired length. Glue bow to center front of upper bodice; glue rem rose over center of bow.

Apply blusher to cheeks.

Popcorn Cranberry Garland

Design by Colleen Sullivan

Trim the Christmas tree with a pretty garland of popcorns and cranberry-colored beads. It's quick and easy to crochet and lots of fun to hang!

Experience Level: Beginner

Finished Measurement: Any length desired

Materials

※ Worsted weight yarn: 3¾ yds white makes popcorn

※ Size G/6 crochet hook or size needed to obtain gauge

※ 5 (8mm) red beads for each popcorn

※ Tapestry needle

※ Dental floss or thread for stringing popcorn and beads

Gauge: Popcorn = 1½" in diameter

To save time, take time to check gauge.

Pattern Stitch

Cl: Holding back on hook last lp of each st, work 2 dc in indicated st, yo, draw through all 3 lps on hook.

Popcorn

Row 1: Ch 5, sc in 2nd ch from hook, sc in each rem sc across, turn. (4 sc)

Row 2: Sl st in first st, *ch 2, [cl, sl st] in same st **, sl st in next st, rep from * across, ending last rep at **; working across rem lps of foundation ch, sl st in rem lp at base of last cl made, rep from * across, ending last rep at **, fasten off, leaving a 6" length. (8 cls)

With tapestry needle, weave 6" length through sc sts of Row 1, pull tightly to gather, secure with several small sts, fasten off.

Make as many popcorns as needed for length, allowing for 5 beads between each pair of popcorns.

Finishing

With tapestry needle and dental floss or thread, [string 1 popcorn and 5 beads] rep for desired length, ending with popcorn. ❧

Old-Time Treasures

Designs by Rose Pirrone

These easy-to-crochet ornaments have an unusual woven appearance. Crochet a dozen in various colors and sizes!

Experience Level: Beginner

Finished Measurements

Ornament 1: 2½" x 1¾" oval, excluding top and tassel

Ornament 2: 3" x 2½" oval, excluding top and tassel

Materials

❋ DMC #3 pearl cotton: 1 skein mauve #3687 for Ornament 1, 1 skein garnet #902 for Ornament 2

❋ DMC antique gold metallic thread: 1 spool for Ornament 1

❋ DMC gold metallic thread: 2 spools for Ornament 2

❋ Steel crochet hook size 1

❋ Steel crochet hook size 10

❋ 2½" x 1¾" plastic foam egg for Ornament 1

❋ 3" x 2½" plastic foam egg for Ornament 2

❋ 2 (8mm) corrugated disks (rondels) with large holes by the Beadery (for Ornament 1)

❋ 3 (7mm) gold metallic disks (rondels) by The Beadery (for Ornament 2)

❋ 9mm rosebud antiqued gold-washed bead by The Beadery (for Ornament 1)

❋ 8mm round gold metallic bead #715 by The Beadery (for Ornament 2)

❋ 9" dusty rose rosebud trim #7062-33 H.P. by Novtex (for Ornament 1)

❋ 9" ¼"-wide green and gold holiday trim #7528-36 H.P. by Novtex for ornament 2

❋ Craft glue

❋ 2 straight pins for each ornament

❋ Pearl-head corsage pin

❋ Scissors

❋ Yardstick

❋ Toothpicks

❋ 2½" x 4" piece of cardboard for Ornament 1

❋ 3" x 4" piece of cardboard for Ornament 2

❋ Cotton swabs

Gauge: Work evenly and consistently throughout

Ornament 1

With larger hook and 1 strand pearl cotton and 1 strand metallic thread held tog, make a ch approximately 4½ yds long, do not fasten off.

Assembly

With toothpick, apply dab of glue to top (wide end) of plastic foam egg. Push beg end of ch into top of egg with tip of scissors. Push pearl-head pin into bottom of egg as visual guide to help keep wrapping even. Applying small amount of glue at a time, begin wrapping egg, keeping flat side of ch against egg and ridged side up. Do not stretch ch; lay ch on top of glue, pressing lightly against egg and turning egg with other hand. If glue gets on top of ch, remove lightly with wet cotton swab. If glue gets on fingers, remove glue with damp cloth. If ch does not completely cover egg, work additional chs to cover, fasten off.

If ch is too long, rip out excess chs, fasten off. Remove pearl-head pin from bottom of egg; push end of ch into egg.

Hanging Loop

With metallic thread only and smaller hook, make a ch approximately 7" long, sl st in first ch, fasten off. Tie ends of thread tog with double knot; trim to approximately ¼". Push straight pin through knot. With smaller hook, pull opposite end of lp through rondel and rosebud bead. Apply small amount of glue between rondel and rosebud bead and to bottom of rondel. Coat straight pin with glue and push down into top of egg.

Tassel

Cut 2 (9") lengths metallic thread and lay across longer edge of cardboard. Measure 18-yd length

of gold metallic thread; wrap around shorter width of cardboard over 2 (9") lengths at top. Knot 9" lengths tightly. Cut through strands at bottom of cardboard. Cut 2 (12") lengths metallic thread and wrap 3 or 4 times around tassel approximately ⅜" down from top. Knot tightly and tuck ends inside tassel. Trim ends of tie at top to approximately ¼". Push straight pin through knot at top of tassel, covering head of pin entirely inside tassel. Put dab of

glue on top of tassel and push pin through rondel. Coat pin and top of rondel with glue and push pin into bottom of egg. Trim ends of tassel if necessary.

Finishing
Glue trim around center of egg, cutting off excess if necessary.

Ornament 2

With larger hook and 1 strand pearl cotton and 1 strand metallic thread held tog, make a ch approximately 5½ yds long, do not fasten off. To flatten sides

of plastic foam egg, place egg on hard surface; press down with palm of hand. Rep on opposite side. Follow directions for assembly, hanging lp, tassel and finishing of Ornament 1, with the following exceptions: For hanging lp, make a ch 8" long instead of 7" long, pulling lp at opposite end from double knot through 1 rondel, 8mm gold metallic bead and 2nd rondel; for tassel, cut 20-yd length of gold metallic thread instead of 18-yd length. ❧

Cherub Enchantment

Designs by Sandy Abbate

Capture the enchantment of Christmas with this set of blissfully sleeping cherubs! They make a lovely gift for new parents!

Experience Level: Intermediate

Size: 4½" high

Materials

❋ Fingering weight yarn: 1 skein pink and 1 skein each yellow, white and blue pompadour

❋ Size B/1 crochet hook or size needed to obtain gauge

❋ Size 3 or thin knitting needle

❋ 2 gold pipe cleaners

❋ 1 yd ⅜"-wide red satin ribbon

❋ 12" ⅜"-wide blue satin ribbon

❋ Tapestry needle

❋ Polyester fiberfill

❋ Small amounts blue, red, pink and light tan 6-strand embroidery floss

❋ Small amount cosmetic blusher

❋ Safety pin or other small marker

Gauge: In dc, 6 sts and 3 rows = 1"

To save time, take time to check gauge.

Pattern Note

Join rnds with a sl st unless otherwise stated.

Girl Cherub

Head

Rnd 1: Beg at center back, with pink, ch 2, work 6 sc in 2nd ch from hook, do not join this or rem rnds unless otherwise stated; mark first st of each rnd with safety pin or other small marker. (6 sc)

Rnd 2: 2 sc in each st around. (12 sc)

Rnd 3: [Sc in next st, 2 sc in next st] rep around. (18 sc)

Rnd 4: [Sc in each of next 2 sts, 2 sc in next st] rep around. (24 sc)

Rnds 5–9: Sc in each sc around.

Rnd 10: [Sc in each of next 2 sts, sc dec] rep around. (18 sts)

Rnd 11: [Sc in next st, sc dec] rep around, join in beg sc, fasten off. (12 sts)

Body

Rnd 1: Attach white with a sl st in joining st of last rnd of head at center back, ch 1, beg in same st, sc in each st around, join in beg sc. (12 sc)

Rnd 2: Ch 3 (counts as first dc throughout), 2 dc in next st, [dc in next st, 2 dc in next st] rep around, join in 3rd ch of beg ch-3. (18 dc)

Rnd 3: Ch 3, dc in next st, 2 dc in next st, [dc in each of next 2 sts, 2 dc in next st] rep around, join in 3rd ch of beg ch-3. (24 dc)

Rnd 4: Ch 3, dc in each of next 2 sts, 2 dc in next st, [dc in each of next 3 sts, 2 dc in next st] rep around, join in 3rd ch of beg ch-3. (30 dc)

Rnds 5–7: Ch 3, dc in each rem dc around. (30 dc)

Rnd 8: Ch 3, dc in each of next 2 sts, dc dec, [dc in each of next 3 sts, dc dec] rep around, join in 3rd ch of beg ch-3. (24 sts)

Rnd 9: Ch 4 (counts as first dc, ch-1), sk next st, [dc in next st, ch 1, sk next st] rep around, join in 3rd ch of beg ch-4.

Rnd 10: Sl st into first ch-1 sp, ch 1, beg in same sp, [sc, ch 3, sc] in each ch-1 sp around, join in beg sc, fasten off.

Stuff head and body. Weave 9" length red ribbon through ch-1 sps of Rnd 9 of body; tie in bow at front. Wrap 9" length ribbon around neck; tie in bow at front.

Skirt

With white, ch 36; taking care not to twist ch, join to form a ring, ch 1, sc in same st as joining, ch 3, [sc in next ch, ch 3] rep around, join with a sl st in beg sc, fasten off, leaving an 18" length for sewing. With tapestry needle, sew skirt to body between Rnds 5 and 6.

Arm (*make 2*)

Rnd 1: With white, ch 4, 8 dc in 4th ch from hook, join in 4th ch of beg ch-4. (9 dc, counting last 3 chs of beg ch-4 as first dc)

Rnds 2–4: Ch 3, dc in each rem dc around, join in 3rd ch of beg ch-3. (9 dc)

Rnd 5: Working in front lps only this rnd, ch 1, sc in same st as joining, ch 3, [sc in next st, ch 3] rep around, join in beg sc, fasten off.

Stuff arm lightly.

Hand

Working in rem lps of Rnd 4 of arm, attach pink with a sl st in any rem lp, ch 3, dc in each rem st around, join in 3rd ch of beg ch-3, fasten off, leaving an 8" length. With tapestry needle, weave 8" length through tops of sts, pull tightly to gather, fasten off.

Sew 1 arm at each side of body over Rnd 2.

Hair

Wrap lengths of yellow yarn closely around knitting needle until needle is completely covered, wet yarn and place in oven on low setting for approximately 20 minutes; let cool and remove from needle when yarn is dry.

Cut curls in 1" lengths. Using crochet hook, pull curls through sts at top of head; make knot at center. Cover top, back and sides of head with curls, leaving opening off-center at right side of head for face. Cut 6" length red ribbon; tie in bow through st at top right of head between curls.

Wings
First Wing

Row 1: With white, ch 6, join to form a ring, ch 6 (counts as first dc, ch-3), [dc, ch 1, dc, ch 3, dc] in ring, turn.

Row 2: Ch 5, sc in first ch-3 sp, ch 5, sc in next dc, ch 5, sc in next ch-1 sp, ch 5, sc in next dc, ch 5, sc in next ch-6 sp, ch 5, sc in 3rd ch of ch-6, turn.

Row 3: [Ch 5, sc in next ch-5 sp] 6 times, ch 2, dc in top of end st of Row 1, turn.

Row 4: Ch 1, sc in ch-2 sp, [ch 5, sc in next ch-5 sp] 6 times, do not fasten off.

Second Wing

Row 1: Sl st down side of first wing to ch-6 ring of base of Row 1 of first wing, sl st in ch-6 ring, working on opposite side of

Continued on page 57

Keepsake Ornaments

Continued from page 46

P: Ch 3, sl st in last sc made.

Ornament Cover

Rnd 1: Ch 5, join to form a ring, ch 3 (counts as first dc throughout), 19 dc in ring, join in 3rd ch of beg ch-3. (20 dc)

Rnd 2: Ch 9 (counts as first trtr, ch-3), [trtr in next dc, ch 3] rep around, join in 6th ch of beg ch-9.

Rnd 3: Beg shell in same st as joining, *ch 3, sc in next trtr, ch 3 **, shell in next trtr, rep from * around, ending last rep at **, join in 3rd ch of beg ch-3. (10 shells)

Rnd 4: Sl st in next dc and in shell sp, ch 1, sc in same sp, *ch 15, sl st in 10th ch from hook, ch 5 **, sc in next shell sp, rep from * around, ending last rep at **, join in beg sc.

Rnd 5: *Sc in each of next 5 chs, sl st in next ch at base of ch-9 lp, sc in first ch of ch-9 lp, [2 sc in next ch, {sc, p} in next ch] 3 times, 2 sc in next ch, sc in last ch of ch-9 lp, sl st in next ch at base of ch-9 lp, sc in each of next 5 chs **, sl st in next sc, rep from * around, ending last rep at **, join in joining st of last rnd, fasten off.

Rnd 6: Attach thread with a sl st in center p of 3-p group on any ch-9 lp, ch 1, sc in same st, ch 7, [sc in center p of next 3-p group, ch 7] rep around, join in beg sc.

Rnd 7: Ch 1, sc in same st as joining, *ch 3, shell in 4th ch of next ch-7 sp, ch 3 **, sc in next sc, rep from * around, ending last rep at **, join in beg sc.

Slip ornament inside cover.

Rnd 8: Sl st in each of next 3 chs, in each of next 2 dc and in

Golden Ball

Materials

❋ Size 30 crochet cotton: 35 yds ecru
❋ Size 10 steel crochet hook or size needed to obtain gauge
❋ 2¾"-diameter gold satin ornament
❋ 2 feathers
❋ 14" 1¼"-wide gold wire-edge ribbon
❋ 7" ⅜"-wide burgundy satin ribbon
❋ 6 (1¼)" pink satin roses with leaves
❋ 4 (½") white satin rosebuds with leaves
❋ Several small sprigs dried baby's breath
❋ 2½" burgundy silk tassel
❋ Sewing needle and gold sewing thread
❋ Craft glue

Gauge: 10 sc = 1"

To save time, take time to check gauge.

shell sp, ch 6 (counts as first trtr), trtr in same sp, ch 1, [2 trtr in next shell sp, ch 1] rep around, join in 6th ch of beg ch-6.

Rnd 9: Sl st in next trtr and in ch-1 sp, ch 1, sc in same sp, sc in each rem ch-1 sp around, join in beg sc, fasten off.

Finishing

Glue ends of ⅜"-wide ribbon to top of ornament to form hanging lp. Cut 1¼"-wide ribbon into 2 (7") lengths. Fold ends on 1 length to center; sew across center with sewing needle and gold thread. Pull thread to gather and form bow. Rep for rem length. Glue 1 bow to top of ornament on each side of hanging lp. Using photo as a guide, glue 1 feather between ends of bows on each side; glue 1 pink rose, 2 white rosebuds and sprigs of dried baby's breath on each side. Glue silk tassel to bottom center of ornament; glue rem 4 pink roses around top of tassel. ❧

Snow Crystals

Designs by Vicki Blizzard

You'll always enjoy a white Christmas with this set of sparkling snowflake ornaments! Stitch a dozen to adorn your tree!

Experience Level: Intermediate

Finished Measurement: Approximately 5½" across widest point

Materials

Makes 1 snowflake

※ Size 10 crochet cotton: small amount white

※ Size D/3 crochet hook or size needed to obtain gauge

※ 1"-diameter white plastic ring

※ Clear thread for hanging lp

※ Ultra-fine iridescent glitter

※ Commercial fabric stiffener

※ Cardboard or plastic foam board

※ Rustproof pins

※ Plastic wrap

※ Safety pin or other small marker

Gauge: Rnds 1 and 2 of Snowflake 1 = 2¼" in diameter

To save time, take time to check gauge.

Pattern Notes

Join rnds with a sl st unless otherwise stated.

All snowflakes are worked with 2 strands cotton held tog throughout.

Pattern Stitches

Picot 3 (p3): Ch 3, sl st in 3rd ch from hook.

Picot 5 (p5): Ch 5, sl st in 5th ch from hook.

Picot 7 (p7): Ch 7, sl st in 7th ch from hook.

Picot 8 (p8): Ch 8, sl st in 8th ch from hook.

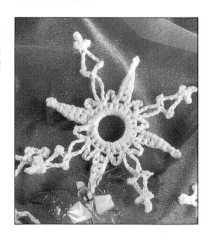

Snowflake 1

Rnd 1: Attach white to plastic ring with a sl st, ch 1, 24 sc over ring, join in beg sc. (24 sc)

Rnd 2: Ch 1, sc in same st as joining, ch 4, [sk next sc, sc in next sc, ch 4] rep around, ending with sk last sc, join in beg sc. (12 ch-4 lps)

Rnd 3: *Ch 6, p7, place marker at base of p7 just made, [p5] 3 times, p7, sl st in marked st, ch 6, sl st in next sc, ch 3, p3, ch 3 **, sl st in next sc, rep from * around, ending last rep at **, join in joining st of Rnd 2, fasten off.

Snowflake 2

Rnd 1: Rep Rnd 1 of Snowflake 1.

Rnd 2: *Ch 5, sk next 2 sc, [sl st, ch 4, p3, ch 4, p3, place marker at base of p3 just made, {p3} twice, sl st in marked st, ch 4, p3, ch 4, sl st] in next st, ch 5, sk next 2 sc **, [sl st, ch 8, p8, ch 8, sl st] in next st, rep from * around, ending last rep at **, [sl st, ch 8, p8, ch 8, sl st] in joining st of Rnd 1, fasten off.

Snowflake 3

Rnd 1: Rep Rnd 1 of Snowflake 1.

Rnd 2: *Ch 10, sl st in 5th ch from hook, sc in next ch, hdc in next ch, dc in each of next 3 chs, sk next sc on Rnd 1, sl st in next sc, ch 5, sk next sc on Rnd 1, [sl st, ch 4, p3, ch 2, p3, place marker at base of p3 just made, {p3} twice, sl st in marked st, ch 2, p3, sl st at base of next p3, ch 4, sl st] in next sc on Rnd 1, ch 5, sk next sc on Rnd 1 **, sl st in next sc, rep from * around, ending last rep at **, join in joining st of Rnd 1, fasten off.

Finishing

Cover cardboard or plastic foam board with plastic wrap. Apply commercial fabric stiffener to 1 side of each snowflake and pin to board with wet side up. While wet, sprinkle snowflakes lightly with iridescent glitter. When dry, remove snowflakes from board; apply fabric stiffener to opposite sides. Pin snowflakes to board; sprinkle with glitter while wet. Let dry thoroughly. Attach clear thread at tip of any point on last rnd of each snowflake for hanging lp. ❧

Cherub Enchantment

Continued from page 54

ring, ch 6, [dc, ch 1, dc, ch 3, dc] in ring, turn.

Rows 2–4: Rep Rows 2–4 of first wing; at end of Row 4, fasten off.

Hanger

Attach white with a sl st in ch-6 ring between wings on either side, ch 40, sl st in beg sl st in ring, fasten off. With hanger at top, sew wings to center back of body just below neck.

Finishing

Using photo as a guide, embroider 2 eyes with blue embroidery floss, nose with pink embroidery floss, and mouth with red embroidery floss. Bend pipe cleaner into circle for halo, leaving ½" free at 1 end; insert end into head at back.

Apply blusher to cheeks. Tie bow with rem piece of red ribbon over dc at center back body above ruffle and below wings; trim ends to desired length.

Boy Cherub

Head

Rnds 1–11: Rep Rnds 1–11 of head for Girl Cherub.

Body

Rnds 1–10: With blue, rep Rnds 1–10 of body for Girl Cherub.

Stuff head and body. Weave 9" length blue ribbon through ch-1 sps of Rnd 9 of body; tie in bow at front; trim ends to length.

Neck Ruffle

With blue, ch 19, sc in 2nd ch from hook, [ch 3, sc in next ch] rep across, do not fasten off; place ruffle around cherub's neck, join in beg sc, fasten off.

Arm *(make 2)*

Rnds 1–5: With blue, rep Rnds 1–5 of arm for Girl Cherub.

Stuff arms lightly.

Hand

Work as for hand for Girl Cherub. Sew 1 arm at each side of body over Rnd 2.

Hair

Work as for hair for Girl Cherub, covering top of head, leaving sides and back uncovered.

Wings

Work as for wings for Girl Cherub.

Hanger

Work as for hanger for Girl Cherub.

Using photo as a guide, embroider 2 straight sts with light tan embroidery floss for eyes.

Tack cherub's left hand to area on face where mouth would be. Apply blusher to cheeks. Make halo with gold pipe cleaner as for Girl Cherub and insert in top of head. ❧

Skirts & Stockings

Delight your loved ones by making each of them a special crocheted stocking to use year after year! And, a handsome tree skirt makes the perfect background for a mountain of sparkling presents!

Americana Set

Designs by Heléne Rush

Crocheted with rich, flecked yarn in warm country colors, this handsome tree skirt and stocking set will add to the pleasant look and feel of your holiday home.

Experience Level: Intermediate

Finished Measurements

Tree skirt: Approximately 64" in diameter

Stocking: Approximately 18" long

Materials

❋ Red Heart Super Saver worsted weight yarn (6 oz per skein): 3 skeins each hunter fleck #4389 (A), burgundy fleck #4376 (B) and buff fleck #4334 (C)

❋ Size J/10 crochet hook or size needed to obtain gauge

❋ Tapestry needle

Gauge: 13 sts and 16 rows = 4" in sc

To save time, take time to check gauge.

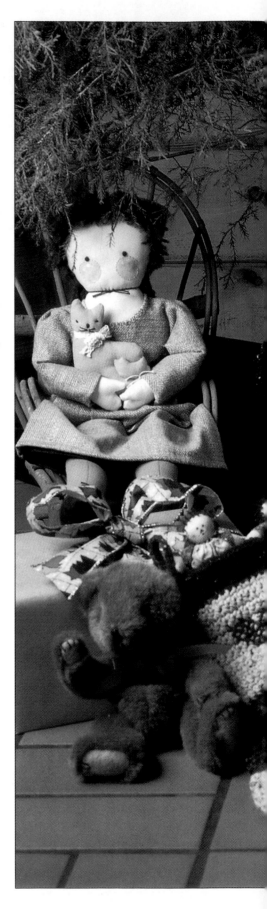

Pattern Notes

To change color in sc, insert hook in last st before color change, yo with working color, draw up a lp, drop working color to WS, yo with or pick up dropped lp of next color, complete sc.

To change color in dc, work last dc before color change until last 2 lps before final yo rem on hook, drop working color to WS, yo with next color, complete dc.

Tree Skirt

Panel *(make 6)*

Row 1: With B, ch 20, sc in 2nd ch from hook, [ch 2, sk next 2 chs, sc in next ch] rep across, changing to A in last sc, do not fasten off B; turn. (6 ch-2 sps)

Row 2 (RS): Ch 3 (counts as first dc throughout), [3 dc in next sp] rep across, ending with dc in last sc, remove hook from lp, do not turn. (20 dc)

Row 3: Insert hook in top of beg ch-3, yo with B, draw through st on hook, ch 1, sc in same st, [ch 3, sk next 3 dc, sc between 3rd sk dc and next dc] rep across to last 4 sts, ending with ch 3, sk next 3 dc, sc in last dc, changing to A, do not fasten off B; turn. (6 ch-3 sps)

Row 4: Ch 3, 2 dc in first sc, [3 dc in next ch-3 sp] rep across, ending with 3 dc in last sc, remove hook from lp, do not turn. (24 dc)

Row 5: Insert hook in top of beg ch-3, yo with B, draw through st on hook, ch 1, sc in same st, ch 2, sk next 2 dc, sc between 2nd sk dc and next dc, [ch 3, sk next 3 dc, sc between 3rd sk dc and next dc] rep across to last 3 dc, ch 2, sk next 2 dc, sc in last dc, changing to A, do not fasten off B; turn. (8 sps)

Row 6: Ch 3, [3 dc in next sp] rep across, ending with dc in last

sc, remove hook from lp, do not turn. (26 dc)

Rows 7–46: Rep Rows 3–6 alternately, at end of Row 46, fasten off A. (86 dc at end of Row 46)

Panel border

Row 1: Insert hook in top of beg ch-3, yo with B, draw through st on hook, ch 1, sc in same st, sc in each rem st across, changing to C in last st, fasten off B, ch 1, turn. (86 sc)

Row 2: Sc in each sc across, ch 1, turn.

Row 3: Sc in each sc across, working 2 sc in first and last sc of row, ch 1, turn. (88 sc)

Rows 4 & 5: Rep Row 2.

Rows 6–17: Rep Rows 3–5 alternately, fasten off at end of Row 17. (96 sc on each of last 3 rows)

Assembly

With WS tog, sc panels tog on RS across long edges with B. Do not join 2nd long edge of first panel to 2nd long edge of last panel for back opening.

Edging & Ties

Row 1: With RS facing, attach B with a sl st at top left back opening, working over ends of rows, [ch 30 for tie, sl st in 2nd ch from hook and in each rem ch across, sc evenly sp ¼ of the way down back opening] 4 times, 3 sc in corner st, sc across bottom, working 3 sc at each seam, 3 sc in next corner, sc evenly sp across row ends up right back opening, working 4 ties to correspond to placement of ties on left back opening, fasten off.

Row 2: With RS facing, attach B with a sl st in corner sc at bottom right corner, ch 1, sc in same st, ch 2, *[sk 2 sc, sc in next sc, ch

2] rep across to 3 sc at seam, adjusting number of sts sk at end of rep if necessary so pattern rep comes out even, sc in first of 3 sc, ch 2, sk next sc, sc in next sc, ch 2, rep from * across, ending   with [sk 2 sc, sc in next sc, ch 2] rep across to opposite bottom corner, adjusting number of sts sk at end of rep if necessary so pattern rep comes out even, sc in corner st, changing to A, fasten off B, turn.

Row 3: Ch 3, [3 dc in next sp] rep across, dc in last sc, changing to B, fasten off A, ch 1, turn.

Row 4: Sc in first st, [ch 4, sk next 3 dc, sc between 3rd sk dc and next dc] rep across to last 4 dc, ch 4, sk next 3 dc, sc in last dc, fasten off.

Finishing
Embroidery

Chart A

```
COLOR AND STITCH KEY
⊠ A (cross-stitch)
⊙ B (cross-stitch)
☐ C (sc)
```

Following the chart above, work cross-stitch on last 16 rows of panel border on each panel as follows: Center first heart on any panel, placing lowest st on 7th row from bottom of panel border, then alternate [tree, heart, tree] on each side of center heart, leaving 4 sts free between each. Place lowest st of tree on 4th row from bottom of panel border.

Stocking
Cuff

Row 1 (RS): With C, ch 50, sc in 2nd ch from hook and in each rem ch across, ch 1, turn. (49 sc)

Rows 2–16: Sc in each sc across, ch 1, turn, at end of Row 16, change to B in last sc, fasten off C, ch 1, turn.

Upper Stocking

Row 17: Sc in first st and in each rem st across, ch 1, turn. (49 sc)

Row 18: Sc in first st, [ch 2, sk 2 sc, sc in next sc] rep across, changing to A in last sc, do not fasten off B; turn. (16 ch-2 sps)

Row 19: Ch 3 (counts as first dc throughout), [3 dc in next sp] rep across, dc in last sc, remove hook from lp, do not fasten off, do not turn. (50 dc)

Row 20: Insert hook in 3rd ch of beg ch-3, yo with B, draw through st on hook, ch 1, sc in same st, [ch 3, sk next 3 dc, sc between 3rd sk dc and next dc] rep across to last 4 dc, ch 3, sk next 3 dc, sc in last dc, changing to A, do not fasten off B, turn.

Rep Rows 19 and 20 until piece measures 10½" from beg of cuff, ending with a Row 19, fasten off A and B.

Heel
First Half

Row 1: With RS facing, attach C in first st of last row, ch 1, sc in same st and in each of next 11 sts, ch 1, turn.

Rows 2–6: Sc in each sc across, ch 1, turn. (12 sc)

Shape heel

Row 7: Sc in each of first 5 sts, sc dec, leaving rem sts unworked, ch 1, turn. (6 sts)

Continued on page 69

Little Stockings Set

Designs by Ann E. Smith

You'll love using this charming tree skirt with matching stocking year after year! Dainty stockings and a pretty edging make them a delight to crochet and display.

Experience Level: Intermediate

Finished Measurements

Stocking: 13" long

Tree Skirt: 22" deep

Materials

❊ J. & P. Coats Luster Sheen 100 percent acrylic yarn (1¾ oz per ball): 11 balls rally red #910 (MC) and 10 balls white/pearl #0001P (CC)

❊ Size E/4 crochet hook or size needed to obtain gauge

❊ Tapestry needle

Gauge: 21 sts and 24 rows = 4" in sc

To save time, take time to check gauge.

Pattern Notes

Join rnds with a sl st unless otherwise stated.

To change color in sc, insert hook in indicated st, yo with working color, draw up a lp, drop working color to WS, yo with next color, complete sc. Do not carry color not in use across WS of work. Use bobbins or wind small balls of yarn for each separate color section.

When working from charts, read even-numbered (RS) rows from right to left, read odd-numbered (WS) rows from left to right.

Pattern Stitches

Puff st: [Yo, draw up a lp] 5 times in indicated st, yo, draw through all 11 lps on hook.

X-st: Sk next unworked st, hdc in next st, hdc in sk st.

Tree Skirt

Panel (*make 5*)

Border

Row 1 (WS): Beg at lower edge with MC, ch 129, sc in 2nd ch from hook and in each rem ch across, ch 1, turn. (128 sc)

Row 2: Sc in each of first 41 sc with MC, changing to CC in last st, sc in each of next 3 sc with CC, changing to MC in 3rd st, [sc in each of next 21 sc with MC, changing to CC in last st, sc in each of next 3 sts with CC, changing to MC in 3rd st] twice, sc in each of last 36 sts with MC, ch 1, turn. (128 sc)

Row 3: Work from chart A (page 64).

Row 4: Sc dec, work from the chart across to last 2 sts, sc dec, ch 1, turn. (126 sts)

Rows 5–18: Follow chart A, working decs as indicated; at end of Row 18, fasten off. (118 sts on Row 18)

Body

Row 1: With RS facing, attach MC with a sl st in first sc of last row at right edge, ch 2 (counts as first hdc throughout), [X-st over next 2 sts] rep across, ending with hdc in last st, ch 1, turn. (58 X-sts; 1 hdc at each edge)

Row 2: Sk first st, sl st in next st, ch 2, [X-st over next 2 hdc] rep across to last 2 sts, hdc in next st, leave last st unworked, fasten off, turn. (57 X-sts; 1 hdc at each edge)

Row 3: With RS facing, attach CC with a sl st in 2nd st at right edge, ch 2, [X-st over next 2 hdc] rep across to last 2 sts, hdc in next st, leave last st unworked, ch 1, turn. (56 X-sts; 1 hdc at each edge)

Row 4: Rep Row 2. (55 X-sts; 1 hdc at each edge)

Row 5: With MC, rep Row 3. (54 X-sts; 1 hdc at each edge)

Row 6: Rep Row 2. (53 X-sts; 1 hdc at each edge)

Rows 7–44: Rep Rows 3–6 alternately, ending with a Row 4; at end of Row 44, fasten off. (15 X-sts with 1 hdc at each edge at end of Row 44)

Assembly

Matching stripes, weave panels tog with tapestry needle. Do not sew 2nd edge of 5th panel to 2nd edge of 1st panel.

Top Edging

With RS facing, attach MC with a sl st in first hdc at right edge, ch 3 (counts as first dc), dc in each hdc across, fasten off.

Bottom Edging

Row 1: With RS facing, attach MC with a sl st in first rem lp of

Chart A
(left half)

Row 15

Row 5

Row 3

Row 1

foundation ch of border at right edge, ch 1, sc in same st as join, *ch 5, sc in each of next 5 sts, rep from * across, ending with ch 5, sc in last st, adjusting number of sts sk at end of row, if necessary, so there is an uneven number of ch-5 lps, ch 1, turn.

Row 2: Sc in first sc, *ch 3, 3 sc in next ch-5 lp, ch 3**, 7 dc in next ch-5 lp, rep from * across, ending last rep at **, sc in last sc, ch 1, turn.

Row 3: Sc in first sc, 3 sc in ch-3 lp, *sk 1 sc, sc in next sc**, ch 4, holding back on hook last lp of each st, dc in each of next 7 dc, yo, draw through all 8 lps on hook, ch 4, rep from * across, ending last rep at **, 3 sc in ch-3 lp, sc in last sc, fasten off.

Tie

With MC, ch 300, fasten off. Fold tie in half and tie 2 loose

ends tog with overhand knot. Weave doubled tie through groups of 5 dc across top edging.

Stocking
Cuff

Row 1 (WS): Beg at bottom of cuff with MC, ch 59, sc in 2nd ch from hook and in each rem ch across, ch 1, turn. (58 sc)

Rows 2–16: Follow Chart B (below), working from A to D twice, then from A to C once for each even-numbered (RS) row and from C to A once, then from D to A twice for each odd-numbered (WS) row; at end of Row 16, fasten off.

Cuff Edging

Row 1: With RS facing, attach

STITCH AND COLOR KEY
☐ MC sc
☒ CC sc
⬤ CC puff st

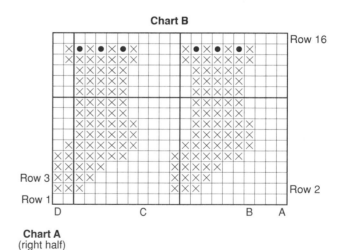

Chart B

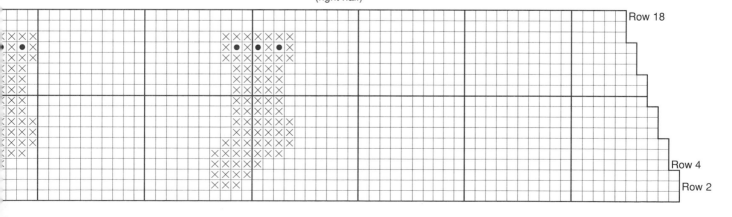

Chart A
(right half)

MC with a sl st in first rem lp of foundation ch at right edge at bottom of cuff, ch 1, sc in same st and in each rem st across, fasten off. (58 sc)

Row 2: With RS facing, working in front lps only this row, attach MC with a sl st in first sc of last row, ch 1, sc in same st and in each of next 3 sc, [ch 5, sc in each of next 5 sc] rep across to last 4 sts, ch 5, sc in each of last 4 sc, ch 1, turn.

Rows 3 & 4: Rep Rows 2 and 3 of bottom edging for tree skirt; do not fasten off at end of Row 4; ch 1, turn.

Row 5: Sc in each of first 2 sc, *6 sc in next ch-4 sp, [ch 5, sl st in 5th ch from hook] 3 times, 6 sc in next ch-4 sp, sc in next sc, rep from * across, ending with sc in each of last 2 sc, fasten off.

Upper Stocking

Row 1: With RS facing, attach MC with a sl st in first rem lp on Row 1 of cuff edging, ch 1, sc in same st and in each rem st across, ch 1, turn. (58 sc)

Row 2: 2 sc in first st, sc in each st across to last st, 2 sc in last st, turn. (60 sc)

Row 3: Ch 2 (counts as first hdc throughout), [X-st over next 2 sts] rep across to last st, hdc in last st, turn.

Row 4: Rep Row 3; fasten off, turn.

Row 5: With RS facing, attach CC with a sl st in first st of last row, rep Row 3.

Row 6: Rep Row 4.

Row 7: With RS facing, attach MC with a sl st in first st of last row, rep Row 3.

Rows 8–16: Rep Rows 4–7 alternately, ending with a Row 4, fasten off.

Heel

Row 1: With RS facing, sk first

46 sts of last row, attach MC with a sl st in next st, ch 1, sc in same st and in each of next 13 rem sts, bring beg of Row 16 of upper stocking around, sc in each of first 14 sts at beg of Row 16, ch 1, turn. (28 sc)

Row 2: Sc in each of first 17 sts, ch 1, turn.

Row 3: Sc in each of next 6 sts, ch 1, turn.

Row 4: Sc in each st across last row, sc in next unworked sc of Row 1, ch 1, turn. (7 sc)

Row 5: Sc in each st across last row, sc in next unworked sc of Row 2, ch 1, turn. (8 sc)

Rows 6–25: Rep Rows 4 and 5 alternately, fasten off at end of Row 25. (28 sts at end Row 25)

Foot

Row 1: With RS facing, attach CC with a sl st in 15th sc from right edge of heel, ch 2, [X-st over next 2 sts] 6 times, sk last heel st, hdc in next st on upper stocking, hdc in sk st on heel, [X-st over next 2 sts] 15 times, sk next st, hdc in next st on heel, hdc in sk st, [X-st over next 2 sts on heel] 6 times, hdc in last st, turn.

Rows 2–6: Continue in established striped X-st pattern on 60 sts; fasten off at end of Row 6.

Toe

Rnd 1: With RS facing, attach MC with a sl st in first st at right edge, ch 1, sc in same st and in each rem st around, join in beg sc, ch 1, turn. (60 sc)

Rnd 2: Sc in each of first 4 sts, sc dec, [sc in each of next 8 sts, sc dec] rep around to last 4 sts, sc in each of last 4 sts, join in beg sc, ch 1, turn. (54 sts)

Rnds 3, 5, 7, 9 & 11: Sc in each st around, join in beg sc, ch

1,turn.

Rnd 4: Sc in each of first 4 sts, sc dec, [sc in each of next 7 sts, sc dec] rep around to last 3 sts, sc in each of last 3 sts, join in beg sc, ch 1, turn. (48 sts)

Rnd 6: Sc in each of first 3 sts, sc dec, [sc in each of next 6 sts, sc dec] rep around to last 3 sts, sc in each of last 3 sts, join in beg sc, ch 1, turn. (42 sts)

Rnd 8: Sc in each of first 3 sts, sc dec, [sc in each of next 5 sts, sc dec] rep around to last 2 sts, sc in each of last 2 sts, join in beg sc, ch 1, turn. (36 sts)

Rnd 10: Sc in each of first 2 sts, sc dec, [sc in each of next 4 sts, sc dec] rep around to last 2 sts, sc in each of last 2 sts, join in beg sc, ch 1, turn. (30 sts)

Rnd 12: [Sc dec] rep around, join in beg st, ch 1, turn. (15 sts)

Rnd 13: Sc in each st around, join in beg sc, fasten off, leaving long end for sewing. With tapestry needle, weave end through sts of last rnd, pull tightly to close, secure with several small sts.

Finishing

Sew seams down back of stocking and across bottom of foot.

Top Edging

Rnd 1: With RS facing, attach MC with a sl st at back seam at top of cuff, ch 1, sc in each st around, join in beg sc.

Rnd 2: Ch 1, beg in same st as joining, sc in each sc around, join in beg sc.

Rnd 3: Ch 1, sl st in each sc around, join in beg sl st, [ch 20, sl st in joining st] 4 times, fasten off. ❧

Touch of Gold Tree Skirt

Design by Colleen Sullivan

Worked in the beautiful Victorian Gold yarn and trimmed with sparkling gold bows, this enchanting tree skirt will complement your christmas tree!

Experience Level: Intermediate

Finishsed Measurement: 41" in diameter

Materials

❋ Caron Victorian Christmas Gold worsted weight yarn (1¾ oz per skein): 9 skeins cranberry #1900 (A), 7 skeins balsam #1901 (B) and 2 skeins lace #1902 (C)

❋ Size H/8crochet hook or size needed to obtain gauge

❋ 17 gold metallic bows, 2½" wide x 2¼" long

❋ 48" ¼"-wide gold metallic ribbon

❋ Tapestry needle

Gauge: Rnds 1–3 of motif = 4" in diameter

To save time, take time to check gauge.

Pattern Note

Join rnds with a sl st unless otherwise stated.

Pattern Stitches

Cl: Holding back on hook last lp of each st, dc in each of next 4 indicated sts, yo, draw through all 5 lps on hook.

Beg cl: Ch 3, holding back on hook last lp of each st, dc in each of next 3 indicated sts, yo, draw through all 4 lps on hook.

Shell: [3 dc, ch 2, 3 dc] in indicated st or sp.

Motif *(make 35)*

Rnd 1: With C, ch 2, 12 sc in 2nd ch from hook, join in beg sc, fasten off C.

Rnd 2: Join A with a sl st in any sc, ch 3 (counts as first dc throughout), dc in same st, 2 dc in next sc, ch 2, [2 dc in each of next 2 sc, ch 2] rep around, join in 3rd ch of beg ch-3. (24 dc)

Rnd 3: Beg cl over next 3 dc, ch 3, sl st in next ch-2 sp, ch 3, [cl over next 4 dc, ch 3, sl st in next ch-2 sp, ch 3] rep around, join in top of beg cl, fasten off A.

Rnd 4: Attach B with a sl st in top of any cl, [shell in next ch-2 sp of Rnd 2, sl st in top of next cl] rep around, join in top of beg cl, fasten off B.

Rnd 5: Attach A with a sl st in joining st of Rnd 4, ch 3, 2 dc in same st, [shell in next shell sp, 3 dc in sl st at top of next cl] rep around, ending with shell in last shell sp, join in 3rd ch of beg ch-3, fasten off A.

Rnd 6: Attach B with a sl st in any shell sp, ch 1, 3 sc in same sp, *[sc in each of next 3 dc, dc in center dc of next 3-dc group in Rnd 4] twice, sc in each of next 3 dc **, 3 sc in next shell sp, rep from * around, ending last rep at **, join in beg sc, fasten off, leaving long end for sewing.

Half-Motif *(make 2)*

Row 1 (RS): With C, ch 2, 6 sc in 2nd ch from hook, fasten off C.

Row 2: With RS facing, attach A with a sl st in first sc of last row, ch 3 (counts as first dc), dc in same st, 2 dc in next st, [ch 2, 2 dc in each of next 2 sts] twice, turn. (12 dc)

Row 3: Beg cl over next 3 dc, ch 3, sl st in next ch-2 sp, ch 3, cl over next 4 dc, ch 3, sl st in next ch-2 sp, ch 3, cl over next 4 sts, ch 3, sl st in same st as last dc of last cl, fasten off A.

Row 4: With RS facing, attach B with a sl st in same st as last sl st of last row, ch 3, 2 dc in same st, [sl st in top of next cl, shell in next ch-2 sp of Row 2] twice, sl st in top of next cl, 3 dc over ch-3 of beg cl at beg of Row 3, fasten off B.

Row 5: With RS facing, attach A with a sl st in 3rd ch of ch-3 at beg of last row, ch 3, 2 dc in same st, [3 dc in sl st at top of next cl, shell in next shell sp] twice, 3 dc in sl st at top of next cl, sk 2 dc, 3 dc in last dc, fasten off A.

Rnd 6: With RS facing, attach B with a sl st in 3rd ch of ch-3 at beg of last row, ch 1, sc in same st and in each of next 2 dc, dc in 3rd st of Row 4, *sc in each of next 3 dc on working row, dc in center dc of next 3-dc group on Row 4, sc in each of next 3 dc, 3 sc in next shell sp, sc in each of next 3 dc, dc in center dc of next 3-dc group on Row 4, rep from * once, sc in each of next 3 dc, dc in center dc of next 3-dc

group on Row 4, sc in each of next 3 dc, working over row ends, sc evenly sp across straight edge of half-motif to beg sc, join in beg sc, fasten off, leaving a long end for sewing.

Assembly

Following Assembly Diagram, using tapestry needle and B, sew motifs tog on WS through back lps, leaving back opening as indicated on diagram.

Border

Rnd 1: With RS facing, attach C with a sl st in top right corner at back opening, ch 1, sc in same st, sc in each st and hdc in each joining seam across to bottom corner, 3 sc in corner st, sc in each st across to first point, 3 sc in center sc of point, sc in each st across to joining seam, sk joining seam, continue in sc across bottom to next corner, working 3 sc in center sc of each point and skipping each joining

ASSEMBLY DIAGRAM
Back Opening

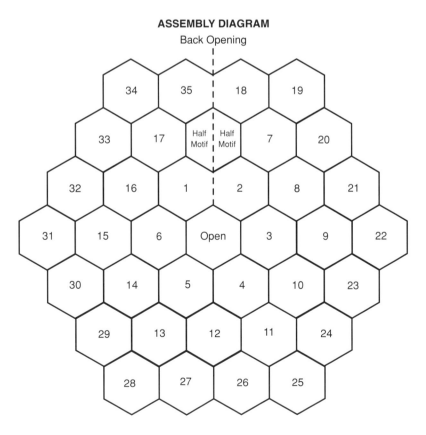

seam, 3 sc in corner st, sc in each st and hdc in each joining seam across back opening to top corner, 3 sc in corner st, sc in each st across to next corner, skipping each joining seam, 2 sc in same st as beg sc, join in beg sc, fasten off.

Rnd 2: With RS facing, attach A with a sl st in joining st of last rnd, [ch 3, sk next st, sl st in next st] rep around, ending with ch 3, join in beg sl st, fasten off.

Finishing

Block skirt lightly by pressing under a pressing cloth. Attach 1 bow at each joining seam across bottom of skirt. Cut 48" length of ribbon into 3 (16") lengths. Draw each 16" length through a ch-3 sp at top, center and bottom of back opening. Tie in bows to close.

Americana Set

Continued from page 62

Row 8: Sc in each st across, ch 1, turn.

Row 9: Sc in each of next 5 sts, work sc dec over next st and next unworked sc of Row 6, ch 1, turn. (6 sts)

Rows 10–17: Rep Rows 8 and 9 alternately, fasten off at end of Row 17.

Second Half

Row 1: With WS facing, attach C with a sl st in first st on last row of upper stocking, rep Row 1 of first half.

Row 2–17: Rep Rows 2–17 of first half.

Foot

Row 1: With RS facing, attach B with a sl st in first st on last row of first half of heel, ch 1, sc in same st, [ch 2, sk 2 sts or 2 rows, sc in next st or next row] 3 times, [ch 3, sc between next 2 3-dc groups on last row of upper

stocking] 9 times, ch 3, sk 2 rows on 2nd half of heel, sc in next row, [ch 2, sk 2 sts or 2 rows, sc in next st or row] 3 times, changing to A in last st, do not fasten off B; turn. (16 sps)

Rows 2–8: Rep Rows 19 and 20 of upper stocking alternately, ending with a Row 19.

Row 9: Rep Row 20 of upper stocking, replacing ch-3 sps with ch-2 sps.

Row 10: Rep Row 19 of upper stocking, working 2 dc in each sp instead of 3 dc. (34 dc)

Row 11: Insert hook in 3rd ch of beg ch-3, yo with B, draw through st on hook, ch 1, sc in same st, [ch 1, sk next 2 dc, sc between 2nd sk dc and next dc] rep across to last 3 dc, ch 1, sk next 2 dc, sc in last dc, do not change to A at end of row, ch 1, turn.

Row 12: Sc in each sc and ch-1 sp across, changing to C at end of row, fasten off A and B, ch 1, turn. (33 sc)

Toe

Rows 1 & 2: Sc in each st across, ch 1, turn.

Row 3: [Sc dec, sc in next st] rep across, ch 1, turn. (22 sts)

Rows 4–6: Rep Row 1.

Row 7: [Sc dec] rep across, ch 1, turn. (11 sts)

Row 8: Rep Row 1, fasten off, leaving end for sewing.

Cuff Trim

Row 1: With RS facing, working in rem lps of foundation ch, attach B with a sl st in first rem lp, ch 1, sc in same st and in each rem lp across, ch 1, turn. (49 sc)

Row 2: Sc in first st, [ch 2, sk 2 sc, sc in next sc] rep across, changing to A in last st, fasten off B, turn. (16 ch-2 sps)

Row 3: Ch 3, 3 dc in each sp across, dc in last sc, do not turn, fasten off A.

Row 4: With RS facing, attach B with a sl st in 3rd ch of beg ch-3, [ch 4, sk next 3 dc, sc between 3rd sk dc and next dc] rep across to last 4 dc, ch 4, sk 3 dc, sc in last dc, fasten off.

Finishing
Embroidery

Following chart (page 62), work cross-stitch, alternating trees and hearts across Rows 1–16 of cuff. Place first tree 4 sts from right edge, with lowest st on Row 13, and leave 4 sts between each design. Place lowest st of heart on Row 10.

Assembly

Weave end at toe in and out of tops of sts of last row; pull tightly to close. Sew back seam of stocking with matching colors.

Hanging Loop

With RS facing, attach B with a sl st at top of back seam, ch 20, sl st in 2nd ch from hook and in each rem ch across, fasten off. Fold ch in half and secure loose end to back seam.

Old-Time Filet Stocking

Design by Alma Shields

Capture the richest sentiments of the holiday season with this pretty filet stocking. May it bring love, joy and peace to your family!

Experience Level: Intermediate

Finished Measurement: 16½" long

Materials

❊ Size 20 crochet cotton: 250 yds white

❊ 6-strand embroidery floss: 13 yds green and 4 yds red

❊ Size 8 steel crochet hook or size needed to obtain gauge

❊ Size 10 steel crochet hook

❊ ⅜ yd red velvet or desired fabric for stocking

❊ ⅜ yd white satin or desired fabric for lining

❊ Sewing needle and white, green and red sewing thread

❊ Tracing paper

❊ Pencil

Gauge: 13 sps and 11 rows = 3" in filet mesh with white and larger hook

To save time, take time to check gauge.

Pattern Notes

Join rnds with a sl st unless otherwise stated.

Read all odd-numbered (RS) rows of chart from right to left; read all even-numbered (WS) rows from left to right.

Pattern Stitches

Trtr: Yo 4 times, insert hook in indicated st, yo, draw up a lp, [yo, draw through 2 lps on hook] 5 times.

Block (bl): Tr in each of next 3 sts.

Sp: Ch 2, sk next 2 tr or next ch-2 sp, tr in next tr.

Beg sp: Ch 6, sk next 2 tr or ch-2 sp, tr in next tr.

Bl over a bl: Tr in each of next 3 tr.

Bl over a sp: 2 tr in next ch-2 sp, tr in next tr.

Sp over a bl: Ch 2, sk next 2 tr, tr in next tr.

Sp over a sp: Ch 2, tr in next tr.

Inc 1 sp at beg of row: Ch 8, tr in next tr.

Inc 2 sps at beg of row: Ch 11, tr in 9th ch from hook, ch 2, tr in next tr.

Inc 1 sp at end of row: Ch 2, trtr in same st in which last tr was made.

Dec sp(s) at beg of row: Sl st across sp(s) to be dec.

Dec sp(s) at end of row: Leave sp(s) to be dec unworked.

Stocking

Row 1 (RS): With larger hook and white, ch 81, tr in 9th ch from hook, [ch 2, sk 2 chs, tr in next ch] rep across, turn. (25 sps)

Row 2: Beg sp, [sp over a sp] 24 times, turn. (25 sps)

Rows 3–58: Work from chart (page 72); do not fasten off at end of Row 58; turn.

Edging

Rnd 1: Working back across last row, ch 3 (counts as first dc), 2 dc in first sp, ch 1, 3 dc in next sp, [ch 3, sk next sp, 3 dc in next sp, ch 1, 3 dc in next sp] 5 times, ch 3, sk next sp, [3 dc, ch 1, 3 dc] over end sp, [ch 3, {3 dc, ch 1, 3 dc} over end sp of next row] twice, ch 3, 3 dc over end sp of next row, ch 1, 3 dc over end sp of next row, ch 3, [3 dc, ch 1, 3 dc] over end sp of next row, [ch 3, sk next row, 3 dc over end sp of next row, ch 1, 3 dc over end sp of next row] twice, ch 3, 3 dc over end sp of next row, ch 1, 3 dc over end sp of next row, ch 3, [3 dc, ch 1, 3 dc] over end sp of next row, *ch 3, 3 dc over end sp of next row, ch 1, 3 dc over end sp of next row, ch 3, 3 dc over next sp, ch 1, 3 dc over end sp of next row *, ch 3, [3 dc, ch 1, 3 dc] over end sp of next row, rep from * to * once, [ch 3, {3 dc, ch 1, 3 dc} over end sp of next row] twice, ch 3, 3 dc over end sp of next row, ch 1, 3 dc over end sp of next row, [ch 3, sk next row, 3 dc over end sp of next row, ch 1, 3 dc over end sp of next row] 10 times, **ch 3, [3 dc, ch 1, 3 dc, ch 3, 3 dc] over end sp of Row 1, ch 1 **, 3 dc over next sp, [ch 3, sk next sp, 3 dc over next sp, ch 1, 3 dc over next sp] 7 times, rep from ** to **, 3 dc

from hook} 3 times, 2 tr] in next ch-3 sp, sc in next ch-1 sp] rep around, join in beg sc, fasten off.

Holly Leaf Pair *(make 5)*

Cut 90" length of green embroidery floss. Separate into 2 3-strand lengths, and use 1 length for each leaf.

First leaf

Rnd 1: With smaller hook, ch 12, sc in 2nd ch from hook, *hdc in each of next 2 chs, dc in each of next 2 chs, tr in next ch, dc in each of next 2 chs, hdc in each of next 2 chs *, [sc, ch 3, sc] in last ch; working in rem lps across opposite side of foundation ch, rep from * to *, sc in last ch, ch 2, join in beg sc.

Rnd 2: Ch 1, sc in same st as joining, ch 3, sl st in last sc made for p *[sc in each of next 3 sts, p] 3 times *, sc in next sc and in each of next 2 chs, p, sc in next ch and in each of next 2 sts, p rep from * to *, [sc, ch 5, sl st] in ch-2 sp, join in beg sc, fasten off.

Second leaf

Rnd 1: Rep Rnd 1 of first leaf.

Rnd 2: Rep Rnd 2 of 2nd leaf until last p before ch-2 sp is made, sc in ch-2 sp, ch 2, sl st in ch-5 sp on Rnd 2 of first leaf, ch 2, sl st in same ch-2 sp on working leaf as last sc, join in beg sc, fasten off.

Holly Berry Cluster *(make 5)*

Cut 40" length of red embroidery floss. Separate into 3 2-strand lengths and use 1 length for each berry. With smaller hook, ch 5, join to form a ring, ch 1, 12 sc in ring, join in beg sc, [ch 6, join in 5th ch from hook to form a ring, holding previous berry at back of work, ch 1, 12 sc in ring, join in beg sc] twice, fasten off.

Finishing

Lightly starch and block stocking.

over end sp of next row, [ch 3, sk next row, 3 dc over end sp of next row, ch 1, 3 dc over end sp of next row] 13 times, [ch 3, 3 dc over end sp of next row, ch 1, 3 dc over end sp of next row] 6 times, ch 3, [3 dc, ch 1, 3 dc]

over end sp of next row, [ch 3, 3 dc over end sp of next row, ch 1, 3 dc over next sp] 3 times, ch 3, join in 3rd ch of beg ch-3.

Rnd 2: Sl st in each of next 2 dc and in ch-1 sp, ch 1, sc in same sp, [2 tr, {ch 3, sl st in 3rd ch

Using photo as a guide, sew holly leaves and berries to stocking.

Using stocking as a guide, make a paper pattern, adding ½" to top for hem and ¼" around rem of stocking for seam allowance. Using paper pattern, cut 2 pieces of red velvet. Cut ½" off top edge of paper pattern. Using paper pattern, cut 2 pieces of white satin.

With RS tog, sew 2 red pieces tog ¼" from edge, leaving top open. Trim seams and turn RS out. With RS tog, sew 2 white pieces tog ⅜" from edge, leaving top open. Do not turn RS out. Insert white lining into red stocking. Turn ½" of fabric down at top of red stocking to inside over white fabric lining. Turning up a narrow hem on red fabric,

sew red fabric to white lining.

Cut a 6" x 2" piece of red fabric. Fold in half lengthwise and press. Open and fold raw edges to center line. Fold in half with raw edges inside, stitch down length to close. Sew to top back of stocking.

With sewing needle and white thread, sew crocheted stocking to red fabric. ❧

Chart A

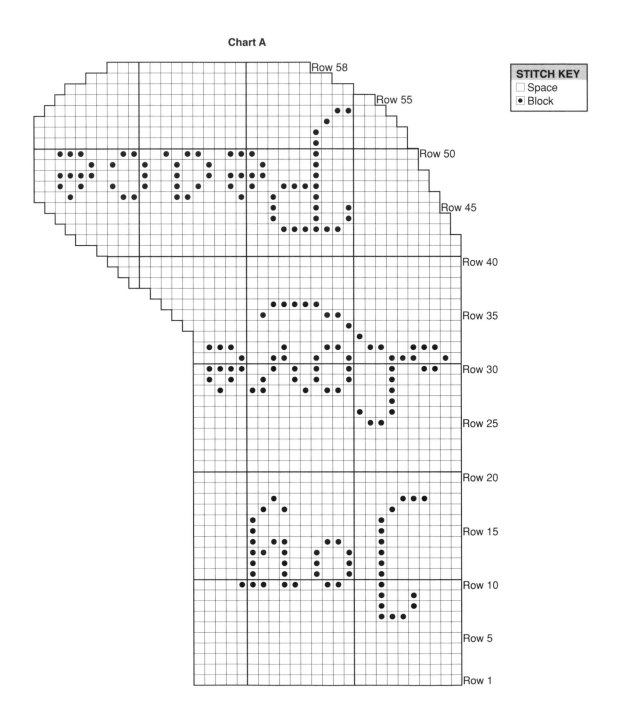

STITCH KEY
☐ Space
● Block

Christmas Rosebuds

Designs by Tammy C. Hildebrand

Crocheted with mohairlike yarn and accented with tiny crocheted rosebuds, this set will add a pretty, delicate touch to your holiday decor.

Experience Level: Intermediate

Finished Measurements

Tree Skirt: Approximately 21" long including ruffle

Stocking: 14" long x 9" wide

Tree Skirt
Materials

❊ Lion Brand Jiffy yarn (3 oz per skein): 9 skeins fisherman (MC), 1 skein each forest green #0131 (A) and wine #0189 (B)

❊ Size I/9 crochet hook or size needed to obtain gauge

❊ Tapestry needle

Gauge: 12 sts and 7 rows = 4" in dc

To save time, take time to check gauge.

Stocking
Materials

❊ Lion Brand Jiffy Yarn (3 oz per skein): 1 skein fisherman #0099 (MC), small amounts each forest green #0131 (A) and wine #0189 (B)

❊ Size I/9 crochet hook or size needed to obtain gauge

Gauge: 9 sts and 6 rows = 4" in dc

To save time, take time to check gauge.

Tree Skirt
Pattern Notes

Join rnds with a sl st unless otherwise stated.

To change color in dc, work last dc before color change until last 2 lps before final yo rem on hook, drop working color to WS, yo with next color, complete dc.

When working cls, work over MC on WS with color in use.

To change color in cl, work cl until last 4 lps before final yo rem on hook, drop working color to WS, yo with next color, complete cl.

Pattern Stitches

Cl: Holding back on hook last lp of each st, work 3 dc in indicated st, yo, draw through all 4 lps on hook.

Popcorn (pc): [Ch 3, 4 dc] in indicated st or sp, remove hook from lp, insert hook from RS to WS in 3rd ch of ch-3, pick up dropped lp and draw through st on hook.

Crossed dc: Sk next unworked st, dc in next st, dc in sk st.

Crossed dc1: Sk next unworked st, dc in next st, ch 1, dc in sk st.

Shell (sh): [2 dc, ch 1, 2 dc] in indicated st or sp.

Joining sh: 2 dc in indicated st, remove hook from lp, insert hook in ch-1 sp on corresponding sh, pick up dropped lp and draw through sp, 2 dc in same st as last 2 dc.

First Panel

Row 1 (RS): Beg at bottom, with MC, ch 42, dc in 4th ch from hook and in each of next 17 chs, crossed dc, dc in each of next 19 rem chs, turn. (1 crossed dc with 19 dc on each side, counting last 3 chs of foundation ch as first dc)

Row 2: Ch 3 (counts as first dc throughout), dc in next dc and in each rem dc across to crossed dc, crossed dc1 over crossed dc, dc in each rem st across, turn.

Row 3: Sl st in each of first 2 sts, ch 3, dc in next dc and in each rem dc across to crossed dc1, changing to A in last dc, sk first dc of crossed dc1, [cl, ch 2, cl] in ch-1 sp, changing to MC in 2nd cl, sk next dc of crossed dc1, dc in each rem st across to last st, leave last st unworked, remove hook from lp, with RS facing, working over ch-2 sp between cls, attach B with a sl st in ch-1 sp between cls, work pc, fasten off B, pick up dropped lp of MC, turn.

Row 4: Ch 3, dc in next dc and

in each rem dc across to first cl, sk cl, 2 sc in top of pc, sk next cl, dc in each rem st across, turn. (38 sts)

Row 5: Sl st in each of first 2 sts, ch 3, dc in next st and in each rem st across to first sc, crossed dc over next 2 sc, dc in each st across to last st, leave last st unworked, turn. (1 crossed dc with 17 dc on each side)

Rows 6–25: Rep Rows 2–5 alternately. (1 crossed dc with 7 dc on each side on Row 25)

Row 26: Ch 3, dc in next st and in each rem st across to crossed dc, crossed dc over crossed dc, dc in each rem st across, turn.

Row 27: Sl st in each of first 2 sts, ch 3, dc in next dc and in each rem dc across to crossed dc, crossed dc over crossed dc, dc in each rem st across to last st, leave last st unworked, ch 1, do not fasten off, do not turn. (1 crossed dc with 6 dc on each side)

First panel border

Rnd 1: Working over row ends, 2 sc over end st of last row, [2 sc over end st of next row] rep across to bottom corner, ch 1, working in rem lps of foundation ch, sc in each st across to next corner, ch 1, [2 sc over end st of next row] rep across to top corner, ch 1, sc in each st across last row of panel, ch 1, join in beg sc, fasten off. (162 sc)

Rnd 2: With RS facing, attach A with a sl st in ch-1 sp at upper right-hand corner, ch 1, sc in same sp, sc in each sc across to next ch-1 sp, sc in ch-1 sp, sl st in next sc, sh in next sc, [sk 3 sc, sh in next sc] 13 times, [sc, ch 1] in next ch-1 sp, [sc, ch 1] in each sc across to next ch-1 sp, [sc, ch 1] in ch-1 sp, sk next sc, sh in next sc, [sk 3 sc, sh in

next sc] 13 times, join in beg sc, fasten off.

Rem 3 Panels

Rows 1–27: Rep Rows 1–27 of first panel.

Rem 3 Panel Borders

Rnd 1: Rep Rnd 1 of first panel border.

Joining Rnd 2: With RS facing, attach A with a sl st in ch-1 sp at upper right-hand corner, ch 1, sc in same sp, sc in each sc across to next ch-1 sp, sc in ch-1 sp, sl st in next sc, joining sh in next sc on working panel to first sh at upper right-hand corner of previous panel, [sk 3 sc on working panel, joining sh in next sc] 13 times, continue around as for Rnd 2 of first panel border.

Ruffle

Row 1: With RS facing, attach MC with a sl st in last dc of last sh at bottom right corner of end panel, ch 1, sc in same st, *ch 3, [sc in next ch-1 sp, ch 3] rep across to opposite edge of same panel **, sk 2 sh, sc in next ch-1 sp on next panel, rep from * across to opposite end panel, ending last rep at **, sc in last dc of last sh at bottom corner of same panel, ch 1, turn.

Row 2–9: Sl st in first ch-3 sp, ch 1, sc in same sp, [ch 3, sc in next ch-3 sp] rep across, ch 1, turn. Fasten off at end of Row 9.

Stocking

Pattern Notes

Join rnds with a sl st unless otherwise stated.

To change color in dc, work last dc in working color until last 2 lps before final yo rem on hook, drop working color to WS, yo with next color, complete dc. To change color in cl, work cl in working color until last 4 lps

before final yo rem on hook, drop working color to WS, yo with next color, draw through all 4 lps on hook. Carry MC loosely across back of work when not in use, working over it with CC in use.

Pattern Stitches

Cl: Holding back on hook last lp of each st, 3 dc in indicated st or sp, yo, draw through all 4 lps on hook.

Popcorn (pc): [Ch 3, 4 dc] in indicated st or sp, remove hook from lp, insert hook from RS to WS in 3rd ch of ch-3, pick up dropped lp, draw through st on hook.

Crossed dc: Sk next 2 sts or next st and next sp, dc in next st, ch 1, dc in first sk st.

Front

Row 1 (RS): With MC, ch 27, dc in 4th ch from hook and in each rem ch across, turn. (25 dc, counting last 3 chs of foundation ch as first dc)

Row 2: Ch 3 (counts as first dc throughout), dc in each of next 2 sts, crossed dc, dc in each of next 18 sts, 2 dc in last st, turn.

Row 3: Ch 3, dc in first dc and in each of next 19 sts, changing to A in last st, sk next dc, [cl, ch 2, cl] in next ch-1 sp, changing to MC in 2nd cl, sk next dc, dc in each of last 3 sts, remove hook from lp, working over ch-2 sp between cls, attach B with a sl st between cls in ch-1 sp, work pc, fasten off B, pick up dropped lp of MC, turn.

Row 4: Ch 3, dc in each of next 2 sts, 3 sc in top of center back st of pc, dc in each rem dc across, ch 1, turn. (27 sts)

Row 5: Sl st in each of first 2 sts, ch 3, dc in each of next 19 sts,

crossed dc, dc in each of last 3 sts, turn.

Row 6: Ch 3, dc in each of next 2 sts, crossed dc, dc in each of next 19 sts, leave last st unworked, ch 1, turn.

Row 7: Sl st in each of first 2 sts, sc in next st, hdc in next st, dc in each of next 15 sts, changing to A in last dc, sk next dc, [cl, ch 2, cl] in ch-1 sp, changing to MC in 3rd dc of 2nd cl, sk next dc, dc in each of last 3 sts, remove hook from lp, working over ch-2 sp between cls, attach B with a sl st between cls in ch-1 sp, work pc, fasten off B, pick up dropped lp of MC, turn.

Row 8: Ch 3, dc in each of next 2 dc, 3 sc in top of center back st of pc, dc in each of next 13 dc, leave rem sts unworked, turn. (19 sts)

Row 9: Ch 3, dc in each of next 12 sts, crossed dc, dc in each of last 3 sts, turn.

Row 10: Ch 3, dc in each of next 2 sts, crossed dc, dc in each of last 13 sts, turn.

Row 11: Ch 3, dc in each of next 12 sts, changing to A in last dc, sk next st, [cl, ch 2, cl] in ch-1 sp, changing to MC in 2nd cl, sk next dc, dc in each of last 3 sts, remove hook from lp, working over ch-2 sp between cls, attach B with a sl st between cls in ch-1 sp, work pc, fasten off B, pick up dropped lp of MC, turn.

Rows 12–21: Rep Rows 8–11 twice, then rep Rows 8 and 9; at end of Row 21, fasten off.

Back

Row 1 (WS): With MC, ch 27, dc in 4th ch from hook and in each rem ch across, turn. (25 dc,

counting last 3 chs of foundation ch as first dc)

Row 2: Ch 3, dc in each of next 23 sts, 2 dc in last st, turn. (26 dc)

Row 3: Ch 3, dc in first dc and in each rem dc across, turn. (27 dc)

Row 4: Ch 3, dc in each rem dc across, ch 1, turn. (27 dc)

Row 5: Sl st in each of first 2 dc, ch 3, dc in each rem dc across, turn. (26 dc)

Row 6: Ch 3, dc in each rem dc across to last st, leave last st unworked, ch 1, turn. (25 dc)

Row 7: Sl st in each of first 2 sts, sc in next st, hdc in next st, dc in each of next 21 sts, turn.

Row 8: Ch 3, dc in each of next 18 sts, leave rem sts unworked, turn. (19 dc)

Rows 9–21: Ch 3, dc in each rem st across, turn, at end of Row 21, fasten off. (19 dc)

Join Front & Back

Holding front and back with WS tog, beg at back top of stocking, attach MC with a sl st over end st of Row 21, ch 1, sc over same st, 5 dc over end st of next row, [sc over end st of next row, 5 dc over end st of next row] 9 times, ch 1, sc in each rem lp of foundation row across, ch 1, [sc over end st of next row, ch 1] 6 times, sc across first 6 unworked sts of Row 7, [ch 1, sc over end st of next row] 14 times, sl st over end st of same row as last sc, fasten off.

Top Edging

With RS facing, attach B with a sl st at top of back seam, ch 11 for hanging lp, sl st in same st as last sl st, sc in next dc of Row 21, [ch 1, sc in next dc] rep around top of stocking, ending with sc in first ch of ch-11, [ch 1, sc in next ch] 10 times, join in beg sc, fasten off. ✌

Aran Elegance

Designs by Ann E. Smith

Styled after the classic Aran patterns of Ireland, this lovely tree skirt and stocking set will suit every decor, from simple sophistication to cozy country.

Experience Level: Advanced

Finished Measurements

Stocking: 19" long

Tree Skirt: 21" deep

Materials

✳ Red Heart Super Saver worsted weight yarn (8 oz per skein): 5 skeins Aran #313

✳ Size H/8 crochet hook or size needed to obtain gauge

✳ Size G/6 crochet hook

✳ 2 safety pins or other small markers

✳ Yarn needle

Gauge: 11 sts and 8 rows = 4" in hdc with larger hook

To save time, take time to check gauge.

Pattern Notes

Join rnds with a sl st unless otherwise stated.

Do not work into top of same st over which fpdc or bpdc has been worked unless otherwise stated.

Pattern Stitches

Hdc dec: [Yo, draw up a lp in next st] twice, yo, draw through all 5 lps on hook.

Bobble: 4 dc in indicated st, remove hook from lp, insert hook from RS to WS in top of first of last 4 dc made, pick up dropped lp, draw through st on hook, ch 1 to secure.

Skirt Cable Pattern (worked over 12 sts)

Row 1 (RS): Fpdc over next st, hdc in each of next 3 sts, sk next 2 sts, fpdc over each of next 2 sts, fpdc over first sk st, fpdc over next sk st, hdc in each of next 3 sts, fpdc over next st.

Row 2: Bpdc over first post st, hdc in each of next 3 hdc, bpdc over each of next 4 post sts, hdc in each of next 3 hdc, bpdc over next post st.

Row 3: Fpdc over first post st, hdc in each of next 2 hdc, sk next hdc, fpdc over each of next 2 post sts, hdc in top of same st over which last fpdc st was made, hdc in top of next st, fpdc over same post st in which last hdc was made, fpdc over next post st, sk next hdc, hdc in each of next 2 hdc, fpdc over next post st.

Row 4: Bpdc over first post st, hdc in each of next 2 hdc, [bpdc over each of next 2 post sts, hdc in each of next 2 hdc] twice, bpdc over next post st.

Row 5: Fpdc over first post st, hdc in next hdc, sk next hdc, fpdc over each of next 2 post sts, hdc in top of same post st over which last fpdc was made, hdc in each of next 2 hdc, hdc in top of next post st, fpdc over same post st in which last hdc was made, fpdc over next post st, sk next hdc, hdc in next hdc, fpdc over next post st.

Row 6: Bpdc over first post st, hdc in next hdc, bpdc over each of next 2 post sts, hdc in each of next 4 hdc, bpdc over each of next 2 post sts, hdc in next hdc, bpdc over next post st.

Row 7: Fpdc over first post st, hdc in next hdc, hdc in top of next post st, fpdc over same post st, fpdc over next st, sk next hdc, hdc in each of next 2 hdc, sk next hdc, fpdc over each of next 2 post sts, hdc in top of same st over which last fpdc was worked, hdc in next hdc, fpdc over next post st.

Row 8: Rep Row 4.

Row 9: Fpdc over first post st, hdc in each of next 2 hdc, hdc in top of next post st, fpdc over same post st, fpdc over next post st, sk next 2 hdc, fpdc over each of next 2 post sts, hdc in top of same post st over which last fpdc was worked, hdc in each of next 2 hdc, fpdc over next post st.

Row 10: Bpdc over first post st, hdc in each of next 3 hdc, bpdc over each of next 4 post sts, hdc in each of next 3 hdc, bpdc over next post st.

Row 11: Fpdc over first post st, hdc in each of next 3 hdc, sk next 2 post sts, fpdc over each of next 2 post sts, fpdc over first sk st, fpdc over next sk st, hdc in each of next 3 hdc, fpdc over next post st.

Stocking Cable Pattern

Row 1 (RS): Fpdc over first st, hdc in next st, sk next st, fpdc over each of next 2 sts, hdc in top of same st over which last fpdc was made, hdc in top of next st, fpdc

over same st in which last hdc was made, fpdc over next st, sk next st, hdc in next st, fpdc over next st.

Row 2: Bpdc over first post st, hdc in next hdc, bpdc over each of next 2 post sts, hdc in each of next 2 hdc, bpdc over each of next 2 post sts, hdc in next hdc, bpdc over next post st.

Row 3: Fpdc over first post st, sk next hdc, fpdc over each of next 2 post sts, hdc in top of same st over which last fpdc was worked, hdc in each of next 2 hdc, hdc in top of next post st, fpdc over same post st, fpdc over next post st, sk next hdc, fpdc over next post st.

Row 4: Bpdc over each of first 3 post sts, hdc in each of next 4 hdc, bpdc over each of next 3 post sts.

Row 5: Fpdc over first post st, hdc in top of next post st, fpdc over same post st, fpdc over next post st, sk next hdc, hdc in each of next 2 hdc, sk next hdc, fpdc over each of next 2 post sts, hdc in top of same post st over which last fpdc was worked, fpdc over next post st.

Row 6: Rep Row 2.

Row 7: Fpdc over first post st, hdc in next hdc, hdc in top of next post st, fpdc over same post st and over next post st, sk 2 hdc, fpdc over each of next 2 post sts, hdc in top of same st over which last fpdc was made, hdc in next hdc, fpdc over next post st.

Row 8: Bpdc over first post st, hdc in each of next 2 hdc, bpdc over each of next 4 post sts, hdc in each of next 2 hdc, bpdc over next post st.

Row 9: Fpdc over first post st, hdc in each of next 2 hdc, sk next 2 post sts, fpdc over each of next 2 post sts, fpdc over first sk post st, fpdc over next sk post st, hdc in each of next 2 hdc, fpdc over next post st.

Row 10: Rep Row 8.

Tree Skirt

Panels 1–5

Row 1: With larger hook, ch 13, sc in 2nd ch from hook and in each rem ch across, turn. (12 sc)

Row 2: Ch 2 (counts as first hdc throughout), hdc in first st, hdc in each rem sc across to last sc, 2 hdc in last sc, turn. (14 hdc)

Row 3: Ch 2, hdc in first st; marking first and last sts of Skirt Cable Pattern with safety pin or other small marker, work Row 1 of Skirt Cable Pattern over next 12 sts, 2 hdc in last st, turn. (16 sts)

Row 4: Ch 2, hdc in first st, hdc in each hdc across to first marked st, continuing to mark first and last sts of Skirt Cable Pattern, work next row of Skirt Cable Pattern across next 12 sts, hdc in each rem hdc across to last hdc, 2 hdc in last hdc, turn. (18 sts)

Rows 5–17: Rep Row 4; after first 11 rows of Skirt Cable Pattern have been worked, beg again with Row 2 of Skirt Cable Pattern. (44 sts at end of Row 17)

Rows 18–33: Continue pattern as established, working incs at beg and end of row on RS rows only, ending with Row 11 of Skirt Cable Pattern; at end of Row 33, ch 1, turn. (60 sts at end of Row 33)

Row 34: Sc in each st across, ch 1, turn. (60 sc)

Row 35: Sc in each of first 5 sc, [bobble in next st, sc in each of next 4 sts] rep across, ch 1, turn.

Row 36: 2 sc in first st, sc in each sc and bobble across to last st, 2 sc in last st, turn. (62 sc)

Row 37: Ch 4 (counts as first tr throughout), *sk next 3 sts, tr in each of next 3 sts, working behind 3 tr just made, tr in first sk st, tr in each of next 2 sk sts, rep from * across, ending tr in last st, ch 1, turn.

Row 38: Sc across, working 2 sc in first and last sts of row, turn. (64 sc)

Row 39: Ch 4, tr in next st, rep Row 37 from * across to last 2 sts, tr in each of last 2 sts, ch 1, turn.

Row 40: Rep Row 38. (66 sc)

Row 41: Ch 4, tr in each of next 2 sts, rep Row 37 from * across to last 3 sts, tr in each of last 3 sts, ch 1, turn.

Row 42: Rep Row 38, fasten off. (68 sc)

Left side border for panels 1–5

Row 1: With RS facing, using larger hook, attach yarn with a sl st at top of left edge of panel, ch 1, beg in same st, work 62 sc evenly sp over row ends across, ch 1, turn.

Row 2: Sc in each of first 5 sts, bobble in next st, [sc in each of next 4 sts, bobble in next st] rep across to last st, sc in last st, fasten off.

Right side border for panels 1–5

Row 1: With RS facing, using larger hook, attach yarn with a sl st at bottom of right edge, ch 1, beg in same st, work 62 sc evenly sp over row ends across edge, fasten off.

Panel 6

Rows 1–42: Rep Rows 1–42 of panels 1–5.

Left side border for panel 6

Rows 1 & 2: Rep Rows 1 and 2 of left side border for panels 1–5.

Right side border for panel 6

Row 1: Rep Row 1 of right side border for panels 1–5, do not fasten off; ch 1, turn.

Row 2: Sc in first sc, [bobble in next sc, sc in each of next 4 sc] rep across, ending with sc in last sc, fasten off.

Assembly

With tapestry needle and yarn, beg with panel 1 at left side, sew 6 panels tog; do not sew

2nd edge of 6th panel to first edge of first panel.

Top Edging

With RS facing, using larger hook, attach yarn with a sl st in first rem lp of foundation ch at top right corner, ch 1, beg in same st, sc evenly sp across, fasten off.

Bottom Edging

With RS facing, using larger hook, attach yarn with a sl st at lower right corner, ch 1, sc in same st, bobble in next st, *[sc in each of next 4 sts, bobble in next st] 13 times **, sc to center of seam, bobble at center of seam, rep from * across, ending last rep at **, sc in each st across to next-to-last st, bobble in next st, sc in last st, fasten off.

Stocking

Cuff

Row 1: With larger hook, ch 45, sc in 2nd ch from hook and in each rem ch across, ch 1, turn. (44 sc)

Row 2 (RS): Sc in first sc, *bobble in next sc **, sc in each of next 3 sc, rep from * across, ending last rep at **, sc in each of last 2 sc, ch 1, turn.

Row 3: Sc in each sc and bobble across, turn. (44 sc)

Row 4: Rep Row 37 of panels 1–5 for Tree Skirt.

Row 5: Sc in each st across, turn. (44 sc)

Rows 6 & 7: Rep Rows 4 and 5; at end of Row 7, ch 1, turn.

Row 8: Rep Row 2; do not ch 1 at end of row; turn.

Upper Stocking

Row 1: Ch 2 (counts as first hdc throughout), hdc in each sc and bobble across, turn. (44 hdc)

Row 2: Ch 2, hdc in each of next 8 hdc, fpdc over next hdc (place marker in top of this st), hdc in each of next 2 hdc, sk next 2 hdc, fpdc over each of next 2 hdc, fpdc over first sk hdc, fpdc over next sk hdc, hdc in each of next 2 hdc, fpdc over next hdc (place marker in top of this st), hdc in each of next 25 hdc, turn.

Row 3: Ch 2, hdc in each hdc and bpdc over each post st across, placing markers in top of first and last bpdc worked, turn. (44 sts)

Row 4: Ch 2, hdc in each hdc across to first marked st, marking first and last sts of Stocking Cable Pattern, work Row 1 of Stocking Cable Pattern across next 10 sts, hdc in each rem hdc across, turn.

Row 5: Ch 2, hdc in each hdc across to first marked st, continuing to mark first and last sts of Stocking Cable Pattern, work next row of Stocking Cable Pattern across next 10 sts, hdc in each rem hdc across, turn.

Rows 6–17: Rep Row 2; after first 10 rows of Stocking Cable Pattern have been worked, beg again with Row 1 of Stocking Cable Pattern; leaving markers in sts, fasten off at end of Row 17. (44 sts)

Heel

Row 1: With RS facing, using larger hook, sk first 35 sts of Row 17 of upper stocking, attach yarn with a sl st in next st, ch 1, sc in same st and in each of next 8 sts, bring beg of row around, sc in each of first 9 sk sts, ch 1, turn. (18 sc)

Row 2: Sc in each of first 11 sts, ch 1, turn. (11 sc)

Row 3: Sc in each of first 5 sts, ch 1, turn. (5 sc)

Row 4: Sc in each st across last row, sc in next unworked sc on Row 1, ch 1, turn. (6 sc)

Row 5: Sc in each st across last row, sc in next unworked sc on Row 2, ch 1, turn. (7 sc)

Rows 6–16: Rep Rows 4 and 5 alternately, ending with Row 4; fasten off at end of Row 16. (18 sc on Row 16)

Foot

Rnd 1: With RS facing, using smaller hook, attach yarn with a sl st in 10th sc from right-hand edge on last row of heel, ch 2, hdc in each of next 8 sts, beg in next marked st on last row of upper stocking and continuing to mark first and last sts of Stocking Cable Pattern, work Row 5 of Stocking Cable Pattern across next 10 sts, hdc in each of next 16 hdc, hdc in each of next 9 rem sts on heel, join in 2nd ch of beg ch-2, turn.

Note: Turn at end of each rem rnd unless otherwise stated.

Rnds 2–13: Continue in established pattern, working Rows 6–10 of Stocking Cable Pattern over 10 marked sts, then working Rows 1–7 of Stocking Cable Pattern, at the same time dec 4 hdc evenly sp over hdc section every RS rnd 3 times, then dec 2 hdc evenly sp over hdc section on next RS rnd; continue in established pattern on 30 sts.

Rnd 14: Ch 1, sc dec around, join in beg sc dec, ch 1, turn. (15 sts)

Rnd 15: Ch 1, sc around to first post st, fpdc over first post st, bobble in next st, fpdc over next post st, sc in each rem st around, join in beg sc, fasten off, leaving end for sewing.

With tapestry needle, weave end through sts of last rnd; pull to close. Secure with several small sts. Sew back seam and close opening at heel.

Top Edging

With RS facing, using larger hook, attach yarn with a sl st at top back seam, ch 1, sl st evenly sp around top, ending [ch 2, sl st in top back seam] 3 times, fasten off. 🌿

Comfort & Joy

Worked in favorite Christmas motifs—from beautiful poinsettias to sweet gingerbread men—and cheery holiday colors, each of these afghans and pillows is as pleasing to the eyes as to the soul.

Timeless Poinsettias Afghan

Design by Darla J. Fanton

Crochet this breathtaking afghan to warm your heart, body and home during the holidays. With its rich, vibrant colors, you just may want to use it all year-round!

Experience Level: Intermediate

Finished Measurements: Approximately 54" x 63"

Materials

* ❋ Spinrite Bernat Berella "4" worsted weight yarn (3.5 oz per skein): 8 skeins winter white #8941 (MC), 2 skeins each scarlet #8933 (A), hunter green #8981 (B) and light tapestry gold #8886 (C), and 1 skein medium lagoon #8821 (D)
* ❋ 6-strand embroidery floss: small amount gold
* ❋ Size J/10 crochet hook or size needed to obtain gauge
* ❋ Yarn needle
* ❋ Bobbins (optional)

Gauge: 10 sts and 9 rows = 3" in hdc

To save time, take time to check gauge.

Pattern Notes

To change color in hdc, work last hdc before color change in working color until last 3 lps before final yo rem on hook, drop working color to WS, yo with next color, complete hdc.

Carry yarn not in use across WS, working over it with color in use for not more than 4 sts. For color sections separated by more than 4 sts, wind separate ball of yarn or use bobbin.

When working from chart, read all odd-numbered (RS) rows from right to left; read all even-numbered (WS) rows from left to right.

Panel A (make 3)

Row 1 (RS): With MC, ch 30, hdc in 3rd ch from hook and in each rem ch across, turn. (29 hdc, counting last 2 chs of foundation ch as first hdc)

Row 2: Ch 2 (counts as first hdc throughout), hdc in each of next 18 sts, changing to B in last st, hdc in each of next 2 sts, changing to MC in last st, hdc in each of last 8 sts, turn.

Rows 3–65: Work from Chart A (page 86).

Rows 66–193: Working from Chart A, rep Rows 2–65 alternately twice, fasten off at end of Row 193.

Panel A Edging

Left side edging

Row 1: With RS facing, attach B with a sl st over end st of Row 193, ch 2, [hdc over end st of next row] rep across to bottom, turn. (193 hdc)

Row 2: Ch 2, hdc in each rem st across, changing to A in last st, turn.

Row 3: Ch 3 (counts as first hdc, ch-1), sk next st, hdc in next st, [ch 1, sk next st, hdc in next st] rep across, changing to C in last st, turn.

Row 4: Ch 2, [hdc over ch-1 sp into next st on Row 2, hdc in next hdc on working row] rep across, fasten off.

Right side edging

Row 1: With RS facing, attach B with a sl st over end st of Row 1, work as for Row 1 of left side edging.

Rows 2–4: Rep Rows 2–4 of left side edging.

Panel B (make 2)

Row 1: Rep Row 1 of panel A.

Rows 2–33: Work Rows 34–65 of Chart A.

Rows 34–161: Working from Chart A, rep Rows 2–65 alternately twice.

Rows 162–193: Work Rows 2–33 of Chart A, fasten off at end of Row 193.

Panel B Edging

Left side edging

Rows 1–4: Rep Rows 1–4 of left side edging for Panel A edging.

Right side edging

Rows 1–4: Rep Rows 1–4 of right side edging for panel A edging.

Assembly

With yarn needle and C, beg with panel A and alternating panels A and B, sew panels tog on WS. ❧

Chart A

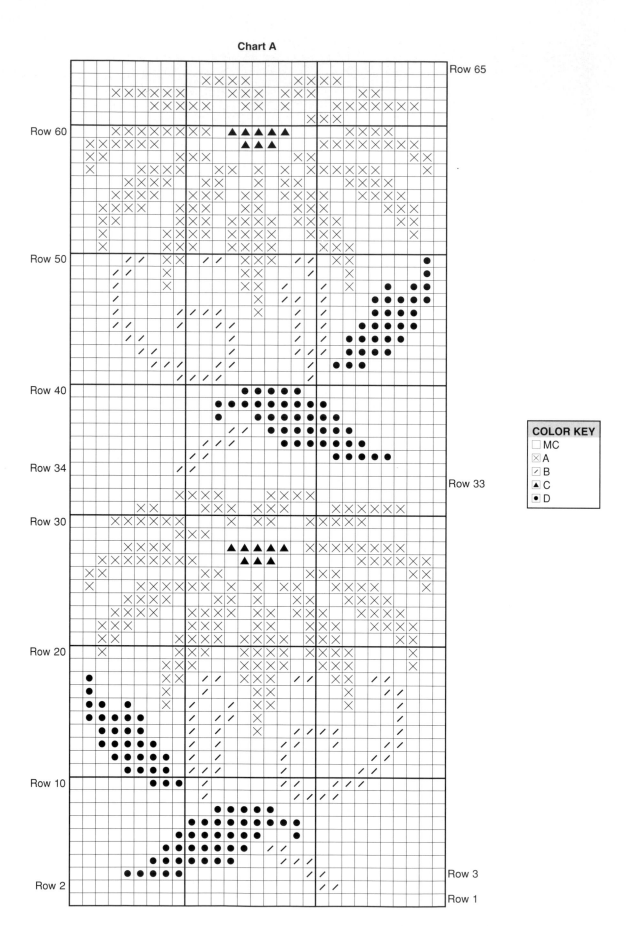

COLOR KEY
☐ MC
☒ A
☑ B
▲ C
● D

Candy Stripe Baby Afghan

Design by Loa Ann Thaxton

Celebrate Baby's first Christmas by crocheting a cuddly soft holiday afghan. The bright colors will keep Baby entertained while the soft yarn will keep the little one warm and cozy.

Experience Level: Advanced

Finished Measurements: Approximately 30" x 35"

Materials

❋ Worsted weight yarn: 12 oz white, 6 oz each green and red

❋ Size G/6 crochet hook or size needed to obtain gauge

Gauge: 3 sc = 1"

To save time, take time to check gauge.

Pattern Notes

Join rnds with a sl st unless otherwise stated.

To change color in sc, insert hook in indicated st, yo with working color, draw up a lp, drop working color to WS, yo with next color, complete sc. Do not fasten off color not in use at end of row unless otherwise stated. Carry color not in use up side of afghan until needed again.

Always sk st on working row that is directly behind a dc or fpdtr that has been worked into a st on a row below before working next st on working row.

Pattern Stitches

Front post dtr (fpdtr): Yo 3 times, insert hook from front to back to front around post of indicated st, yo, draw up a lp, complete dtr.

Cable twist: Sk next 2 sts on 4th row below, fpdtr over each of next 2 sts on 4th row below, fpdtr over each of 2 sk sts on 4th row below.

Afghan

Row 1 (RS): With red, ch 96, sc in 2nd ch from hook and in each rem ch across, ch 1, turn. (95 sc)

Row 2: Sc in each st across, changing to white in last st, ch 1, turn. (95 sc)

Row 3: Sc in first st, dc in next st on row before last, sc in next st on working row, dc in next st on row before last, [sc in each of next 2 sts on working row, dc in each of next 4 sts on row before last] twice, sc in each of next 2 sts on working row, [dc in next st on row before last, sc in next st on working row] 30 times, sc in next st on working row, [dc in each of next 4 sts on row before last, sc in each of next 2 sts on working row] twice, [dc in next st on row before last, sc in next st on working row] twice, ch 1, turn.

Row 4: Rep Row 2, changing to green in last st, ch 1, turn. (95 sc)

Row 5: Sc in each of first 2 sts, dc in next st on row before last, sc in next st on working row, dc in each of next 2 sts on row before last, [sc in each of next 4 sts on working row, dc in each of next 2 sts on row before last] twice, [sc in next st on working row, dc in next st on row before last] 29 times, sc in next st on working row, [dc in each of next 2 sts on row before last, sc in each of next 4 sts on working row] twice, dc in each of next 2 sts on row before last, sc in next st on working row, dc in next st on row before last, sc in each of last 2 sts on working row, ch 1, turn.

Row 6: Rep Row 2.

Row 7: With white, sc in first st, dc in next st on row before last, sc in next st on working row, dc in next st on row before last, sc in each of next 2 sts on working row, *[cable twist, sc in each of next 2 sts on working row] twice *, [dc in next st on row before last, sc in next st on working row] 30 times, sc in next st on working row, rep from * to *, dc in next st on row before last, sc in next st on working row] twice, ch 1, turn.

Row 8: Rep Row 2, changing to red in last st.

Rows 9 & 10: Rep Rows 5 and 6.

Row 11: Sc in first st, [dc in next st on row before last, sc in next st on working row] twice, sc in next st on working row, *[fpdtr over each of next 4 fpdtr, sc in each of next 2 sts on working row] twice *, [dc in next st on row before last, sc in next st on working row] 30 times, sc in next st on working row, rep from * to *, [dc in next st on row before last, sc in next st on working row] twice, ch 1, turn.

Row 12: Rep Row 4.

Rows 13–138: Rep Rows 5–12 alternately, ending with a Row 10; at end of Row 138, ch 1 with white, turn.

Border

Rnd 1: Sc in each st across to last st, 3 sc in last st, sc evenly sp over row ends to next corner, 3 sc in corner st, sc in each rem lp across foundation ch to next corner, 3 sc in corner st, sc evenly sp over row ends to next corner, 2 sc in same st as beg sc, join in beg sc, ch 1, do not turn.

Rnd 2: Rev sc in each sc around, join in beg rev sc, fasten off. ❧

Reindeer in the Snow Afghan

Design by Darla J. Fanton

Get cozy Northwoods-style in this abundant afghan. The cool blue tones and the close stitch will keep the heat in and the cold out—with the reindeer.

Experience Level: Intermediate

Finished Measurements: Approximately 50" x 69"

Materials:

※ Patons Canadiana knitting worsted weight yarn (3.5 oz per skein): 10 skeins medium decorator blue #143 (MC) and 7 aran #104 (CC)

※ Size J/10 crochet hook or size needed to obtain gauge

Gauge: 7 sts and 6 rows = 2" in hdc

To save time, take time to check gauge.

Pattern Note

To change color in hdc, work last hdc before color change in working color until last 3 lps before final yo rem on hook, drop working color to WS, yo with next color, complete hdc. Do not carry color not in use across WS of work; attach a new ball or bobbin of yarn for each color section.

Afghan

Row 1 (RS): With MC, ch 184, hdc in 3rd ch from hook and in each rem ch across, changing to CC in last st, fasten off MC, turn. (183 hdc, counting last 2 chs of foundation ch as first hdc)

Row 2: Ch 2 (counts as first hdc throughout), hdc in next st, [ch 3, sk 3 sts, hdc in next st] rep across to last st, hdc in last st, changing to MC, fasten off CC, turn. (48 hdc; 45 ch-3 sps)

Row 3: Ch 2, hdc in next st, [working in front of next ch-3, dc in each of next 3 sts on row before last, hdc in next hdc on last row] rep across to last st, hdc in last st on last row, changing to CC, fasten off MC, turn. (183 sts)

Row 4: Ch 4 (counts as first hdc, ch-2), sk next 2 sts, hdc in next st, [ch 3, sk 3 sts, hdc in next st] rep across to last 3 sts, ch 2, sk 2 sts, hdc in last st, changing to MC, fasten off CC, turn. (47 hdc; 46 sps)

Row 5: Ch 2, working in front

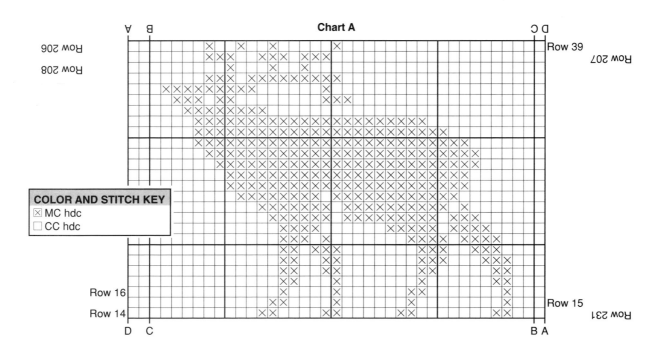

Chart A

COLOR AND STITCH KEY
⊠ MC hdc
☐ CC hdc

Row 206
Row 208
Row 16
Row 14

Row 39
Row 207
Row 15
Row 231

Rows 10 & 11: Rep Rows 2 and 3, do not change to CC at end of Row 11; turn.

Row 12: Ch 2, hdc in each rem st across, changing to CC in last st, fasten off MC, turn. (183 hdc)

Row 13: Ch 2, hdc in each rem st across, turn. (183 hdc)

Row 14: Continuing to work in hdc, following chart and changing colors as indicated, work from D to B once, work from C to B 3 times, work from C to A once, turn.

Row 15: Continuing to follow chart, work from A to C once, work from B to C 3 times, work from B to D once, turn.

Rows 16–39: Continuing to work from chart, rep Rows 14 and 15 alternately.

Row 40: With CC, rep Row 13, changing to MC in last st, fasten off CC, turn. (183 hdc)

Row 41: Rep Row 13, changing to CC in last st, turn.

Rows 42-202: Rep Rows 2–5 alternately, ending with a Row 2.

Row 203: Rep Row 3, do not change to CC at end of row; turn.

Rows 204 & 205: Rep Rows 12 and 13.

Row 206: With chart upside down, work from A to C once, from B to C 3 times, and from B to D once, turn.

Row 207: Continuing to follow chart, work from D to B once, from C to B 3 times, and from C to A once, turn.

Rows 208–231: Continuing to work from chart, rep Rows 206 & 207 alternately.

Rows 232 & 233: Rep Rows 40 and 41.

Rows 234–244: Rep Rows 2–12; do not change to CC at end of Row 244; fasten off. ❧

of next ch-2, dc in each of next 2 sts on row before last, hdc in next hdc on last row, [working in front of next ch-3, dc in each of next 3 sts on row before last, hdc in next hdc on last row] rep across to last 3 sts, dc in each of next 2 sts on row before last, hdc in 2nd ch of turning ch-4, changing to CC, fasten off MC, turn. (183 sts)

Rows 6–9: Rep Rows 2–5.

Christmas Patchwork Afghan

Design by Laura Gebhardt

Worked in blocks reminiscent of traditional quilt blocks, this vibrant afghan combines the look of quilting with crochet.

Experience Level: Intermediate

Finished Measurements: Approximately 50" x 55"

Materials

❈ Worsted weight yarn: 36 oz white, 8 oz each red and green, and 3 oz gold

❈ Size J/10 afghan hook or size needed to obtain gauge

❈ Size H/8 crochet hook

❈ Tapestry needle

Gauge: 16 sts and 14 rows = 4" with afghan hook in afghan stitch

To save time, take time to check gauge.

Pattern Note

Join rnds with a sl st unless otherwise stated.

Pattern Stitches

Basic Afghan St

Row 1: Retaining all lps on hook, draw up a lp in 2nd ch from hook and in each rem ch across (first half of row); *yo, draw though 1 lp on hook, [yo, draw through 2 lps on hook] rep across until 1 lp rems (2nd half of row; lp which rems counts as first st of next row).

Row 2: Retaining all lps on hook, sk first vertical bar, [insert hook under next vertical bar, yo, draw up a lp] rep across, ending with insert hook under last vertical bar and 1 strand directly behind it, yo, draw up a lp for last st (first half of row); rep Row 1 from * across for 2nd half of row.

Rep Row 2 for basic afghan st.

Shell: [3 dc, ch 2, 3 dc] in indicated st or sp.

Beg shell: [Ch 3, 2 dc, ch 2, 3 dc] in indicated st or sp.

Block (make 9)

With afghan hook and white, ch 50.

Rows 1–50: Work in basic afghan st on 50 sts.

Row 51: Sk first vertical bar, [insert hook under next vertical bar, work sl st (1 lp rems on hook)] rep across, fasten off.

Block Border

Rnd 1: With RS facing, using crochet hook, attach red with a sl st in upper right corner of block, beg shell in same st, *[ch 1, sk 2 sts, 3 dc in next st] 15 times, ch 1, shell in corner st, working over ends of rows, [ch 1, sk 2 rows, 3 dc over end of next row] 16 times, ch 1 *, shell in first rem lp of foundation ch, rep from * to *, join in 3rd ch of beg ch-3, fasten off.

Rnd 2: With RS facing, using crochet hook, attach white with a sl st in beg shell sp at upper right corner, beg shell in same sp, *[ch 1, 3 dc in next ch-1 sp] rep across to corner shell, ch 1 **, shell in corner shell sp, rep from * around, ending last rep at **, join in 3rd ch of beg ch-3, fasten off.

Rnd 3: With RS facing, using crochet hook, attach green with a sl st in beg shell sp at upper right corner, beg shell in same sp, [3 dc in next ch-1 sp] rep across to corner shell **, shell in corner shell sp, rep from * around, ending last rep at **, join in 3rd ch of beg ch-3, fasten off.

Rnd 4: With RS facing, using crochet hook, attach white with a sl st in beg shell sp at upper right corner, ch 1, beg in same sp, [3 sc in corner shell sp, sc in each dc across to next corner shell] rep around, join in beg sc, fasten off.

Work cross-stitch on 5 blocks from Chart A (page 93); work cross-stitch on rem 4 blocks from Chart B.

Assembly

With tapestry needle, working from WS, sew blocks tog through back lps only in 3 rows of 3 blocks each, beg with block A in upper right corner and alternating B and A across and up and down.

Edging

Rnd 1: With RS facing, using crochet hook, attach white with a sl st in upper right corner, ch 3 (counts as first dc), 2 dc in same st, dc in each rem sc and seam around, working 3 dc in each corner sc, join in 3rd ch of beg ch-3.

Rnd 2: Ch 1, rev sc in each st around, join in beg rev sc, fasten off. ❧

Chart A

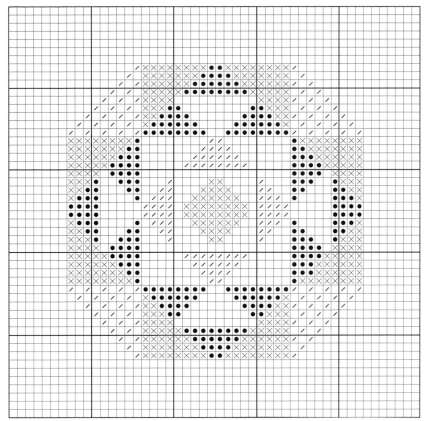

COLOR KEY
- ● Red
- ⊠ Gold
- ⁄ Green

Chart B

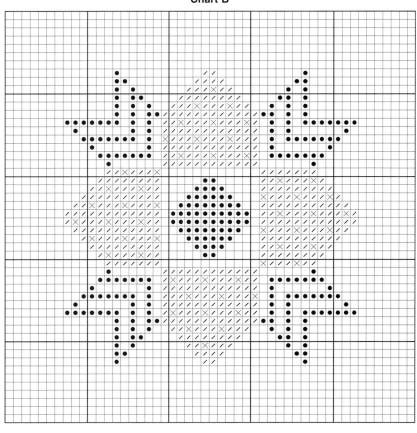

Gingerbread Boy Pillow

Design by Michele Wilcox

Placed on a couch or overstuffed chair, this darling pillow will please friends and family who visit during the holidays.

Experience Level: Intermediate

Finished Measurements: Approximately 10½" x 12"

Materials:

❋ Spinrite Bernat Berella "4" worsted weight yarn (3.5 oz per skein): 1 skein each medium lagoon #8821 (A), scarlet #8933 (B), winter white #8941 (C) and honey #8795 (D)

❋ Size F/5 crochet hook or size needed to obtain gauge

❋ 2 (⅜") black buttons

❋ 3 (½") white buttons

❋ Tapestry needle

❋ Sewing needle and thread

❋ Polyester fiberfill

❋ Bobbins (optional)

Gauge: 17 sc = 4"

To save time, take time to check gauge.

Pattern Notes

Join rnds with a sl st unless otherwise stated.

To change color in sc, insert hook in indicated st, yo with working color, draw up a lp, drop working color to WS, yo with next color, complete sc. Do not carry color not in use across WS of work; use bobbins or wind small balls of yarn for each separate color section.

When working from chart, read all odd-numbered (RS) rows from right to left, all even-numbered (WS) rows from left to right.

Pillow Back

Row 1 (RS): With A, ch 46, sc in 2nd ch from hook and in each rem ch across, ch 1, turn. (45 sc)

Rows 2–55: Sc in each sc across, ch 1, turn; at end of Row 55, do not fasten off; ch 1, do not turn. (45 sc)

Back border

*Sc evenly sp over row ends to corner, 3 sc in corner st *, sc evenly sp in each rem lp across foundation ch to last st, 3 sc in last st, rep from * to *, sc across last row to last st, 3 sc in last st, join in beg sc fasten off.

Pillow Front

Row 1: With B, ch 46, sc in 2nd ch from hook and in each rem ch across, ch 1, turn.

Rows 2–8: Sc in each sc across, ch 1, turn. (45 sc)

Continued on page 96

Christmas Tree Pillow

Design by Michele Wilcox

Crocheted with a sparkling worsted weight yarn, this festive pillow makes a welcome decoration or gift.

Experience Level: Intermediate

Finished Measurements: Approximately 13" x 17"

Materials

❋ Caron Victorian Christmas Gold worsted weight yarn (3.5 oz per skein): 5 skeins lace #1902, 2 skeins balsam #1901 and 1 skein cranberry #1900

❋ Size G/6 crochet hook or size needed to obtain gauge

❋ Polyester fiberfill

❋ 6" piece of cardboard

❋ Bobbins (optional)

Gauge: 11 sc = 3"

To save time, take time to check gauge.

Pattern Notes

Join rnds with a sl st unless otherwise stated.

To change color in sc, insert hook in indicated st, yo with working color, draw up a lp, drop working color to WS, yo with next color, complete sc. Do not carry color not in use across WS of work; use bobbins or wind small balls of yarn for each separate color section.

When working from chart, read all odd-numbered (RS) rows from right to left, all even-numbered (WS) rows from left to right.

Pillow Back

Row 1 (RS): With lace, ch 50, sc in 2nd ch from hook and in each rem ch across, ch 1, turn. (49 sc)

Rows 2–70: Sc in each sc across, ch 1, turn; at end of Row 70, do not ch 1; fasten off.

Pillow Front

Rows 1 & 2: Rep Rows 1 and 2 of pillow back.

Row 3: Sc in each of first 20 sc, changing to balsam in last st, sc in each of next 9 sc, changing to 2nd ball of lace in last sc, sc in each of next 20 sc, ch 1, turn.

Rows 4–70: Continuing in sc, work from Chart A; at end of Row 70, fasten off.

Assembly

Holding pillow front and pillow back with WS tog, attach lace with sl st in any corner, ch 1, 3 sc in same st, sc evenly sp around 3 sides, working 3 sc in each corner, stuff pillow with polyester fiberfill, sc rem side tog, join in beg sc, fasten off.

Tassel *(make 4)*

Wrap cranberry around cardboard 50 times; cut open across 1 edge. Tie 1 strand of cranberry at center of 50 strands held tog. Pull sides down; tie 2nd strand of cranberry around tassel approximately 1" down from top. Trim ends evenly. Tie 1 tassel to each corner of pillow. ❧

Gingerbread Boy Pillow

Continued from page 94

Row 9: Sc in each of first 5 sc with B, changing to C in 5th sc, sc in each of next 35 sc with C, changing to 2nd ball of B in last sc, sc in each of next 5 sc with B, ch 1, turn. (45 sc)

Rows 10–55: Continuing in sc, work from Chart A; at end of Row 55, do not fasten off; ch 1, do not turn. (45 sc)

Front border

Rep back border.

With sewing needle and thread, using photo as a guide, sew 2 black buttons on face for eyes; sew 3 buttons down front chest. With tapestry needle and B, work French knot for nose; work mouth in straight st.

Assembly

With WS tog, working through both thicknesses, attach A with a sl st in any corner on border, ch 1, 3 sc in same st, sc around 3 sides, working 3 sc in each corner, stuff pillow with polyester fiberfill, sc last side tog, join in beg sc, fasten off.

Tassel *(make 4)*

With A, [ch 35, sl st in first ch] 12 times, fasten off, leaving end for sewing. With tapestry needle, sew 1 tassel in each corner. ❧

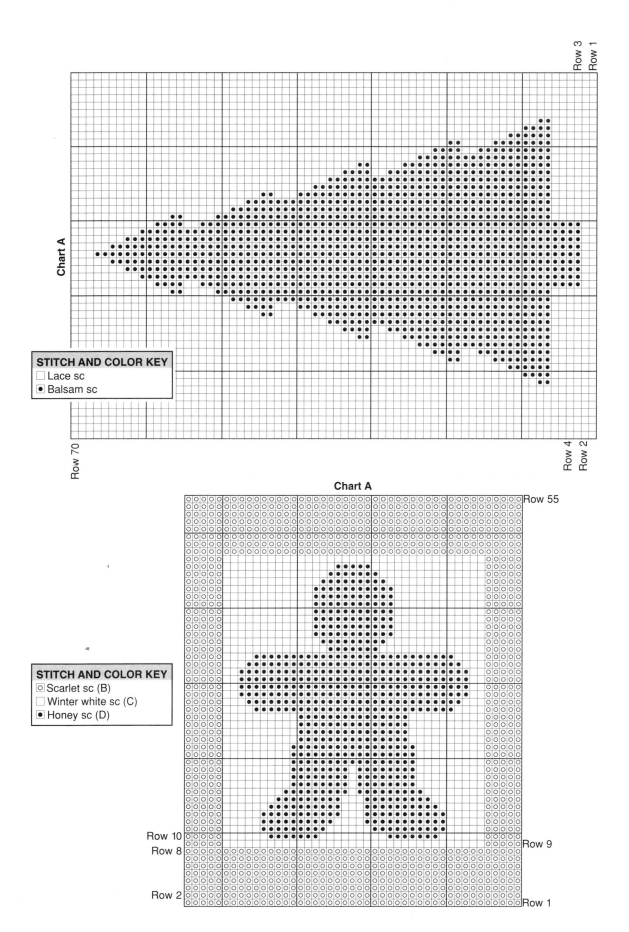

Row 3
Row 1

Chart A

STITCH AND COLOR KEY
☐ Lace sc
⦿ Balsam sc

Row 70

Row 4
Row 2

Chart A

Row 55

STITCH AND COLOR KEY
⊙ Scarlet sc (B)
☐ Winter white sc (C)
⦿ Honey sc (D)

Row 10

Row 8

Row 9

Row 2

Row 1

Lush Snowballs

Design by Loa Ann Thaxton

Pretty ripples come together in this eye-catching afghan. Fluffy pompoms look like perfect snowballs on the edges!

Experience Level: Intermediate

Finished Measurements: Approximately 34" x 65"

Materials:

❊ Worsted weight yarn: 24 oz white (MC), 12 oz dark green (A), and 5 oz each red (B) and light green (C)

❊ Size H/8 crochet hook or size needed to obtain gauge

Gauge: 2¾" across widest point of each ripple

To save time, take time to check gauge.

Pattern Note

To change color in sc, insert hook in indicated st, yo with working color, draw up a lp, drop working color to WS, yo with next color, complete sc.

Afghan

Row 1 (RS): With A, ch 338, sc in 2nd ch from hook, sk next ch, [sc, ch 2, sc] in next ch, *[sk 2 chs, {sc, ch 2, sc} in next ch] 3 times, sk 2 chs, [sc, ch 2, sc, ch 3, sc, ch 2, sc] in next ch, [sk 2 chs, {sc, ch 2, sc} in next ch] 3 times, sk 2 chs **, sc in next ch, sk 3 chs, sc in next ch, rep from * across to last 3 chs, ending last rep at **, [sc, ch 2, sc] in next ch, sk next ch, dc in last ch, ch 1, turn. (11 complete ripples; ½ ripple at each end)

Row 2: Sc in first dc, sc in next ch-2 sp, [{sc, ch 2, sc} in next ch-2 sp] 4 times, *[sc, ch 2, sc, ch 3, sc, ch 2, sc] in next ch-3 sp, [{sc, ch 2, sc} in next ch-2 sp] 3 times **, [sc in next ch-2 sp] twice, [{sc, ch 2, sc} in next ch-2 sp] 3 times, rep from * across, ending last rep at **, [sc, ch 2, sc] in next ch-2 sp, sc in

last ch-2 sp, dc in last sc, changing to C in last st, ch 1, turn.

Row 3: Rep Row 2, do not change color at end of row; ch 1, turn.

Row 4: Rep Row 2, changing to B in last st, ch 1, turn.

Rows 5 & 6: Rep Rows 3 and 4 with B, changing to A in last sc of Row 6, ch 1, turn.

Rows 7 & 8: Rep Rows 3 and 4 with A, changing to MC in last sc of Row 8; ch 1, turn.

Rows 9–13: Rep Row 3.

Row 14: Rep Row 4, changing to A in last st, ch 1, turn.

Rows 15 & 16: Rep Rows 3 and 4, changing to C in last sc of Row 16, ch 1, turn.

Rows 17–106: Rep Rows 3–16 alternately, ending with Row 8; at end of Row 106, do not change to MC in last st, do not ch 1; fasten off.

Finishing

With MC, make 23 (2"-diameter) pompoms and attach 1 to the tip of each complete ripple along edge of afghan. ❧

Cradled Bobble Afghan

Design by Mary Lamb Becker

Crocheted in vibrant Christmas colors, this pretty afghan is just right for curling up in on Christmas eve!

Experience Level: Intermediate

Finished Measurements: Approximately 52" x 65" without fringe

Materials

❋ Spinrite Bernat Berella "4" worsted weight yarn (3.5 oz per skein): 9 skeins hunter green #8981 (MC), 4 skeins geranium #8929 (A) and 1 skein each natural #8940 (B) and medium lagoon #8821 (C)

❋ Size I/9 crochet hook or size needed to obtain gauge

Gauge: 16 dc = 5"

To save time, take time to check gauge.

Pattern Note

After working bptr and fpdtr, always sk st directly behind bptr and fpdtr on last row before working next st.

Pattern Stitches

Bobble: Holding back on hook last lp of each st, work 4 dc in indicated st, yo, draw through all 5 lps on hook.

Back post tr (bptr): Yo twice, insert hook from back to front to back around post of indicated st, yo, draw up a lp, complete tr.

Front post dtr (fpdtr): Yo 3 times, insert hook from front to back to front around post of indicated st, yo, draw up a lp, complete dtr.

Afghan

Row 1 (RS): With MC, ch 165, dc in 4th ch from hook and in each rem ch across, turn. (163 dc, counting last 3 chs of foundation ch as first dc)

Rows 2–6: Ch 3 (counts as first dc throughout), dc in each rem st across, fasten off at end of Row 6, turn. (163 dc)

Row 7: With RS facing, attach B with a sl st in top of first dc, ch 1, sc in same st and in each of next 8 sts, bobble in next st, [sc in each of next 23 sts, bobble in next st] rep across to last 9 sts, sc in each of last 9 sts, fasten off, turn. (163 sts)

Row 8: With WS facing, attach C with a sl st in first sc, ch 1, sc in same st and in each of next 8 sts, bptr over next dc in row before last, [sc in each of next 23 sts, bptr over next dc in row before last] rep across to last 9 sts, sc in each of last 9 sts, fasten off, turn. (163 sts)

Row 9: With RS facing, attach A with a sl st in first sc, ch 1, sc in same st and in each of next 9 sts, work fpdtr directly below bptr over same dc in 3rd row below as bptr, [sc in each of next 23 sts, fpdtr directly below bptr over same dc in 3rd row below as bptr] rep across to last 8 sts, sc in each of last 8 sts, turn.

Row 10: Ch 3, dc in each rem st across, fasten off, turn. (163 sts)

Row 11: With RS facing, attach MC with a sl st in first dc of last row, ch 3, dc in each rem st across, turn. (163 dc)

Rows 12–16: Rep Rows 2–6.

Row 17: With RS facing, attach B with a sl st in first st, ch 1, sc in same st and in each of next 20 sts, bobble in next st, [sc in each of next 23 sts, bobble in next st] rep across, ending with sc in each of last 21 sts, fasten off, turn. (163 sts)

Row 18: With WS facing, attach C with a sl st in first sc, ch 1, sc in same st and in each of next 20 sts, bptr over next dc in row before last, [sc in each of next 23 sts, bptr over next dc in row before last] rep across, ending with sc in each of last 21 sts, fasten off, turn. (163 sts)

Row 19: With RS facing, attach A with a sl st in first sc of last row, ch 1, sc in same st and in each of next 21 sts, fpdtr directly below bptr over same dc in 3rd row below as bptr, [sc in each of next 23 sts, fpdtr directly below bptr over same dc in 3rd row below as bptr] rep across, ending with sc in each of last 20 sts, turn. (163 sts)

Row 20: Rep Row 10.

Row 21: Rep Row 11.

Rows 22–136: Rep Rows 2–21 alternately, ending with a Row 16, fasten off at end of Row 136.

Fringe

Cut 5 (18") lengths of A for every other st across each short end of afghan. Holding 5 strands tog, fold in half, insert hook from WS to RS in first st on either short end, pull folded end of strands through st on hook to form a lp, draw cut ends through lp and pull to tighten. Rep for every other st across each short end of afghan. ❧

Holidays at Home

Turn your home-sweet-home into a cozy, winter-wonderland this Christmas season! Festive decorations for every room in the house will add sparkle and cheer while delighting friends and family.

Victorian Christmas Tree

Design by Maggie Petsch Chasalow

This beautiful tree will elicit "oohs" and "aahs" from family and friends. Display it in a window or on a table where everyone can enjoy it.

Experience Level: Intermediate

Finished Measurements: For an 18"-tall artificial tree

Materials:

❊ J & P Coats Metallic Knit-Cro-Sheen crochet thread (100 yds per ball): 1 ball white/silver #1S (A)

❊ J. & P. Coats Knit-Cro-Sheen crochet cotton size 10 (150 yds per ball): 1 ball shaded flamingo #16 (B)

❊ Kreinik Blending Filament (55 yd per spool): 2 spools silver #001HL-BF

❊ Size 7 steel crochet hook or size needed to obtain gauge

❊ Safety pin or other small marker

❊ 18"-tall artificial tree

❊ 37 (15mm) jingle bells

❊ 12 (⅛") pearls

❊ 16" ¼"-wide pink satin ribbon

❊ Small amount polyester fiberfill

❊ Sewing needle and white thread

❊ Commercial fabric stiffener

Gauge: Rnds 1–3 of star = 1" in diameter

To save time, take time to check gauge.

Pattern Notes

Join rnds with a sl st unless otherwise stated.

To change color when joining rnds, work last st of rnd in working color, drop working color to WS, insert hook in indicated st, complete sl st with next color.

Pattern Stitches

Front post tr (fptr): Yo twice, insert hook from front to back to front around post of indicated st, yo, draw up a lp, complete tr.

3-dc cl: Holding back on hook last lp of each st, 3 dc in indicated st or sp, yo, draw through all 4 lps on hook.

Beg 3-dc cl: Ch 2, holding back on hook last lp of each st, 2 dc in indicated st or sp, yo, draw through all 3 lps on hook.

Tree Skirt

Rnd 1 (RS): With A, ch 100; being careful not to twist, join to form a ring, ch 5 (counts as first tr, ch-1 throughout), sk next st, [tr in next st, ch 1, sk next st] rep around, join in 4th ch of beg ch-5. (50 ch-1 sps)

Rnd 2: [{Dc, tr, dc} in next tr, sl st in next tr] rep around, join in same st as joining st of Rnd 1, fasten off.

Rnd 3: With RS facing, working in rem lps of foundation ch, attach B with a sl st in rem lp at base of any tr, beg 3-dc cl in same st, ch 4, [sk next 3 sts, 3-dc cl in rem lp at base of next tr, ch 4] rep around, ending with ch 2, hdc in top of beg 3-dc cl to form last ch-4 sp. (25 3-dc cls)

Rnd 4: Beg 3-dc cl in sp just formed, ch 4, *[3-dc cl in next sp, ch 4] 3 times **, [3-dc cl, ch 4] twice in next sp, 3-dc cl in next sp, ch 4, rep from * around, ending last rep at **, [3-dc cl, ch 4, 3-dc cl] in last sp, ch 2, hdc in top of beg 3-dc cl to form last sp. (30 3-dc cls)

Rnds 5–7: Beg 3-dc cl in sp just formed, [ch 4, 3-dc cl in next sp] rep around, ending with ch 2, hdc in top of beg 3-dc cl to form last sp.

Rnd 8: Rep Rnd 5, ending with ch 4, sl st in top of last 3-dc cl, fasten off.

Rnd 9: With RS facing, attach A with a sl st in any ch-4 sp, ch 1, sc in same sp, *[tr, ch 1] 4 times in next sp, tr in same sp **, sc in next sp, rep from * around, ending last rep at **, join in beg sc, fasten off.

Star (*make 2*)

Rnd 1 (RS): With B, ch 1 (for center ch), ch 2 (counts as first hdc), 9 hdc in center ch, join in 2nd ch of beg ch-2. (10 hdc)

Rnd 2: Ch 3 (counts as first dc), dc in same st as joining, 2 dc in

each rem hdc around, join in 3rd ch of beg ch-3, changing to A, do not fasten off B. (20 dc)

Rnd 3: Ch 1, 2 sc in same st as joining, fptr over first hdc of Rnd 1, *sk dc behind fptr just made **, 2 sc in next dc, fptr over next hdc on Rnd 1, rep from * around, ending last rep at **, join in back lp only of beg sc. (30 sts)

Rnd 4: Working in back lps only this rnd, *ch 9, sc in 2nd ch from hook, dc in next ch, tr in each of next 2 chs, dtr in each of next 4 chs, sk next 5 sts of Rnd 3 **, sl st in next st, rep from * around, ending last rep at **, join in beg sc of Rnd 3 with B, fasten off A. (5 arms)

Rnd 5: Ch 1, sc in rem lps of each of next 8 chs of ch-9, *3 sc over end of next sc, sc in top of same sc, sc in each of next 6 sts **, draw up a lp in next dtr, in next sl st, and in rem lp of first ch of next ch-9, yo, draw through all lps on hook, sc in rem lps of each of next 7 chs of ch-9, rep from * around, ending last rep at **, draw up a lp in next dtr and in next sl st, yo, draw through all lps on hook, join in beg sc, fasten off.

Holding both pieces with WS tog, using tapestry needle and B and beg at tip of any arm, sew both pieces tog until 3 arms are joined on both sides, sew first half of next arm tog to tip, leaving half of same arm and half of first arm open.

Garland

With B and blending filament held tog, *[ch 4, {yo, insert hook in first ch of last ch-4 made, yo, draw up a lp to top of ch-4, yo, draw through 2 lps on hook} 4 times, yo, draw through all 5 lps on hook] 5 times **, sl st in metal lp at top of jingle bell, rep

from * until all 37 jingle bells have been strung, ending last rep at **, fasten off.

Icicle (make 12)

With A, ch 12, 2 sc in 2nd ch from hook and in each rem ch across, ch 9 for hanging lp, sl st over side of last sc made, fasten off.

Grasp bottom of icicle and twist into spiral.

Snowflake (make 12)

With A, ch 1 (for center ch), [ch 5, sl st in 3rd ch from hook, sl st in each of next 2 chs, sl st in center ch, ch 4, sl st in 3rd ch from hook, sl st in next ch, sl st in center ch] 3 times, ch 14, sl st in 10th ch from hook for hanging lp, sk next ch, sl st in each of next 3 chs, sl st in center ch, ch 4, sl st in 3rd ch from hook, sl st in next ch, sl st in center ch, fasten off.

Rosebud & Lace Ornament (make 12)

Rnd 1: With B, ch 2, 6 sc in 2nd ch from hook, join in front lp only of beg sc. (6 sc)

Rnd 2: Ch 2, working in front lps only this rnd, [sl st in next sc, ch 2] rep around, ending with ch 2, join in beg sc of Rnd 1, fasten off. (6 ch-2 lps)

Rnd 3: Attach A with a sl st in any rem lp of Rnd 1, working in rem lps behind ch-2 lps of last

rnd, [ch 5, sl st in same st, ch 5, sl st in next st] rep around, join in same st as beg ch-5, ch 10 for hanging lp, sl st in 10th ch from hook, fasten off. (12 ch-5 lps)

Sew 1 pearl at center of Rnd 1.

Pink Ball Ornament (make 12)

Note: *Do not join rnds unless otherwise stated; mark first st of each rnd with safety pin or other small marker.*

Rnd 1: With B, ch 2, 6 sc in 2nd ch from hook. (6 sc)

Rnd 2: 2 sc in each sc around. (12 sc)

Rnd 3: [Sc in next sc, 2 sc in next sc] rep around. (18 sc)

Rnds 4–8: Sc in each sc around. (18 sc)

Rnd 9: [Sc dec, sc in next sc] rep around. (12 sts)

Stuff ornament firmly.

Rnd 10: [Sc dec] 6 times, join in beg sc, fasten off, leaving 18" end.

Weave 18" end through sts of last rnd, pull to tighten, secure with knot, do not cut end.

Hanging Loop

Insert hook into top center of ornament, yo with 18" end, draw up a lp, ch 10, sl st into top of ornament at base of ch-10, fasten off.

Finishing

Weave 16" length of ribbon through ch-1 sps on Rnd 1 of tree skirt. Slip skirt over base of tree; pull ribbon ends to tighten top of skirt around base of tree, adjusting fullness evenly around. Tie ribbon into bow; trim ends to desired length. Coat star, icicles, snowflakes, and rosebud-and-lace ornaments lightly with fabric stiffener. Allow to dry. Place star on top of tree. Beg at top of tree, wind garland around tree to bottom. Using photo as a guide, hang ornaments on tree. ❦

Festive Banner

Design by Colleen Sullivan

Adorned with everyone's favorite Christmas motifs, this merry Noel wall hanging is a lively holiday decoration all will enjoy.

Experience Level: Intermediate

Finished Measurements: Approximately 13½" wide x 34½" long

Materials

❋ Worsted weight yarn: 5 oz white, 4 oz red, 3 oz green, and small amounts each dark blue, light blue and yellow

❋ Size G/6 crochet hook or size needed to obtain gauge

❋ Size E/4 crochet hook

❋ Tapestry needle

❋ 14½" ⅝"-diameter wooden dowel

❋ 2 (⅞") wooden balls with ⅝" holes to fit dowel

Gauge: 9 sts and 10 rows = 3" in sc with larger hook

To save time, take time to check gauge.

Pattern Notes

Join rnds with a sl st unless otherwise stated.

To change color in sc, insert hook in indicated st, yo with working color, draw up a lp, drop working color to WS, yo with next color, complete sc.

Do not carry color not in use across WS of work; wind small balls of yarn or use bobbins for each separate section of color.

When working from chart, read all odd-numbered (RS) rows from right to left, all even-numbered (WS) rows from left to right.

Center Panel

Row 1 (RS): With larger hook and white, ch 17, sc in 2nd ch from hook and in each rem ch across, ch 1, turn. (16 sc)

Rows 2–4: Sc in each sc across, ch 1, turn. (16 sc)

Row 5: Sc in first sc with white, changing to red, sc in each of next 14 sc with red, changing to white in 14th red sc, sc in last sc with white, ch 1, turn. (16 sc)

Rows 5–80: Continuing in sc, work from Chart A (page 109); at end of Row 80, do not fasten off; ch 1, turn.

Center panel border

Rnd 1 (RS): Sc in first st, sc in each st across last row to last st, 3 sc in last st, sc evenly sp over row ends to next corner, 3 sc in first rem lp of foundation ch, sc in each st across foundation ch to last st, 3 sc in last st, sc evenly sp over row ends to next corner, 2 sc in same st as beg sc, join in beg sc, fasten off white.

Rnd 2: With RS facing, using larger hook, attach green with a sl st in any corner sc, ch 1, 3 sc in same st, sc around, working 3 sc in each corner st, join in beg sc, fasten off.

Side Panel *(make 2)*

Row 1 (RS): With larger hook and white, ch 9, sc in 2nd ch from hook and in each rem ch across, ch 1, turn. (8 sc)

Rows 2–11: Sc in each sc across, ch 1, turn; at end of Row 11, change to green in last sc, ch 1, turn. (8 sc)

Row 12: With green, sc in each sc across, changing to white in last sc, ch 1, turn.

Rows 13–23: With white, sc in each sc across, ch 1 turn; at end of Row 23, change to green in last sc, ch 1, turn.

Rows 24–107: Rep Rows 12–23 alternately; at end of Row 107, do not change to green, do not ch 1; fasten off.

Center Square *(make 4)*

Rows 1–11: Rep Rows 1–11 of side panel, changing to green in last sc of Row 11, ch 1; don't turn.

Center square border

Working over row ends, sc evenly sp down side to corner, 3 sc in corner st, sc across rem lps of foundation ch to next corner, 3 sc in corner st, sc evenly sp over row ends to next corner, fasten off.

Panel Assembly

Left side panel

With RS facing, using larger hook, attach green with a sl st at bottom corner of long edge on right-hand side of either side panel, ch 1, sc evenly sp over row ends to top corner, fasten off.

With tapestry needle and green, letting first and last 11 rows of side panel extend beyond top and bottom edges of center panel, sew right-hand edge of side panel to left edge of center panel from RS, working through back lps only.

Right side panel

With RS facing, using larger hook, attach green with a sl st at

corner, 3 sc in corner st, sc evenly sp over row ends to top corner, sc in same st as beg sc, join in beg sc.

Rnd 2: Ch 1, sc in each st around, working 3 sc in each corner st, join in beg sc, fasten off.

Appliqués

Heart (*make 4*)

Row 1 (RS): With smaller hook and red, ch 2, 3 sc in 2nd ch from hook, ch 1, turn. (3 sc)

Row 2: Sc in each sc across, ch 1, turn. (3 sc)

Row 3: 2 sc in first sc, sc in next sc, 2 sc in last sc, ch 1, turn. (5 sc)

Row 4: Rep Row 2. (5 sc)

First half of top

Row 5: Sc in each of first 2 sc, ch 1, turn. (2 sc)

Row 6: Rep Row 2. (2 sc)

Row 7: Sc dec, fasten off.

Second half of top

Row 5: With RS facing, using smaller hook, sk next st on Row 4, attach red with a sl st in next st, ch 1, sc in same st and in next st, ch 1, turn. (2 sc)

Rows 6 & 7: Rep Rows 6 and 7 of first half of top; do not fasten off at end of Row 7; ch 1, do not turn.

Sc evenly sp around heart, join in beg sc, fasten off, leaving long end for sewing.

Wreath (*make 4*)

Rnd 1: With smaller hook and green, ch 8, join to form a ring, ch 1, 2 sc in each ch around, join in beg sc, fasten off. (16 sc)

Tie 9" length of red into bow at bottom of wreath; trim ends to desired length.

Candy Cane (*make 4*)

With smaller hook, holding 1 strand red and 1 strand white tog, ch 12, fasten off, leaving long end for

top corner of long edge on left side of rem side panel, ch 1, sc evenly sp over row ends to bottom corner, fasten off.

With tapestry needle and green, sew left edge of side panel to right edge of center panel as for left side panel.

Join Center Squares to Center Panel

With tapestry needle and green, sew 2 center squares tog across either long edge from RS through back lps only. Matching green edge across bottom of center squares to green edge at top of center panel, sew sides and

bottom of center squares into opening at top of center panel between side panels.

Rep for 2 rem center squares, joining to opening at bottom of center panel between side panels.

Border

Rnd 1: With RS facing, using larger hook, attach green with a sl st in upper right corner, ch 1, 2 sc in same st, sc in each sc and seam across top to corner, 3 sc in corner st, sc evenly sp over row ends across to bottom corner, 3 sc in corner st, sc in rem lps of foundation ch and in each seam across bottom to

sewing. Tie 10" length of green into bow halfway down candy cane.

Stocking (make 4)

Row 1: Beg at top of stocking, with smaller hook and light blue, ch 4, sc in 2nd ch from hook, sc in each of next 2 chs, ch 1, turn. (3 sc)

Rows 2–7: Sc in each sc across, ch 1, turn; at end of Row 7, do not ch 1 or turn. (3 sc)

Foot

Row 8: Sc over end of last row and end of next row, ch 1, turn.

Row 9: Sc in each of first 3 sts, ch 1, turn.

Row 10: Draw up a lp in each of next 3 sts, yo, draw through all 4 lps on hook, do not fasten off or turn.

Ch 1, sc evenly sp around entire stocking, working 3 sc in each corner, join in beg sc, fasten off, leaving long end for sewing.

Candle (make 3)

Row 1 (RS): With smaller hook and dark blue, ch 4, sc in 2nd ch from hook and in each of next 2 chs, ch 1, turn. (3 sc)

Rows 2–5: Sc in each sc across, ch 1, turn; do not fasten off or turn at end of Row 5.

Sc evenly sp around, working 3 sc in each corner, join in beg sc, fasten off, leaving long end for sewing.

With smaller hook, attach yellow in center st at top of candle, ch 3, holding back on hook last lp of each st, 2 dc in same st, yo, draw through all 3 lps on hook, fasten off, leaving end for sewing.

Bell (make 1 each red, green & yellow)

Row 1: With smaller hook, ch 4, sc in 2nd ch from hook and in each rem ch across, ch 1, turn. (3 sc)

Rows 2–4: Sc in each sc across, ch 1, turn.

Row 5: Sc across, working 2 sc in first and last sts of row, ch 1, turn. (5 sc)

Row 6: Rep Row 5, do not fasten off or turn. (7 sc)

Sc evenly sp around bell, join in beg sc, fasten off, leaving long end for sewing.

Hanging Tab

First hanging tab

Row 1: With RS facing, using larger hook, attach green with sl st in first st on Rnd 2 of border at upper right corner, ch 1, sc in same st and in each of next 2 sts, ch 1, turn.

Rows 2–6: Sc in each sc across, ch 1, turn; at end of Row 6, do not ch 1; fasten off, leaving long end for sewing.

Fold tab to back of wall hanging, sew to top of border with tapestry needle.

Rem 4 tabs

Work as for Rows 1–6 of first hanging tab over each seam across top of wall hanging and over first 3 sts at upper left corner.

Hanger

With larger hook and green, ch 70, fasten off.

Insert dowel through hanger tabs. Tie ends of hanger to ends of dowel. Slip 1 wooden ball over each end of dowel.

Finishing

With tapestry needle, using photo as a guide, sew appliqués to white boxes around outer edge of wall hanging, shaping candy canes as shown in photo. ❧

STITCH AND COLOR KEY
☐ White sc
▣ Red sc

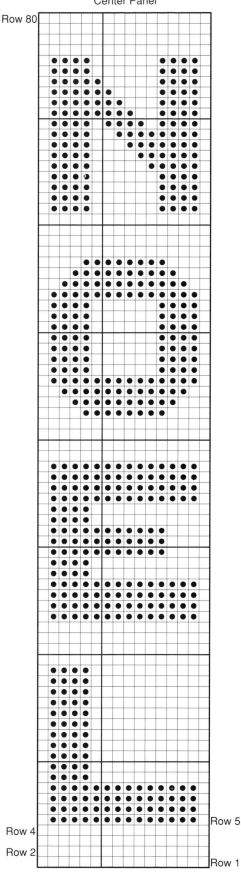

Chart A
Center Panel

Row 80

Row 5

Row 4

Row 2

Row 1

Pattern Note

Join rnds with a sl st unless otherwise stated.

Cross

Rnd 1: Ch 4, join to form a ring, ch 18, sl st in 16th ch from hook (counts as first dc, ch-15 lp), [6 dc in ring, ch 15, sl st in top of last dc made] twice, 6 dc in ring, ch 29, sl st in top of last dc made, 5 dc in ring, join in 3rd ch of beg ch-18. (24 dc in ring)

Rnd 2: Ch 1, *sc in first ch of next ch-15 lp, [2 sc in next ch, sc in next ch] 3 times, 3 sc in next ch, sc in next ch, [2 sc in next ch, sc in next ch] 3 times, sl st in sl st at base of ch-15 lp, sc in each of next 5 dc **, sl st in next dc at base of ch-15 lp, rep from * twice, ending 2nd rep at **, sl st in next dc at base of ch-29 lp, [sc in next ch, 2 sc in next ch] 7 times, 3 sc in next ch, [2 sc in next ch, sc in next ch] 7 times, sl st in sl st as base of ch-29 lp, sc in each of next 5 dc, join in joining st of Rnd 1.

Rnd 3: Working in back lps only, sl st in each of first 3 sc on next ch-15 lp, ch 1, sc in same st as last sl st, *[ch 3, sk next sc, sc in next sc] 4 times, ch 4, sk next sc, sc in next sc, [ch 3, sk next sc, sc in next sc] 4 times, ch 2, sk next 4 sc, sc in both lps of center sc of 5-sc group, ch 3, sl st in last sc made for p, ch 2, sk 4 sc **, working in back lps only, sc in 3rd sc on next ch-15 lp, rep from * twice, ending 2nd rep at **; working in back lps only, sc in 3rd sc on next ch-29 lp, [ch 3, sk next 2 sc, sc in next sc] 5 times, [ch 3, sk next sc, sc in next sc] twice, ch 4, sk next sc, sc in next sc, [ch 3, sk next sc, sc in next sc] twice, [ch 3, sk next 2 sc, sc in next sc] 5 times, ch 2, sk 4 sc, sc in both lps of center sc of 5-sc group, p, ch 2, join in beg sc, fasten off.

Apply fabric stiffener. ❧

Christmas Cross

Design by Jo Ann Maxwell

For many, Christmas is a time of devotion and reflection as well as festivity. Make this lacy cross a lasting symbol of your faith this Christmas season.

Experience Level: Intermediate

Finished Measurements: Approximately 5½" tall x 4¼" wide

Materials

❋ Size 10 crochet cotton: 20 yds cream

❋ Size 5 steel crochet hook or size needed to obtain gauge

❋ Commercial fabric stiffener

Gauge: 24 dc at center of Rnd 1 = 1" in diameter

To save time, take time to check gauge.

Detergent Bottle Apron

Design by Nancy Hearne

Add a touch of Christmas cheer to your kitchen sink with this charming dish detergent bottle apron!

Experience Level: Intermediate

Finished Measurements: Fits average kitchen detergent bottle

Materials

❋ DMC Baroque bedspread weight crochet cotton (400 yds per skein): 1 skein each ecru #0002 (MC), Christmas red #0666 (A) and Christmas green #0699 (B)

❋ Size 5 steel crochet hook or size needed to obtain gauge

❋ 1 yd ¼"-wide red satin ribbon

Gauge: 9 sps = 2⅝"; 9 rows = 2¼" in filet mesh

To save time, take time to check gauge.

Pattern Notes

When working from chart, read odd-numbered (RS) rows from right to left; read even-numbered (WS) rows from left to right.

To change color in dc, work last dc before color change with working color until last 2 lps before final yo rem on hook, drop working color to WS, yo with next color, complete dc.

To change color in pc, work pc with working color until 4th dc is completed, work 5th dc with working color, changing to next color, complete pc with next color.

Carry MC across WS of work when not in use, working over it with A or B until it is needed again.

To carry color not in use across a sp, wrap color not in use around working cotton while working each ch st of sp.

Pattern Stitches

See Instructions for Filet Crochet on page 175.

Cl: Holding back on hook last lp of each st, 3 dc in indicated st or sp, yo, draw through all 4 lps on hook.

Beg cl: Ch 2, holding back on hook last lp of each st, 2 dc in indicated st or sp, yo, draw through all 3 lps on hook.

Popcorn (pc): 5 dc in indicated st or sp, remove hook from lp, insert hook from RS to WS in top of first of 5 dc made, pick up dropped lp, draw through st on hook, ch 1 tightly to secure.

Pc bl: Pc in next st, sk next st, dc in next dc.

Pc bl over a bl: Pc in next dc, sk next dc, dc in next dc.

Pc bl over a sp: Pc in next ch, sk next ch, dc in next dc.

Pc bl over a pc bl: Pc in top of next pc, dc in next dc.

Sp over a pc bl: Ch 2, sk pc, dc in next dc.

V-st: [Dc, ch 3, dc] in indicated st or sp.

Beg V-st: [Ch 6, dc] in indicated st or sp.

Bib

Row 1 (RS): Beg at waist, with MC, ch 32, dc in 8th ch from hook, [ch 2, sk 2 chs, dc in next ch] rep across, turn. (9 sps)

Row 2: Beg sp, [sp over sp] 3 times, changing to B in last dc of last sp, bl over sp, changing to MC in last dc of bl, [sp over sp] 4 times, turn.

Rows 3–9: Work from Chart A; at end of Row 9, fasten off.

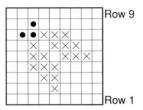

Chart A

Row 9

Row 1

STITCH AND COLOR KEY
☐ MC sp
☒ Christmas green bl
⊡ Christmas red pc bl

Skirt

Row 1: With RS facing, attach MC with a sl st in first sp at bottom of Row 1, ch 6 (counts as first dc, ch-3), [dc, ch 3] twice in same sp, dc in rem lp of foundation ch at base of next dc, [ch 3, dc in next sp, ch 3, dc in rem lp of foundation ch at base of next dc] rep across to last sp, ch 3, [dc, ch 3] twice in last sp, dc in same sp, turn. (20 sps)

Row 2: Sl st in first sp, beg V-st in same sp, V-st in each rem sp across, turn. (20 V-sts)

Rows 3–8: Sl st in first V-st sp, beg V-st in same sp, V-st in each rem V-st sp across, turn. (20 V-sts)

Row 9: Sl st in first V-st sp, [beg cl, ch 5, cl] in same sp, [cl, ch 5, cl] in each rem V-st sp across, do not fasten off at end of row.

Edging

Sc evenly sp across side of apron, side of bib, top of bib, opposite side of bib and opposite side of skirt to opposite bottom corner of skirt, fasten off.

Finishing

Beg at top of bib, insert 1 end of ribbon from RS to WS through first sp at either edge and weave through sps down side to waist. Rep with opposite end of ribbon down opposite edge of bib. Leaving a lp of approximately 5" across top of bib, slip apron over detergent bottle, crisscross ends of ribbon over back of bottle. Bring ends to front of apron and weave each end through sps of Row 1 from side to center. Tie in bow at center and trim ends. ❧

Holiday Welcome Rug

Design by Daria McGuire for Women of Design

Give your holiday guests a warm welcome with this attractive rug. Place it in a hallway or in front of the fireplace for a warm and handsome decoration.

Experience Level: Intermediate

Finished Measurements: Approximately 31½" x 38" including border

Materials

❋ Worsted weight cotton: 22½ oz each dark green (MC) and off-white (CC), 5 oz red, and 2½ oz each black, gold, medium brown and burgundy

❋ Size H/8 crochet hook or size needed to obtain gauge

❋ Tapestry needle

Gauge: 14 sts and 17 rows = 4" in sc

To save time, take time to check gauge.

Pattern Notes

Join rnds with a sl st unless otherwise stated.

To change color in sc, insert hook in indicated st, yo with working color, draw up a lp, drop working color to WS, yo with next color, complete sc. Do not carry color not in use across WS of work; wind small balls of yarn or use bobbins for each separate color section.

When working from chart, read all odd-numbered (RS) rows from right to left; read all even-numbered (WS) rows from left to right.

Bow, pinecone spray and lettering are worked in cross-stitch after rug is completed.

Pattern Stitch

Reverse sc (rev sc): Working from left to right, insert hook in next st to right, yo, draw up a lp, complete sc.

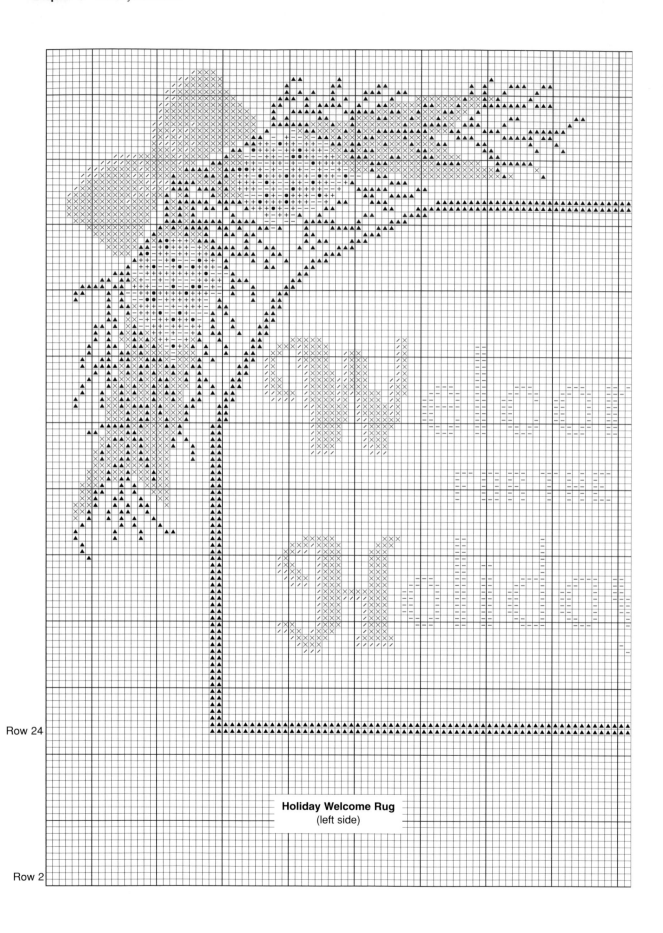

Row 24

Row 2

Holiday Welcome Rug
(left side)

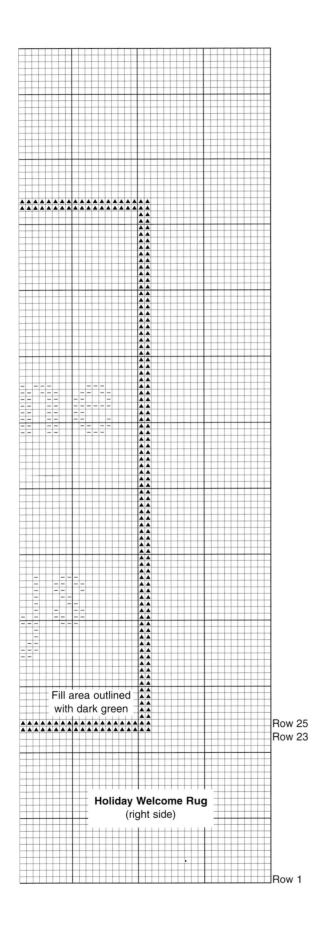

Row 25
Row 23

Fill area outlined with dark green

Holiday Welcome Rug
(right side)

Row 1

Rug

Row 1 (RS): With CC, ch 128, sc in 2nd ch from hook and in each rem ch across, ch 1, turn. (127 sc)

Rows 2–23: Sc in each sc across, ch 1, turn. (127 sc)

Row 24: Sc in each of first 25 sc with CC, changing to MC in 25th sc, sc in each of next 84 sc with MC, changing to CC in 84th sc, sc in each of last 18 sc with CC, ch 1, turn. (127 sc)

Rows 25–127: Continuing in sc, work background and inner border from Chart A; do not fasten off at end of Row 127; ch 1, do not turn.

Note: *Bow, pinecone spray and lettering are worked in cross-stitch after rug is completed.*

Border

Rnd 1: Sc evenly sp around, working 3 sc at each corner, join in beg sc, fasten off.

Rnd 2: With RS facing, attach MC with a sl st in any corner sc, ch 3 (counts as first dc), dc in each rem st around, working 3 dc in each corner sc, join in 3rd ch of beg ch-3.

Rnd 3: Ch 1, rev sc around, join in beg rev sc, fasten off.

Finishing

With tapestry needle, work cross-stitch from chart. ❧

COLOR KEY
▲ Dark green (MC)
☐ Off-white (CC)
☒ Red (A)
● Black (B)
⊟ Gold (C)
⊞ Medium brown (D)
☑ Burgundy (E)

Christmas Colors Runner

Design by Nancy Hearne

Arrange your silverware on this charming runner edged with elegant fringe. It will look festive and beautiful at the same time!

Experience Level: Intermediate

Finished Measurements: Approximately 13" x 24" without fringe

Materials

✳ DMC Cebelia crochet cotton size 20 (50 grams per ball): 2 balls cream #712 (MC), 1 ball each green #699 (A) and burgundy #816 (B)

✳ Size 10 steel crochet hook or size needed to obtain gauge

✳ 14 bobbins (optional)

Gauge: 19 sps and 23 rows = 4" in filet mesh

To save time, take time to check gauge.

Pattern Notes

Join rnds with a sl st unless otherwise stated.

Wind 5 small balls of thread or bobbins each of MC and B; wind 4 small balls of thread or bobbins of A.

Read all odd-numbered (RS) rows from right to left; read all even-numbered (WS) rows from left to right.

To change colors in dc, work last dc before color change with working color until last 2 lps before final yo rem on hook, drop working color to WS, yo with next color and complete dc.

Carry MC across WS of work when not in use, working over it with color in use.

Do not carry color A or B across WS of work for more than 2 bls or sps when not in use; attach

Chart A

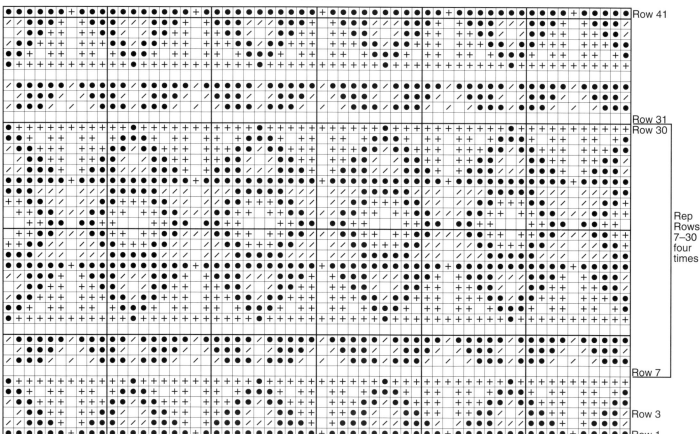

Row 41
Row 31
Row 30
Rep Rows 7–30 four times
Row 7
Row 3
Row 1

separate bobbin or small ball of thread.

To carry color not in use across sp to its next working area, wrap color not in use around working color while working each ch st of sp.

Pattern Stitches

See Instructions for Filet Crochet on page 175.

Runner

Row 1 (RS): With MC, ch 183, dc in 4th ch from hook and in each of next 14 chs, changing to A in last dc, [dc in each of next 3 chs with A, changing to MC in last dc, dc in each of next 33 chs with MC, changing to A in last dc] 4 times, dc in each of next 3 chs with A, changing to MC in last dc, dc in each of last 18 chs

with MC, changing to B in last st, turn.

Row 2: Beg bl over bl, bl over bl, changing to MC in last dc of last bl, *[bl over bl] 3 times, changing to A in last dc of last bl, bl over bl, sp over bl, bl over bl, changing to MC in last dc of last bl, [bl over bl] 3 times, changing to B in last dc of last bl **, [bl over bl] 3 times, changing to MC in last dc of last bl, rep from * across to last bl, ending last rep at **, bl over last bl with B, turn.

Rows 3–30: Work Rows 3–30 from Chart A.

Rows 31–126: Rep Rows 7–30 alternately 4 times.

Rows 127–137: Work Rows 31–41 from chart; at end of Row 137, do not fasten off.

Border

Rnd 1: Ch 6 (counts as first dc, ch-3), dc in top of last dc made, working over row ends, ch 3, dc at base of end st of last row, [ch

3, dc at base of end st of next row] rep across to corner, ch 3, [dc, ch 3] twice in first rem lp of foundation ch, working across foundation ch, [sk 2 sts, dc in next st, ch 3] rep across to next corner, [dc, ch 3] twice in last rem lp of foundation ch, dc in top of end st of first row, ch 3, [dc in top of end st of next row, ch 3] rep across to next corner, [dc, ch 3] twice in first st of last row, [sk 2 sts, dc in next st, ch 3] rep across to next corner, join in 3rd ch of beg ch-6, fasten off.

Fringe

Cut 6 (12") lengths of MC for each ch-3 sp across each short edge. Holding 6 strands tog, fold in half. Insert hook from WS to RS through first ch-3 sp on border at either short edge, draw folded end of strands through sp to form lp, pull cut ends through lp, pull to tighten. Rep for each rem ch-3 sp across each short edge on border of runner. ❧

STITCH AND COLOR KEY
☐ Sp
⦿ Cream bl (MC)
☑ Burgundy bl (B)
⊞ Green bl (A)

Roses in the Snow

Design by Dot Drake

Capture the endless beauty of the rose and winter's first snowfall with this exquisite centerpiece doily.

Experience Level: Advanced

Finished Measurement: 16" in diameter

Materials

❋ J. & P. Coats Knit-Cro-Sheen crochet cotton size 10: 1 (225-yd) ball white #1 (MC) and 1 (150-yd) ball each Spanish red #126 (A) and hunters green #48 (B)

❋ Size 8 steel crochet hook or size needed to obtain gauge

Gauge: Rnds 1–5 of center motif = 1⅞" in diameter

To save time, take time to check gauge

Pattern Note

Join rnds with a sl st unless otherwise stated.

Pattern Stitches

P: Ch 3, sl st in 3rd ch from hook.

Shell: [2 dc, ch 2, 2 dc] in indicated sp or st.

Tr cl: Holding back on hook last lp of each st, work 3 tr in indicated sp or st, yo, draw through all 4 lps on hook.

Beg tr cl: Ch 3, holding back on hook last lp of each st, work 2 tr in indicated sp or st, yo, draw through all 3 lps on hook.

Center Motif

Rnd 1 (RS): With A, ch 6, join to form a ring, ch 1, 12 sc in ring, join in beg sc.

Rnd 2: Ch 1, sc in same st as joining, ch 3, [sk next sc, sc in next sc, ch 3] rep around, join in beg sc. (6 ch-3 lps)

Rnd 3: Sl st in first ch-3 lp, ch 1, beg in same lp, [sc, hdc, 3 dc, hdc, sc] in each ch-3 lp around, do not join. (6 petals)

Rnd 4: Working from behind petals, sl st in first unworked sc of Rnd 2, ch 5, [sl st in next unworked sc of Rnd 2, ch 5] rep around, join in beg sl st. (6 ch-5 lps)

Rnd 5: Sl st in first ch-5 lp, ch 1, beg in same lp, [sc, hdc, 3 dc, p, 3 dc, hdc, sc] in each ch-5 lp around, join in beg sc, fasten off. (6 petals)

Rnd 6: Working behind petals of last rnd, attach B with a sl st to back of post of 2nd hdc on any petal, ch 3, tr at back of first hdc on next petal, ch 12, [holding back on hook last lp of each st, tr at back of next hdc on same petal, tr at back of first hdc on next petal, yo, draw through all 3 lps on hook, ch 12] rep around, join in top of first tr.

Rnd 7: Sl st into first ch-12 lp, ch 1, beg in same lp, work 21 sc in each ch-12 lp around, join in beg sc, fasten off. (126 sc)

Rnd 8: With RS facing, attach MC with a sl st in 6th sc of any 21-sc group, ch 5 (counts as first dc, ch 2), [sk next sc, dc in next sc, ch 2] 5 times, sk next sc, *holding back on hook last lp of each st, dc in next sc, dc in 4th sc of next 21-sc group, yo, draw through all 3 lps on hook **, [ch 2, sk next sc, dc in next sc] 6 times, ch 2, sk next sc, rep from * around, ending last rep at **, ch 2, join in 3rd ch of beg ch-5.

Rnd 9: Ch 3 (counts as first dc), *[2 dc in next sp, dc in next dc] twice, shell in next sp, dc in next dc, [2 dc in next sp, dc in next dc] twice, dc in next sp; holding back on hook last lp of each st, dc in same sp, dc in next sp, yo, draw through all 3 lps on hook, dc in same sp **, dc in next dc, rep from * around, ending last rep at **, join in 3rd ch of beg ch-3, fasten off.

Rnd 10: With RS facing, attach A with a sl st in any shell sp, beg tr cl in same sp, *[ch 3, tr cl in same sp] twice, ch 5, sk next 2 dc of shell and next 2 dc, sc in each of next 13 sts, ch 5 **, tr cl in next shell sp, rep from * around, ending last rep at **, join in top of beg tr cl, fasten off.

Rnd 11: With RS facing, attach MC with a sl st in first sc of any 13-sc group, ch 1, beg in same st, *sc in each of next 13 sc, 7 sc in next ch-5 sp, [5 sc in next ch-3 sp] twice, 7 sc in next ch-5 sp, rep from * around, join in beg sc, fasten off.

First Outer Ring Motif

Rnds 1–10: Rep Rnds 1–10 of center motif.

Rnd 11: With RS facing, attach MC with a sl st in first sc of any 13-sc group, ch 1, beg in same st, sc in each of next 13 sc, 7 sc in next ch-5 sp, 5 sc in next ch-3 sp, 3 sc in in next ch-5 sp, sl st in center sc of any 5-sc group immediately to the right of a 7-sc group on last rnd of center motif,

2 sc in same sp on working motif (first joining to center motif), 4 sc in next ch-5 lp on working motif, sl st in center sc of next 7-sc group on center motif, 3 sc in same lp on working motif, sc in each of next 13 sc, 4 sc in next ch-5 lp, sl st in center sc of next 7-sc group on center motif, 3 sc in same lp on working motif, 3 sc in next ch-5 lp on working motif, sl st in center sc of next 5-sc group on center motif, 2 sc in same lp on working motif, continue around as for Rnd 11 of center motif, fasten off.

Second Outer Ring Motif

Rnds 1–10: Rep Rnds 1–10 of center motif.

Rnd 11: Working first joining to center motif in 2nd unworked 5-sc group on center motif to the right of first joining to center motif of previous outer ring motif, rep Rnd 11 of first outer ring motif until 2nd 5-sc group of working motif has been joined to center motif, 3 sc in

next ch-5 lp, sl st in center sc of corresponding 5-sc group on previous outer ring motif, 2 sc in same lp on working motif, 4 sc in next ch-5 lp on working motif, sl st in center sc of next 7-sc group on previous outer ring motif, 3 sc in same lp on working motif, sc in each of next 13 sc on working motif, 4 sc in next ch-5 lp on working motif, sl st in center sc of next 7-sc group on previous outer ring motif, 3 sc in same lp on working motif, 3 sc in next ch-5 lp on working motif, sl st in center sc of next 5-sc group on previous outer ring motif, 2 sc in same lp on working motif, continue around as for Rnd 11 of center motif, fasten off.

Rem Outer Ring Motifs
(make 4)

Rnds 1–11: Rep Rnds 1–11 of 2nd outer ring motif, also joining right edge of 6th outer ring motif to left edge of first outer ring motif.

Border

Rnd 1: With RS facing, attach MC with a sl st in 4th sc of any 7-sc group immediately to the right of a 5-sc group, ch 1, sc in same st, *ch 5, [sc in 3rd sc of next 5-sc group, ch 5] twice, sc in 4th sc of next 7-sc group, ch 5, sc in 3rd sc of next 13-sc group, sc in each of next 8 sc, ch 5 **, sc in 4th sc of next 7-sc group, rep from * around, ending last rep at **, join in beg sc.

Rnd 2: Sl st in next ch-5 lp, ch 4 (counts as first tr), *p, [ch 2, tr, p] twice in same lp, [ch 2, tr in next ch-5 lp, p, {ch 2, tr, p} twice in same lp] twice, ch 2, [tr, p, ch 2] twice in next lp, holding back on hook last lp of each st, tr in same lp, tr in next lp, yo, draw through all 3 lps on hook, ch 2, [tr, p, ch 2] twice in same lp **, tr in next lp, rep from * around, ending last rep at **, join in 4th ch of beg ch-4, fasten off. ❧

The Christmas Spirit

Nothing says you're in the Christmas spirit quite as much as a wardrobe bursting with holiday cheer! This collection of His and Hers winter warmers, children's sweater sets, festive slippers and more await you in this merriest of chapters!

Winter Berry Cardigan
Instuctions begin on page 125

Fisherman-Style Pullover

Design by Daria McGuire for Women of Design

Display your love for that special man by making this warm and masculine looking sweater. Cuddling up next to him will help you enjoy the warmth and textures as much as he does.

Experience Level: Advanced

Size: Man's size Small(Medium)(Large) Instructions are given for smallest size, with larger sizes in parentheses. When only 1 number is given, it applies to all sizes.

Finished Measurements: Chest: 46(48)(52)"

Length: 26"

Materials

❊ Paton's Canadiana Tweed worsted weight yarn (3.5 oz per ball): 10(12)(14) balls ripe berry

❊ Size I/9 crochet hook or size needed to obtain gauge

❊ Size H/8 crochet hook

Gauge: 18 sts and 10 rows = 5" in dc with larger hook

To save time, take time to check gauge.

Pattern Notes

For each fpdc, bpdc, or fptr worked, sk top of 1 st on last row before working next st on last row.

Join rnds with a sl st unless otherwise stated.

Pattern Stitch

Front post treble crochet (fptr):
Yo twice, insert hook from front to back to front around post of indicated st, yo, draw up a lp, complete tr.

Back Ribbing

Row 1 (RS): With smaller hook, ch 84(90)(96), dc in 4th ch from hook and in each rem ch across, turn. (82, 88, 94 dc, counting last 3 chs of foundation ch as first dc)

Row 2: Ch 3 (counts as first dc throughout), bpdc over each of next 2 sts, [dc in each of next 4 sts, bpdc over each of next 2 sts] rep across, ending with dc in last st, turn.

Row 3: Ch 3, fpdc over each of next 2 sts, [dc in each of next 4 sts, fpdc over each of next 2 sts] rep across, ending with dc in last st, turn.

Row 4: Rep Row 2; do not fasten off; turn.

Back

Row 1: With larger hook, ch 3, dc in each rem st across, turn. (82, 88, 94 dc)

Rep Row 1 until back including ribbing measures 25½" from beg, ending with a WS row; do not fasten off; turn.

First Shoulder

Ch 3, dc in each of next 25(28)(31) dc, fasten off. (26, 29, 32 dc)

2nd Shoulder

Sk next 30 sts on last row of back, attach yarn with a sl st in next st, ch 3, dc in each of last 25(28)(31) sts, fasten off. (26, 29, 32 dc)

With RS facing, using smaller hook, work 1 row sc across last row of each shoulder.

With RS facing, using smaller hook, work 1 row sc evenly sp over row ends across back ribbing and back on each edge.

Front Ribbing

Rows 1–4: Rep Rows 1–4 of back ribbing.

Row 1: Rep Row 1 of back.

Row 2 and all even (WS) rows: Sc in each st across, turn. (82, 88, 94 sc)

Row 3: Ch 3, dc in each of next 10(13)(16) sc, *fptr over next dc on row before last, dc in each of next 5 sc, sk next dc on row before last, fptr over next dc; working behind fptr just made, fptr over sk dc on row before last, dc in each of next 5 sc, fptr over next dc on row before last*, dc in each of next 4 sc, [sk dc on row before last directly beneath last dc worked, fptr over next dc to the right on row before last, fptr over sk dc on row before last, dc in each of next 2 sc on last row] 7 times, rep from * to * once, dc in each of next 11(14)(17) sc, ch 1, turn.

Row 5: Ch 3, dc in each of next 10(13)(16) sc, *fptr over next fptr, dc in each of next 4 sc, fptr over next fptr, dc in each of next 2 sc, fptr over next fptr, dc in each of next 4 sc, fptr over next fptr*, [sk next 2 sts on row before last, fptr over each of next 2 dc, dc in each of next 2 sc] 8 times, rep from * to * once, dc in each of last 11(14)(17) sc, ch 1, turn.

Row 7: Ch 3, dc in each of next

10(13)(16) sc, *fptr over next fptr, dc in each of next 3 sc, fptr over next fptr, dc in each of next 4 sc, fptr over next fptr, dc in each of next 3 sc, fptr over next fptr*, dc in each of next 4 sc, [sk dc on row before last directly beneath last dc worked, fptr over next dc to the right on row before last, fptr over sk dc, dc in each of next 2 sc] 7 times, rep from * to * once, dc in each of last 11(14)(17) sc, ch 1, turn.

Row 9: Ch 3, dc in each of next 10(13)(16) sc, *fptr over next fptr, dc in each of next 2 sc, fptr over next fptr, dc in each of next 6 sc, fptr over next fptr, dc in each of next 2 sc, fptr over next fptr*, [sk next 2 sts on row before last, fptr over each of next 2 dc, dc in each of next 2 sc] 8 times, rep from * to * once, dc in each of last 11(14)(17) sc, ch 1, turn.

Row 11: Ch 3, dc in each of next 10(13)(16) sc, *fptr over next fptr, dc in next sc, fptr over next fptr, dc in each of next 8 sc, fptr over next fptr, dc in next sc, fptr over next fptr*, dc in each of next 4 sc, [sk dc on row before last directly beneath last dc worked, fptr over next dc to the right on row before last, fptr over sk dc, dc in each of next 2 sc] 7 times, rep from *to * once, dc in each of last 11(14)(17) sc, ch 1, turn.

Row 13: Ch 3, dc in each of next 10(13)(16) sc, *fptr over next fptr, dc in each of next 2 sc, fptr over next fptr, dc in each of next 6 sc, fptr over next fptr, dc in each of next 2 sc, fptr over next fptr*, [sk next 2 sts on row before last, fptr over each of next 2 dc, dc in each of next 2 sc] 8 times, rep from * to * once, dc in each of last 11(14)(17) sc, ch 1, turn.

Row 15: Ch 3, dc in each of next 10(13)(16) sc, *fptr over next fptr, dc in each of next 3 sc,

fptr over next fptr, dc in each of next 4 sc, fptr over next fptr, dc in each of next 3 sc, fptr over next fptr*, dc in each of next 4 sc, [sk dc on row before last directly beneath last dc worked, fptr over next dc to the right on row before last, fptr over sk dc, dc in each of next 2 sc] 7 times, rep from * to * once, dc in each of last 11(14)(17) sc, ch 1, turn.

Row 17: Ch 3, dc in each of next 10(13)(16) sc, *fptr over next fptr, dc in each of next 4 sc, fptr over next fptr, dc in each of next 2 sc, fptr over next fptr, dc in each of next 4 sc, fptr over next fptr*, [sk next 2 sts on row before last, fptr over each of next 2 dc, dc in each of next 2 sc] 8 times, rep from * to * once, dc in each of last 11(14)(17) sc, ch 1, turn.

Row 19: Ch 3, dc in each of next 10(13)(16) sc, *fptr over next fptr, dc in each of next 5 sc, [fptr over next fptr] twice, dc in each of next 5 sc, fptr over next fptr*, dc in each of next 4 sc, [sk dc on row before last directly beneath last dc worked, fptr over next dc to the right on row before last, fptr over sk dc, dc in each of next 2 sc] 7 times, rep from * to * once, dc in each of last 11(14)(17) sc, ch 1, turn.

Row 21: Ch 3, dc in each of next 10(13)(16) sc, *fptr over next fptr, dc in each of next 4 sc, sk next fptr, fptr over next fptr, dc in each of next 2 sc; working behind last fptr made, fptr over sk fptr, dc in each of next 4 sc, fptr over next fptr*, [sk next 2 sts on row before last, fptr over each of next 2 dc, dc in each of next 2 sc] 8 times, rep from * to * once, dc in each of last 11(14)(17) sc, ch 1, turn.

Row 22: Rep Row 2.

Rows 23–53: Rep Rows 7–22 alternately, ending with a Row

21; do not fasten off at end of Row 53; ch 1, turn.

First Shoulder

Row 54: Sc in each of first 31 (34)(37) sts, turn. (31, 34, 37 sc)

Row 55: Sl st in each of first 2 sts, ch 3, sk dc on row before last directly beneath ch-3 just made, fptr over next dc to the right on row before last, fptr over sk dc, dc in each of next 2 sc, rep from * to * on Row 15, dc in each of last 11(14)(17) sc, ch 1, turn.

Row 56: Sc in each of first 29(32)(35) sts, turn.

Row 57: Sl st in each of first 2 sts, ch 3, dc in each of next 2 sc, rep from * to * on Row 13, dc in each of last 11(14)(17 sc, ch 1, turn.

Row 58: Sc in each of first 27(30)(33) sts, turn.

Row 59: Sl st in each of first 2 sts, ch 3, rep from * to * on Row 11, dc in each of last 11(14)(17) sc, ch 1, turn.

Row 60: Sc in each of first 26(29)(32) sts, turn.

Row 61: Ch 3, rep from * to * on Row 9, dc in each of last 11(14)(17) sc, fasten off. (26, 29, 32 sts)

2nd Shoulder

Row 54: With WS facing, sk next 20 sts on Row 53, using larger hook, attach thread with a sl st in next st, ch 1, sc in same st and in each rem st across, turn. (31, 34, 37 sc)

Row 55: Ch 3, dc in each of next 10(13)(16) sc, rep from * to * on Row 15, dc in each of next 5 sts, leave last st unworked, turn.

Row 56: Sl st in first dc, sc in each rem st across, turn. (29, 32, 35 sc)

Row 57: Ch 3, dc in each of next 10(13)(16) sc, rep from * to * on Row 13, dc in each of next 3 sc, ch 1, turn.

Row 58: Sl st in first dc, sc in each rem st across, turn. (27, 30, 33 sc)

Row 59: Ch 3, dc in each of next 10(13)(16) sc, rep from * to * on Row 11, dc in next sc, ch 1, turn.

Row 60: Sc in each st across, turn. (26, 29, 32 sc)

Row 61: Ch 3, dc in each of next 10(13)(16) sc, rep from * to * on Row 9, dc in last sc, fasten off. (26, 29, 32 sts)

With RS facing, using smaller hook, work 1 row sc across last row of each shoulder.

With RS facing, using smaller hook, work 1 row sc evenly sp over row ends across front ribbing and front at each edge.

Sleeve (make 2)
Sleeve Ribbing
Row 1: With smaller hook, ch 42, dc in 4th ch from hook and in each rem ch across, turn. (40 dc, counting last 3 chs of foundation ch as first dc)

Rows 2–4: Rep Rows 2–4 of back ribbing.

Sleeve Body
Row 1: With larger hook, ch 3, dc in each rem st across, turn. (40 dc)

Row 2: Ch 3, dc in first st, dc in each rem st across to last st, 2 dc in last st, turn. (42 dc)

Rows 3–35: Rep Rows 1 and 2 alternately, ending with a Row 1; fasten off at end of Row 35. (74 sts on Rows 34 and 35)

With RS facing, using smaller hook, attach thread with a sl st over end st of Row 1 of sleeve ribbing, ch 1, beg in same st, sc evenly sp over row ends to top of sleeve, sc in each st across last row of sleeve, sc evenly sp over row ends to end st of Row 1 of sleeve ribbing on opposite side, fasten off.

Finishing
Sew shoulder seams.

Position top center of sleeve at shoulder seam; sew sleeve in place. Rep for rem sleeve. Sew underarm and side seams.

Neckband
Rnd 1: With RS facing, using smaller hook, attach yarn with a sl st at right shoulder seam, ch 3, work 2 more dc over row end of shoulder, work 30 dc across back neck, 3 dc over row end of next shoulder, 13 dc evenly sp down left neck to front neck, 20 dc across front neck, 13 dc up right front neck, join in 3rd ch of beg ch-3. (82 dc)

Rnd 2: Ch 1, sc in same st as joining and in next st, sc dec, [sc in each of next 3 sts, sc dec] rep around, ending with sc in each of last 3 sts, join in beg sc. (66 sts)

Rnd 3: Ch 3, dc in each of next 3 sts, fptr over each of next 2 dc on rnd before last, [dc in each of next 4 sts on last rnd, fptr over each of next 2 dc on rnd before last] rep around, join in 3rd ch of beg ch-3. (66 sts)

Rnd 4: Ch 1, sc in same st as joining and in each rem st around, join in beg sc, fasten off. ❧

Winter Berry Cardigan

Design by Daria McGuire for Women of Design

This beautifully designed sweater embellished wih fine details will make you feel festive each and every time you wear it.

Experience Level: Intermediate

Size: Woman's size Medium(Large) Instructions are given for smaller size, with larger size in parentheses. When only 1 number is given, it applies to both sizes.

Finished Measurements: Chest: 44(50)"; Length: 25"

Materials
- Paton's Decor worsted weight yarn (3.5 oz per skein): 4(5) skeins hunter green (MC), 3(4) skeins autumn variegated (CC), 1 skein deep coralberry (A), and small amount rich bronze (B)
- Size I/9 crochet hook or size needed to obtain gauge
- Size H/8 crochet hook
- 22" long separating zipper
- 2½" x 5" piece of cardboard
- Tapestry needle

Gauge: [Shell, 2 dc, shell, dc] = 4" in patt st with larger hook

To save time, take time to check gauge.

Pattern Note

To change color in dc, work last dc before color change in working color until last 2 lps before final yo rem on hook, drop working color to WS, yo with next color, complete dc.

Join rnds with a sl st unless otherwise stated.

Pattern Stitch

Shell: 5 dc in indicated st.

Back

Row 1 (RS): With larger hook and MC, ch 71(77) for foundation ch, ch 3 more (counts as first dc), dc in 4th ch from hook, dc in each of next 0(3) chs, *sk 2 chs, shell in next ch, sk 2 chs**, dc in each of next 2 chs, rep from * across to last 2(5) chs, ending last rep at **, dc in each of last 2(5) chs, turn. (10 shells)

Row 2: Ch 3 (counts as first dc throughout), dc in each of next 1(4) dc, shell in center dc of next shell, sk next 2 dc of same shell**, dc in each of next 2 dc, rep from * across, ending last rep at **, dc in each of last 2(5) dc, changing to CC in last st, fasten off MC, turn.

Row 3: Rep Row 2 with CC, do not change color in last st; turn.

Row 4: Rep Row 2, changing to MC in last st, fasten off CC, turn.

Row 5: Rep Row 2 with MC, do not change color in last st; turn.

Row 6: Rep Row 2.

Rows 7–33: Rep Rows 3–6 alternately, ending with a Row 5; do not fasten off at end of Row 33; turn.

Shape Neck

First Shoulder

Row 34: Ch 3, dc in each of next 1(4) dc, [shell in center dc of next shell, sk next 2 dc of same shell, dc in each of next 2 dc] twice, 2 dc in center dc of next shell, changing to CC in last st, fasten off MC, turn.

Row 35: Ch 2, sk first 2 dc, dc in each of next 2 dc, [shell in center dc of next shell, sk next 2 dc of same shell, dc in each of next 2 dc] twice, dc in each of last 0(3) dc, turn.

Row 36: Ch 3, dc in each of next 1(4) dc, [shell in center dc of same shell, dc in each of next 2 dc] twice, changing to MC in last st, fasten off CC, turn.

Row 37: Ch 3, dc in next dc, [shell in center dc of next shell, sk next 2 dc of same shell, dc in each of next 2 dc] twice, dc in each of last 0(3) dc, ch 1, turn.

Row 38: Sc in each of first 2(5) dc, [ch 2, sc in center dc of next shell, ch 2, sk next 2 dc of same shell, sc in each of next 2 dc] twice, ch 1, turn.

Row 39: Sc in each of first 2 sc, [2 sc in next sp, sc in next sc, 2 sc in next sp, sc in each of next 2 sc] twice, sc in each of last 0(3) sc, fasten off.

2nd Shoulder

Row 34: With WS facing, sk next 4 unworked shells on Row 33, using larger hook, attach MC with a sl in center dc of next shell, ch 3, dc in same st, sk next 2 dc of same shell, [dc in each of next 2 dc, shell in center dc of next shell, sk next 2 dc of same shell] twice, dc in each of last 2(5) dc, changing to CC in last st, fasten off MC, turn.

Row 35: Ch 3, dc in each of next 1(4) dc, [shell in center dc of next shell, sk next 2 dc of same shell, dc in each of next 2 dc] twice, turn.

Row 36: Ch 3, dc in next dc, shell in center dc of next shell, sk next 2 dc of same shell, dc in

each of next 2 dc, shell in center dc of next shell, sk next 2 dc of same shell, dc in each of last 2(5) dc, changing to MC in last st, fasten off CC, turn.

Row 37: Ch 3, dc in each of next 1(4) dc, [shell in center dc of next shell, sk next 2 dc of same shell, dc in each of next 2 dc] twice, ch 1, turn.

Row 38: Sc in each of first 2 dc, [ch 2, sc in center dc of next shell, ch 2, sk next 2 dc of same shell, sc in each of next 2 dc] twice, sc in each of last 0(3) dc, ch 1, turn.

Row 39: Sc in each of first 2(5) sc, [2 sc in next ch-2 sp, sc in next sc, 2 sc in next ch-2 sp, sc in each of next 2 sc] twice, fasten off.

Back Edging

Rnd 1: With RS facing, using smaller hook, attach MC with a sl st in first rem lp of foundation ch at bottom right corner, ch 1, sc in same st, [ch 1, sk 1 st, sc in next st] rep across to next corner; working over row ends, [ch 1, sk approximately ¼", sc over edge] rep across to next corner, continue as established across top and down next side, join in beg sc, fasten off.

Left Front

Row 1 (RS): With MC and larger hook, ch 29(32) for foundation ch, ch 3 more (counts as first dc), dc in 4th ch from hook, dc in each of next 0(3) chs, [sk 2 chs, shell in next ch, sk 2 chs, dc in each of next 2 chs] rep across, turn. (4 shells)

Row 2: Ch 3 (counts as first dc throughout), dc in next dc, *shell in center dc of next shell, sk next 2 dc of same shell**, dc in each of next 2 dc, rep from * across to last shell, ending last rep at **, dc in each of last 2(5) dc, changing to CC in last st, fasten off MC, turn.

Row 3: Ch 3, dc in each of next 1(4) dc, [shell in center dc of next shell, sk next 2 dc of same shell, dc in each of next 2 dc] rep across, turn.

Row 4: Rep Row 2, changing to MC in last st, fasten off CC, turn.

Row 5: Rep Row 3 with MC.

Row 6: Rep Row 2.

Rows 7–31: Rep Rows 3–6 alternately, ending with a Row 3.

Shape Neck

Row 32: Ch 1, sc in each of first 2 dc, ch 2, sc in center dc of first shell, ch 2, sk next 2 dc of same shell, dc in each of next 2 dc, *shell in center dc of next shell, sk next 2 dc of same shell**, dc in each of next 2 dc, rep from * across to last shell, ending last rep at **, dc in each of last 2(5) dc, changing to MC in last st, fasten off CC, turn.

Row 33: Ch 3, dc in each of next 1(4) dc, [shell in center dc of next shell, sk next 2 dc of same shell, dc in each of next 2 dc] 3 times, ch 1, turn.

Row 34: Sc in first dc, ch 2, 2 dc in center dc of next shell, sk next 2 dc of same shell, [dc in each of next 2 dc, shell in center dc of next shell, sk next 2 dc of same shell] twice, dc in each of last 2(5) dc, changing to CC in last st, fasten off MC, turn.

Row 35: Ch 3, dc in each of next 1(4) dc, [shell in center of next shell, sk next 2 dc of same shell, dc in each of next 2 dc] twice, sk next dc, dc in next dc, turn.

Row 36: Ch 3, [dc in each of next 2 dc, shell in center dc of next shell, sk next 2 dc of same shell] twice, dc in each of next 2(5) dc, changing to MC in last st, turn.

Row 37: Ch 3, dc in each of

next 1(4) dc, [shell in center dc of next shell, sk next 2 dc of same shell, dc in each of next 2 dc] twice, ch 1, turn.

Rows 38 & 39: Rep Rows 38 and 39 of 2nd shoulder for back.

Left Front Edging

Rnd 1: With RS facing, using smaller hook, attach MC with a sl st in first rem lp of foundation ch at bottom right corner, rep Rnd 1 of back edging across bottom, up side, across shoulder, and down neck and front opening, join in beg sc, fasten off.

Right Front

Row 1 (RS): With MC and larger hook, ch 29(32) for foundation ch, ch 3 more (counts as first dc), dc in 4th ch from hook, *sk 2 chs, shell in next ch, sk 2 chs**, dc in each of next 2 chs, rep from * across to last 2(5) chs, ending last rep at **, dc in each of last 2(5) chs, turn. (4 shells)

Row 2: Ch 3, dc in each of next 1(4) dc, [shell in center dc of next shell, sk next 2 dc of same shell, dc in each of next 2 dc] rep across, changing to CC in last st, fasten off MC, turn.

Row 3: Ch 3, dc in next dc, *shell in center dc of next shell, sk next 2 dc of same shell**, dc in each of next 2 dc, rep from * across to last shell, ending last rep at **, dc in each of next 2(5) dc, turn.

Row 4: Rep Row 2, changing to MC in last st, fasten off CC, turn.

Row 5: Rep Row 3 with MC.

Row 6: Rep Row 2.

Rows 7–31: Rep Rows 3–6 alternately, ending with a Row 3.

Shape Neck

Row 32: Ch 3, dc in each of next 1(4) dc, [shell in center dc of next shell, sk next 2 dc of

same shell, dc in each of next 2 dc] 3 times, dc in center dc of next shell, changing to MC, turn.

Row 33: Ch 2, sk first dc, dc in each of nex 2 dc, *shell in center dc of next shell, sk next 2 dc of same shell**, dc in each of next 2 dc, rep from * across to last shell, ending last rep a **, dc in each of last 2(5) dc, turn.

Row 34: Ch 3, dc in each of next 1(4) dc, [shell in center dc of next shell, sk next 2 dc of same shell, dc in each of next 2 dc] twice, 2 dc in center dc of next shell, sk next 2 dc of same shell and next dc, dc in next dc, changing to CC, fasten off MC, ch 1, turn.

Row 35: Sk first dc, sc in next dc, ch 2, sk next dc, [dc in each of next 2 dc, shell in center dc of next shell, sk next 2 dc of same shell] twice, dc in each of last 2(5) dc, turn.

Row 36: Ch 3, dc in each of next 1(4) dc, [shell in center dc of next shell, sk next 2 dc of same shell, dc in each of next 2 dc] twice, changing to MC in last st, fasten off CC, turn.

Row 37: Ch 3, dc in next dc, [shell in center dc of next shell, sk next 2 dc of same shell, dc in each of next 2 dc] twice, dc in each of last 0(3) dc, ch 1, turn.

Rows 38 & 39: Rep Rows 38 and 39 of first shoulder for back.

Right Front Edging

Rnd 1: With RS facing, using smaller hook, attach MC with a sl st in first rem lp of foundation ch at bottom right corner, rep Rnd 1 of back edging across bottom, up front opening, across neck and top and down side, join in beg sc, fasten off.

Front Band (*make 2*)

Row 1 (RS): With A and smaller hook, ch 8, sc in 2nd ch

from hook and in each rem ch across, ch 1, turn. (7 sc).

Rows 2–78: Ch 1, sc in each sc across, ch 1, turn; at end of Row 78, do not ch 1; fasten off.

Left Front Band Edging

Row 1: With smaller hook and RS facing, working over row ends at right edge of either band, attach MC with a sl st in bottom corner, ch 1, sc in same st, [ch 1, sk approximately ¼", sc over edge] rep evenly sp across edge to top, fasten off.

Sew side of front band with edging to left front.

Right Front Band Edging

Row 1: With smaller hook and RS facing, working over row ends at left edge of rem band, attach MC with a sl st in top corner, rep Row 1 of left front band edging.

Sew side of front band with edging to right front.

Sleeve (make 2)

Row 1 (RS): With MC and smaller hook, ch 31 for foundation ch, ch 3 more (counts as first dc), dc in 4th ch from hook, dc in next ch, *sk 2 chs, shell in next ch, sk 2 chs**, dc in each of next 2 chs, rep from * across to last 3 sts, ending last rep at **, dc in each of last 3 chs, turn. (4 shells; 3 dc at each edge)

Row 2: Ch 3, dc in each of next 2 dc, *shell in center dc of next shell, sk next 2 dc of same shell**, dc in each of next 2 dc, rep from * across to last shell, ending last rep at **, dc in each of last 3 dc, changing to CC in last st, fasten off MC, turn.

Row 3: Ch 3, dc in each rem dc across to first shell, *shell in center dc of next shell, sk next 2 dc of same shell**, dc in each of next 2 dc, rep from * across to last shell, ending last rep at **, dc in each rem dc across, turn.

Row 4: Ch 3, dc in first dc, dc in each rem dc across to first shell, shell in center dc of first shell, *sk next 2 dc of same shell**, dc in each of next 2 dc, shell in center dc of next shell, rep from * across to last shell, ending last rep at **, dc in each rem dc across to last dc, 2 dc in last dc, changing to MC in last dc, fasten off CC, turn. (4 shells; 4 dc at each edge)

Row 5: Rep Row 3 with MC.

Row 6: Rep Row 4, changing to CC in last dc, fasten off MC. (4 shells; 5 dc at each edge)

Rows 7-29: Rep Rows 3–6 alternately, ending with a Row 5. (4 shells, 16 dc at each edge on Rows 28 and 29).

Row 30: Ch 1, sc in each dc across to first shell, ch 2, sk first 2 dc of shell, sc in center dc of next shell, *ch 2, sk next 2 dc of same shell**, sc in each of next 2 dc, ch 2, sc in center dc of next shell, rep from * across to last shell, ending last rep at **, sc in each rem dc across, ch 1, turn.

Row 31: Sc in each sc across to first ch-2 sp, *2 sc in ch-2 sp, sc in next sc, 2 sc in next ch-2 sp**, sc in each of next 2 sc, rep from * across, ending last rep at **, sc in each rem sc across, fasten off.

Sleeve Edging

Row 1: With RS facing, using smaller hook and working over row ends across either edge, attach MC with a sl st at right corner, rep Row 1 of front band edging. Rep on opposite edge of same sleeve.

Cuff

Row 1: With RS facing, using smaller hook, attach A with a sl st in first rem lp of foundation ch at bottom of sleeve, ch 1, sc in same st, work 29 more sc evenly sp across, ch 1, turn. (30 sc)

Rows 2–7: Ch 1, sc in each sc across, ch 1, turn; do not ch 1 at end of Row 7; fasten off. (30 sc)

Cuff Edging

Row 1: With RS facing, using smaller hook and beg over end st of Row 1 and working over row ends, attach MC with a sl st, ch 1, sc in same st, *[ch 1, sk next row, sc over end of next row] 3 times*, sc in each st across to next corner, sc over end st of last row, rep from * to *, fasten off.

Finishing

Sew shoulder seams. Matching center tops of sleeves to shoulder seams, sew sleeves in position. Leaving approximately 1¼" at bottom edges of cuffs free, sew underarm and side seams. Turn back cuffs.

Neckband

Row 1: With RS facing, using smaller hook, attach A with a sl st in upper right corner of front band on right front, ch 1, beg in same st, work 7 sc evenly sp across row ends of front band, 30 sc evenly sp across front neck to shoulder seam, 60 sc evenly sp across back neck to shoulder seam, 30 sc evenly sp across left front neck to front band, 7 sc across row ends of front band, ch 1, turn. (134 sc)

Row 2: Sc in each of first 14 sts, [sc dec, sc in each of next 13 sts] rep across, ch 1, turn. (126 sts)

Row 3: Sc in each of first 17 sts, sc dec, [sc in each of next 16 sts, sc dec] 5 times, sc in each of last 17 sts, ch 1, turn. (120 sts)

Row 4: Sc in each of first 15 sts, [sc dec, sc in each of next 16 sts, sc dec, sc in each of next 15 sts] rep across, ch 1, turn. (114 sts)

Row 5: Sc in each of first 10 sts, [sc dec, sc in each of next 11 sts] rep across, ch 1, turn. (106 sts)

Row 6: Sc in each of first 13 sts, [sc dec, sc in each of next 14 sts, sc dec, sc in each of next 13 sts] rep across, ch 1, turn. (100 sts)

Row 7: Sc in each of first 13 sts, [sc dec, sc in each of next 12 sts, sc dec, sc in each of next 13 sts] rep across, ch 1, turn. (94 sts)

Row 8: Sc in each of first 11 sts, sc dec, [sc in each of next 12 sts, sc dec] 5 times, sc in each of last 11 sts, ch 1, turn. (88 sts)

Row 9: Sc in each of first 10 sts, [sc dec, sc in each of next 11 sts] rep across, ch 1, turn. (82 sts)

Row 10: Sc in each of first 8 sts, *[sc dec, sc in each of next 7 sts] 3 times, sc dec, sc in each of next 8 sts, rep from * across, fasten off. (74 sts)

Border

Rnd 1: With RS facing, using smaller hook, attach MC with a sl st at bottom right corner, ch 1, sc in same st, working in rem lps of foundation ch across bottom of front band, [ch 1, sk next st, sc in next st] 3 times, ch 1, sc in next ch-1 sp at bottom of sweater, [ch 1, sc in next ch-1 sp] rep across to next front band, ch 1, sc in first rem lp of foundation ch at bottom of front band, [ch 1, sk next st, sc in next st] 3 times; working over row ends of front, [ch 1, sk approximately ¼", sc over edge] rep up front band to neck, continue in pat of [sc, ch 1] around neck and down opposite front opening, join in beg sc, do not turn.

Rnd 2: Ch 1, rev sc in next sp to the right, ch-1, [rev sc in next ch-1 sp, ch 1] rep around, join in beg rev sc, fasten off.

Sew zipper to front opening.

Continued on page 139

Christmas Plaid Tunic

Design by Maureen Egan Emlet

Enjoy the holidays with your sweetheart in these brightly colored plaid sweaters. The rows of shells across the bottom will give you a feminine accent when you wear this as a couple with a special man in your life. He will look Dashing in his coordinating vest with the solid-color back and bold buttons.

Experience Level: Intermediate

Size: Woman's small(medium)(large) Instructions are given for smallest size, with larger sizes in parentheses. When only 1 number is given, it applies to all sizes.

Finished Measurements: Chest: 38(42)(48)"; Length: 23(25¼)(27½)" with lace border

Materials

❋ Spinrite Bernat Berella "4" worsted weight yarn (3.5 oz per skein): 3(3)(4) skeins winter white #8941 (A), 2(2)(3) skeins each geranium #8929 (B) and hunter green #8981 (C), and 1(1)(2) skeins deep colonial blue #8860 (D)

❋ Size H/8 crochet hook or size needed to obtain gauge

Gauge: 16 sts and 18 rows = 4" in sc

To save time, take time to check gauge.

Pattern Notes

Tunic is shown with lace border. Instructions are also given for optional ribbing, which may be used instead of lace border. Use 1 less skein A and 1 more skein B(B)(C) if working ribbing.

When working from chart, read all odd-numbered (RS) rows from right to left, all even-numbered (WS) rows from left to right.

To change color in sc, insert hook in indicated st, yo with working color, draw up a lp, drop working color to WS, yo with next color and complete sc.

Join rnds with a sl st unless otherwise stated.

Pattern Stitches

Dc cl: Holding back on hook last lp of each st, work 2 dc in indicated st or sp, yo, draw through all 3 lps on hook.

Cl shell: [Dc cl, ch 2] twice in indicated st or sp, dc cl in same st or sp.

Surface ch: Make sl knot and remove sl knot from hook. With working yarn at WS, insert hook from RS to WS through first indicated sp, pick up sl knot, draw through sp to RS, [insert hook from RS to WS in next indicated sp, yo, draw through sp and through lp on hook] rep as indicated.

Holiday Vest
Instructions begin on page 133

Back

Lace border

Row 1 (RS): With A, ch 76(86)(101), ch 5 more (counts as first dc, ch 2), dc cl in 6th ch from hook, sk 4 chs, [cl shell in next ch, sk 4 chs] rep across to last ch, [dc cl, ch 2, dc] in last ch, ch 1, turn.

Row 2: Sc in first dc, ch 5, [sc in center dc cl of next cl shell, ch 5] rep across, ending with sc in 3rd ch of turning ch-5, turn.

Row 3: Ch 5 (counts as first dc, ch 2 throughout), dc cl in first sc, [cl shell in next sc] rep across to last sc, [dc cl, ch 2, dc] in last sc, ch 1, turn.

Rows 4–13(15)(17): Rep Rows 2 and 3 alternately; at end of Row 13(15)(17), ch 1, do not turn.

Row 14(16)(18): Reverse sc in each dc cl and sp across, fasten off.

Ribbing (optional)

Row 1: With B(B)(C), ch 15, sc in 2nd ch from hook and in each rem ch across, ch 1, turn. (14 sc)

Row 2: Working in back lps only, sc in each sc across, ch 1, turn. (14 sc)

Rep Row 2 until ribbing measures 16(17)(19)", fasten off.

Row 1: With RS facing, attach A with a sl st in first rem lp of foundation ch at right edge of lace border (for ribbing, working across row ends on either long edge, attach A with a sl st in upper right corner), ch 1, beg in same st as joining, work 75(84)(96) sc evenly sp across, changing to B in last st, fasten off A, ch 1, turn.

Row 2: Following Chart A, work from D to B 1(0)(1) times, from C to B 1(4)(2) times, and from C to A 1(0)(1) times; ch 1, turn.

Row 3: Continuing to follow chart, work from A to C 1(0)(1) times, from B to C 1(4)(2) times, and from B to D 1(0)(1) times; ch 1, turn.

Rows 4–17: Rep Rows 2 and 3 alternately, changing colors as indicated on Chart A.

Rows 18–67(73)(79): Rep Rows 2–17 alternately, ending with a Row 3(9)(15).

Neck shaping

Row 1: Work in established pattern across first 28(30)(34) sts, sl st in each of next 19(24)(28) sts, work in pattern across rem 28(30)(34) sts, ch 1, turn.

Row 2: Work in pattern across 25(27)(31) sts, sl st in each of next 25(30)(34) sts, work in pattern across rem 25(27)(31) sts, ch 1, turn.

Row 3: Work in pattern across 23(25)(29) sts, sl st in each of next 29(34)(38) sts, work in pattern across rem 23(25)(29) sts, ch 1, turn.

Row 4: Work in pattern across 22(24)(28) sts, sl st in each of next 31(36)(40) sts, work in pattern across rem 22(24)(28) sts, ch 1, turn.

Row 5: Work in pattern across 21(23)(27) sts, sl st in each of next 33(38)(42) sts, work in pattern across rem 21(23)(27) sts, ch 1, turn.

Row 6: Work in pattern across 20(22)(26) sts, sl st in each of next 35(40)(44) sts, work in pattern across rem 20(22)(26) sts, ch 1, turn.

Row 7: Sc in each sc and in each sl st across, fasten off.

Front

Lace border

Rows 1–18: Rep Rows 1–14(16)(18) of lace border for back.

Ribbing *(optional)*

Rep ribbing for back if using ribbing instead of lace border.

Body

Rows 1–67(73)(79): Rep Rows 1–67(73)(79) of body for back.

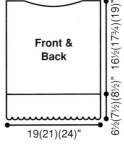

Front & Back

6½(7½)(8½)" 16½(17¾)(19)"

19(21)(24)"

Chart A
Back/Front

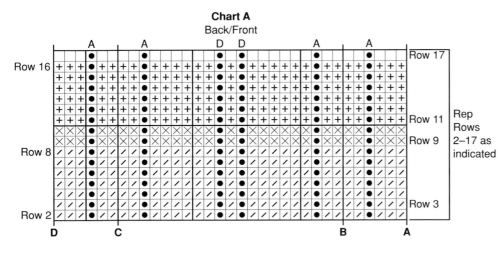

Row 17
Row 16
Row 11
Row 9
Row 8
Row 3
Row 2

D   C   B   A
A   A   D D   A   A

Rep Rows 2–17 as indicated

COLOR AND STITCH KEY

□ Sc with A
☑ Sc with B
⊞ Sc with C
⊠ Sc with D
● Ch-1 in same color as row in progress
A Surface ch with A
D Surface ch with D
Note: A and D surface ch are to be worked after back/front is completed.

Neck shaping

Rows 1–7: Rep Rows 1–7 of neck shaping for back.

Sleeve *(make 2)*

Lace cuff

Row 1: With A, ch 36(41)(51), ch 5 more (counts as first dc, ch-2), dc cl in 6th ch from hook, sk 4 chs, [cl shell in next ch, sk 4 chs] rep across to last ch, [dc cl, ch 2, dc] in last ch, ch 1, turn.

Rows 2 & 3: Rep Rows 2 and 3 of lace border for back.

Rows 4–7: Rep Rows 2 and 3 alternately.

Row 8: Rep Row 14(16)(18) of lace border for back.

Ribbing *(optional)*

Rows 1 & 2: Rep Rows 1 and 2 of ribbing for back if using ribbing instead of lace cuffs.

Rep Row 2 until ribbing measures 5¾(6¼)(7)", fasten off.

Sleeve body

Row 1: With RS facing, attach A with a sl st in first rem lp of foundation ch at right edge of lace cuff (for ribbing, working across row ends on either long edge, attach A with a sl st in upper right corner), ch 1, beg in same st as joining, work

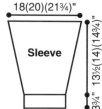

Chart B
Sleeve—Small

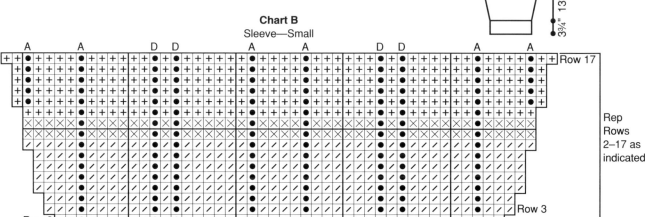

Chart C
Sleeve—Medium

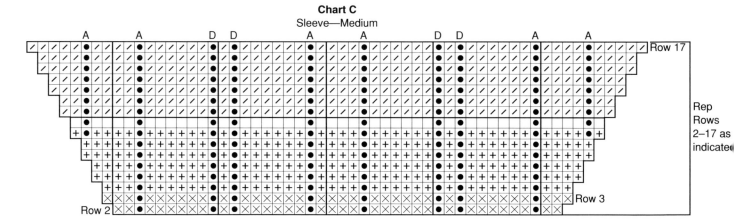

Chart D
Sleeve—Large

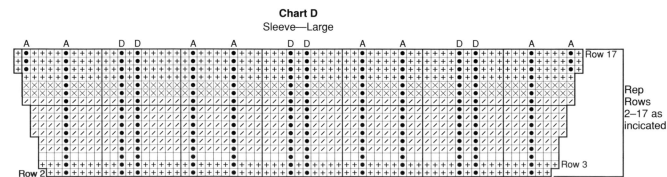

42(42)(63) sc evenly sp across, changing to D in last st for size medium and C in last st for large, fasten off A for sizes medium and large, ch 1 with A(D)(C), turn.

Rows 2–17: Follow Chart B(C)(D), working incs as indicated.

Rows 18–61(63)(67): Rep Rows 2–17 of Chart B(C)(D) alternately; at the same time, continue to inc 1 st at each end of every 2nd row 0(1)(0) more

times and at the end of every 4th row 10(10)(8) more times; work even on 72(80)(87) sts in established pattern after last inc row, fasten off at end of Row 61(63)(67).

Finishing

For front and back, beg in first ch-1 sp at bottom of first column of ch-1 sps at right edge, work surface ch on each column of ch-1 sps, following Chart A for color sequence. For sleeves, beg

in first ch-1 at bottom of first column of ch-1 sps at right edge, work surface ch on each column of ch-1 sps, following Chart B(C)(D) for color sequence.

Sew shoulder seams. Measure 9 (10)(11)" down from shoulder seam on front and back and place markers. Sew sleeve in place between markers. Rep for 2nd sleeve. Sew side and underarm seams. ❧

Holiday Vest

Design by Maureen Egan Emlet
Experience Level: Intermediate

Size: Man's small(medium)(large)(extra-large) Instructions are given for smallest size, with larger sizes in parentheses. When only 1 number is given, it applies to all sizes.

Finished Measurements: Chest: 40(44)(48)(52)"
Length: 25½(27)(28½)(30)"

Materials:

❋ Spinrite Bernat Berella "4" worsted weight yarn (3.5 oz per skein): 4(4)(5)(6) skeins geranium #8929 (A), 1(1)(2)(2) skeins deep colonial blue #8860 (B), 1(1)(2)(2) skeins hunter green #8981 (C) and 1 skein winter white #8941 (D)

❋ Size H/8 crochet hook or size needed to obtain gauge

❋ 5 (11/16)" square blue buttons

Gauge: 16 sts and 18 rows = 4" in sc

To save time, take time to check gauge.

Pattern Notes

When working from charts, read all odd-numbered (RS) rows from right to left, all even-numbered (WS) rows from left to right.

To dec 1 st at beg or end of row, work sc dec over first 2 or last 2 sts of row.

To dec more than 1 st at beg of row, sl st across number of sts to be dec plus 1, ch 1, beg working pattern in same st as last sl st. To

dec more than 1 st at end of row, leave number of sts to be dec unworked, ch 1, turn.

Join rnds with a sl st unless otherwise stated.

Pattern Stitch

Surface ch: Make sl knot and remove sl knot from hook. With working yarn at WS, insert hook from RS to WS through first indicated sp, pick up sl knot, draw through sp to RS, [insert hook from RS to WS in next

indicated sp, yo, draw through sp and through lp on hook] rep as indicated.

Back

Row 1 (RS): With A, ch 79(89)(97)(105), sc in 2nd ch from hook and in each rem ch across, ch 1, turn. (78, 88, 96, 104 sc)

Row 2: Sc in each sc across, ch 1, turn. (78, 88, 96, 104 sc)

Rep Row 2 until back measures 15(15½)(16)(16½)" from beg, ending with a WS row.

Armhole shaping

Continuing in sc, dec 5 sts at the end of each of next 2 rows, dec 2 sts at the end of each of next 4 rows, then dec 1 st at each end of every other row 1(2)(3)(4) times. (58, 66, 72, 78 sts at end of last dec row)

Work even in sc on 58(66)(72)(78) sts until back measures 24¼(25¾)(27¼)(28¾)" from beg.

Shoulder shaping

Continuing in sc, dec 5(6)(6)(7) sts at the end of each of next 4 rows, then dec 6(6)(8)(7) sts at the end of each of next 2 rows, fasten off. (26, 30, 32, 36 sts at the end of last dec row)

Left Front

Row 1 (RS): With A, ch 43(45)(49)(53), sc in 2nd ch from hook and in each rem ch across, ch 1, turn. (42, 44, 48, 52 sc)

Rows 2–18: Follow Chart A, ending each row with ch 1, turn.

Rep Rows 3–18 alternately until left front measures15(15½)(16)(16½)", ending with a WS row.

Armhole & neck shaping

Continuing in established pattern, dec 5 sts at armhole edge once, dec 2 sts at armhole edge every other row twice, then dec 1 st at armhole edge every other row 1(2)(3)(4) times; at the same time, beg on same row as first armhole dec, dec 1 sc at neck edge, then dec 1 sc at neck edge every other row 5(0)(0)(0) times, then dec 1 st at neck edge every 3rd row 10(14)(15)(17) times.

Continue in established pattern on 16(18)(20)(21) sts until left front measures 24¼(25¾)(27¼)(28¾)" from beg.

Shoulder shaping

Dec 5(6)(6)(7) sts at armhole edge every other row twice, then work even on 6(6)(8)(7) sts for 2 rows; fasten off.

Right Front

Row 1: Rep Row 1 of left front.

Rows 2–18: Follow Chart B, ending each row with ch 1, turn.

Rep Rows 3–18 alternately until

Continued on page 139

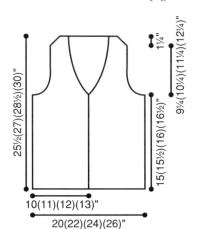

COLOR AND STITCH KEY
- ⊠ Sc with A
- ☑ Sc with B
- ⊞ Sc with C
- ☐ Sc with D
- ● Ch-1 in same color as row in progress
- A Surface ch with A
- D Surface ch with D

Note: *A and D surface ch are to be worked after left/right front is completed.*

Chart A
Left Front

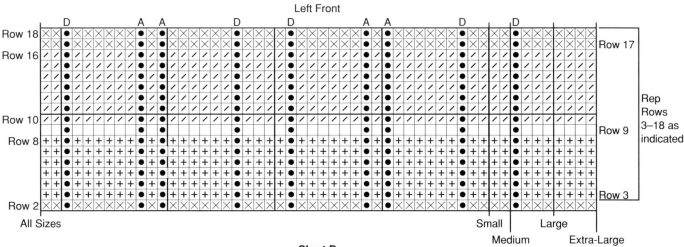

Chart B
Right Front

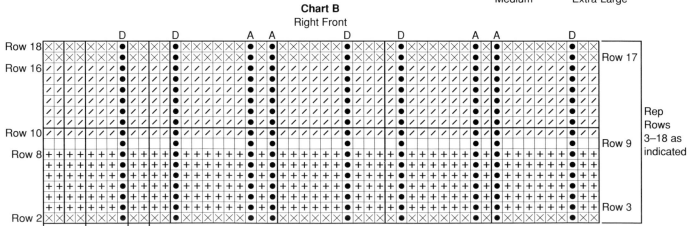

Teen Holiday Hats

Designs by Héléne Rush

Top off your Christmas outfit with these distinctive hats. Their vivid colors and accents will display your holiday cheer as you wear them.

Cloché Hat

Experience Level: Beginner

Finished Measurements: Circumference: 20"

Materials

❊ Sport weight cotton yarn: 4 oz black (A), and 1 oz each red (B) and green (C)

❊ Size H/8 crochet hook or size needed to obtain gauge

❊ Tapestry needle

Gauge: 18 sts and 23 rows = 4" in sc

To save time, take time to check gauge.

Crown-Edge Hat

Experience Level: Intermediate

Finished Measurements: Circumference: 21¾"

Materials

❊ Red Heart Sport sport weight yarn (2½ oz per skein): 1 skein each paddy green #687 (A) and cherry red #912 (B)

❊ Red Heart Baby Sport sport weight yarn (6 oz per skein): 1 skein white pompadour #1001(C)

❊ Size H/8 crochet hook or size needed to obtain gauge

❊ Tapestry needle

Gauge: 15 sc = 4"

To save time, take time to check gauge.

Cloché Hat

Pattern Notes

Join rnds with a sl st unless otherwise stated.

To join with next color, drop working color to WS, insert hook in indicated st, yo with next color, complete sl st.

Hat

Rnd 1: With A, ch 4, join to form a ring, ch 1, 8 sc in ring, join in beg sc. (8 sc)

Rnd 2: Ch 1, beg in same st as joining, 2 sc in each sc around, join in beg sc. (16 sc)

Rnd 3: Ch 1, sc in same st as joining, 2 sc in next sc, [sc in next sc, 2 sc in next sc] rep around, join in beg sc. (24 sc)

Rnd 4: Ch 1, sc in same st as joining, sc in each of next 2 sc, 2 sc in next sc, [sc in each of next 3 sc, 2 sc in next sc] rep around, join in beg sc. (30 sc)

Rnd 5: Ch 1, sc in same st as joining and in each rem sc around, join in beg sc.

Rnd 6: Ch 1, sc in same st as joining, sc in each of next 4 sc, 2 sc in next sc, [sc in each of next 5 sc, 2 sc in next sc] rep around, join in beg sc with B. (35 sc)

Rnd 7: Ch 1, sc in same st as joining, sc in each of next 5 sc, 2 sc in next sc, [sc in each of next 6 sc, 2 sc in next sc] rep around, join in beg sc. (40 sc)

Rnd 8: Ch 1, sc in same st as joining, sc in each of next 6 sc, 2 sc in next sc, [sc in each of next 7 sc, 2 sc in next sc] rep around, join in beg sc with A. (45 sc)

Rnd 9: Ch 1, sc in same st as joining, sc in each of next 3 sc, 2 sc in next sc, [sc in each of next 4 sc, 2 sc in next sc] rep around, join in beg sc. (54 sc)

Rnd 10: Rep Rnd 6, do not change to B. (63 sc)

Rnd 11: Rep Rnd 5. (63 sc)

Rnd 12: Rep Rnd 7. (72 sc)

Rnd 13: Rep Rnd 5, join with C. (72 sc)

Rnd 14: Rep Rnd 8, do not change to A. (81 sc)

Rnd 15: Rep Rnd 5, join with A. (81 sc)

Rnd 16: Rep Rnd 5. (81 sc)

Rnd 17: Ch 1, sc in same st as joining, sc in each of next 7 sc, 2 sc in next sc, [sc in each of next 8 sc, 2 sc in next sc] rep around, join in beg sc. (90 sc)

Rnds 18–20: Rep Rnd 5, at end of Rnd 20, join with B.

join in beg sc. (8 sc)

Rnd 2: Ch 1, [sc, hdc, 3 dc, hdc, sc] in same sc as joining, *sk next sc, [sc, hdc, 3 dc, hdc, sc] in next sc, rep from * around, join in beg sc. (4 petals)

Rnd 3: Working behind petals of last rnd, [ch 4, sl st between next 2 petals] 4 times, fasten off.

Rnd 4: Attach C with a sl st in any ch-4 sp, ch 2 (counts as first hdc), [dc, 3 tr, dc, hdc] in same sp, [hdc, dc, 3 tr, dc, hdc] in each rem sp around, join in 2nd ch of beg ch-2, fasten off.

Center

With A, ch 4, 4 dc in 4th ch from hook, remove hook from lp, insert hook in 4th ch of beg ch-4, pick up dropped lp, draw through st on hook, fasten off.

Place flower center on top of flower and stitch in place at side of hat just above top of brim.

Crown-Edge Hat
Pattern Notes

Join rnds with a sl st unless otherwise stated.

To join with next color, drop working color to WS, insert hook in indicated st, yo with next color, complete sl st.

To change color in sc, work last sc before color change as follows: Insert hook in indicated st, yo with working color, draw up a lp, drop working color to WS, yo with next color, complete sc.

To change color in dc, work last dc before color change until last 2 lps before final yo rem on hook, drop working color to WS, yo with next color, complete dc.

When working from Chart A, carry color not in use across WS of work, working over it with color in use until needed again.

Rnds 21 & 22: Rep Rnd 5, at end of Rnd 22, join with A.

Rnds 23–27: Rep Rnd 5, at end of Rnd 27, join with C

Rnds 28 & 29: Rep Rnd 5, at end of Rnd 29, join with A.

Rnds 30–34: Rep Rnd 5, at end of Rnd 34, join with B.

Rnds 35 & 36: Rep Rnd 5, at end of Rnd 36, join with A.

Rnds 37–39: Rep Rnd 5.

Brim

Rnd 40: Rep Rnd 6, do not change to B. (105 sc)

Rnd 41: Rep Rnd 5.

Rnd 42: Rep Rnd 7. (120 sc)

Rnd 43: Rep Rnd 5. (120 sc)

Rnd 44: Ch 1, sc in same st as joining, sc in each of next 3 sc, [2 sc in next sc, sc in each of next 7 sc] rep around to last 4 sc, 2 sc in next sc, sc in each of last 3 sc, join in beg sc. (135 sc)

Rnds 45–49: Rep Rnd 5, at end of Rnd 49, fasten off.

Flower

Rnd 1: With B, ch 4, join to form a ring, ch 1, 8 sc in ring,

Top

Rnd 1 (RS): With A, ch 4, join to form a ring, ch 1, 8 sc in ring, join in beg sc. (8 sc)

Rnd 2: Ch 2 (counts as first hdc throughout), hdc in same st as joining, 2 hdc in each rem st around, join in 2nd ch of beg ch-2. (16 hdc)

Rnd 3: Ch 1, sc in same st as joining, [2 sc in next st, sc in next st] rep around, ending with 2 sc in last st, join in beg sc. (24 sc)

Rnd 4: Ch 1, sc in same st as joining, sc in next st, [2 sc in next st, sc in each of next 2 sts] rep around, ending with 2 sc in last st, join in beg sc. (32 sc)

Rnd 5: Ch 2, hdc in each of next 2 sts, 2 hdc in next st, [hdc in each of next 3 sts, 2 hdc in next st] rep around, join in 2nd ch of beg ch-2. (40 hdc)

Rnd 6: Ch 1, sc in same st as joining, sc in each of next 3 sts, [2 sc in next st, sc in each of next 4 sts] rep around, ending with 2 sc in last st, join in beg sc. (48 sc)

Rnd 7: Ch 1, sc in same st as joining, sc in each of next 4 sts, 2 sc in next st, [sc in each of next 5 sts, 2 sc in next st] rep around, join in beg sc. (56 sc)

Rnd 8: Ch 2, hdc in each of next 5 sts, 2 hdc in next st, [hdc in each of next 6 sts, 2 hdc in next st] rep around, join in 2nd ch of beg ch-2. (64 hdc)

Rnd 9: Ch 1, sc in same st as joining, sc in each of next 6 sts, 2 sc in next st, [sc in each of next 7 sts, 2 sc in next st] rep around, join in beg sc. (72 sc)

Rnd 10: Ch 1, sc in same st as joining, sc in each of next 7 sts, 2 sc in next st, [sc in each of next 8 sts, 2 sc in next st] rep around, join in beg sc. (80 sc)

Rnd 11: Ch 2, hdc in each rem st around, join in 2nd ch of beg ch-2.

Rnd 12: Ch 1, sc in same st as joining, sc in each of next 8 sts, 2 sc in next st, [sc in each of next 9 sts, 2 sc in next st] rep around, join in beg sc. (88 sc)

Rnd 13: Ch 1, sc in same st as joining, sc in each of next 9 sts, 2 sc in next st, [sc in each of next 10 sts, 2 sc in next st] rep around, join in beg sc. (96 sc)

Rnd 14: Rep Rnd 11.

Rnd 15: Ch 3 (counts as first dc throughout), [bpdc over next hdc] rep around, join in 3rd ch of beg ch-3 with C, fasten off A, turn. (96 sts)

Crown

Note: Work back and forth in rows from now on.

Row 1 (WS): Ch 1, beg in same st as joining, sc in each of first 6 sts, [sc dec, sc in each of next 4 sts] 14 times, sc in each of last 6 sts, turn. (82 sts)

Row 2: Ch 3, dc in each rem st across, changing to A in last st, ch 1, turn. (82 dc)

Rows 3–11: Work in sc following Chart A and changing colors as indicated; at end of Row 11, change to C in last st, turn.

Row 12: Rep Row 2, do not change color in last st; turn.

Row 13 (WS): Working in front lps only this row, ch 3, dc in each of next 7 dc, [dc dec, dc in each of next 11 dc] 5 times, dc dec, dc in each of last 7 dc, turn. (76 sts)

Row 14: Ch 3, fpdc over next st, [dc in next st, fpdc over next st] rep around, join in 3rd ch of beg ch-3, fasten off.

Sew back seam of crown.

With tapestry needle and C, work cross-stitch on crown, following Chart A.

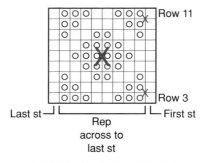

Chart A

Row 11

Last st — Row 3

First st

Rep across to last st

COLOR AND STITCH KEY
☐ Sc with A
⊙ Sc with B
✕ Cross st with C, worked after crown is completed

With 26" length of A and tapestry needle, weave A through dc sts on Row 2 of crown.

Crown points

Rnd 1: With RS facing, working in rem lps of Row 12 of crown, attach A with a sl st in first rem lp, ch 1, sc in same st, [sc in next st, hdc in next st, dc in next st, tr in each of next 2 sts, dc in next st, hdc in next st, sc in next st] rep around to last st, sc in last st, join in beg sc. (10 points)

Rnd 2: Sl st in next sc, [sc in next hdc, hdc in next dc, dc in next tr, tr between same tr and next tr, dc in next tr, hdc in next dc, sc in next hdc, sl st in each of next 2 sc] rep around, join in beg sl st, fasten off.

Popcorns

Leaving a 6" end, attach B with a sl st in tr at center of any point on Rnd 2 of crown points, ch 3, 4 dc in same tr, remove hook from lp, insert hook in 3rd ch of beg ch-3, pick up dropped lp, draw through st on hook, fasten off, leaving 6" end. Tack crown point to crown of hat with 6" ends. Alternating B and C, work 1 popcorn at tip of each crown point around. ❧

Jingle Bell Slippers

Design by Ruth G. Shepherd

SH-H-H-H-H! Whoever plays Santa at your house will not be able to remain anonymous when wearing these slippers. All little ears and eyes will be delighted when they hear and see anyone sporting these slippers!

Experience Level: Intermediate

Size: Woman's small/medium: 5½–6½ (large: 7–8) Instructions are given for smaller size, with larger size in parentheses. When only 1 number is given, it applies to all sizes.

Materials

※ Worsted weight yarn: 3½(4½) oz red, and ½(1) oz each green and white

※ Size G/6 crochet hook or size needed to obtain gauge

※ 20 (½") jingle bells

※ Tapestry needle

Gauge: 10 hdc = 3"

To save time, take time to check gauge.

Pattern Note

Join rnds with a sl st unless otherwise stated.

Slipper *(make 2)*

Instep

Rnd 1 (RS): Beg at toe, with red, ch 8, join to form a ring, ch 2 (counts as first hdc throughout), 9 more hdc in ring, join in 2nd ch of beg ch-2. (10 hdc)

Rnd 2: Ch 2, hdc in same st as joining, 2 hdc in each rem st around, join in 2nd ch of beg ch-2. (20 hdc)

Rnd 3: Ch 2, hdc in same st as joining, hdc in next st, [2 hdc in next st, hdc in next st] rep around, join in 2nd ch of beg ch-2. (30 hdc)

Rnds 4 & 5: Ch 1, sc in same st as joining and in each rem st around, join in beg sc. (30 sc)

Rnds 6 & 7: Ch 2, hdc in same st as joining and in each rem st around, join in 2nd ch of beg ch-2. (30 hdc)

Rnds 8–12(16): Rep Rnds 4–7 alternately, ending with a Rnd 4.

Row 13(17): Ch 1, sc in same st as joining and in each rem sc around, don't join; ch 7, fasten off.

Sides & Heel

Row 1: Ch 8, hdc in 3rd ch from hook and in each of next 5 chs; with RS facing, holding ch-8 at WS of work, yo, insert hook in first sc of last row of instep and in same ch of ch-8 as last hdc, yo, draw up a lp through both thick-nesses, yo, complete hdc, hdc in each rem st across, hdc in each of last 7 chs, turn. (44 hdc, counting last 2 chs of ch-8 as first hdc)

Row 2: Ch 2, hdc in each rem st across, ch 1, turn. (44 hdc)

Row 3: Sc in each st across, ch 1, turn. (44 sc)

Row 4: Sc in each st across, turn. (44 sc)

Row 5: Ch 2, hdc in each rem st across, turn. (44 hdc)

Row 6: Rep Row 2.

Rows 7–12: Rep Rows 3–6 once, then rep Rows 3 and 4.

Row 13: Ch 2, hdc in each of next 17 sts, [hdc dec] 4 times, hdc in each of 18 rem sts, fasten off, leaving end for sewing.

Sew heel seam and instep seam.

Cuff

Rnd 1: With WS facing, attach green with a sl st at center back seam, ch 2, work 29 more hdc evenly sp around ankle opening, join in 2nd ch of beg ch-2. (30 hdc)

Rnd 2: Ch 2, hdc in each rem st around, join in 2nd ch of beg ch-2, fasten off. (30 hdc)

Rnd 3: With WS facing, attach white with a sl st in joining st of Rnd 2, ch 1, sc in same st, ch 3, [sk 2 sts, sc in next st, ch 3] rep around, join in beg sc. (10 ch-3 sps)

Rnd 4: Sl st in first ch-3 sp, ch 1, beg in same sp, [sc, ch 3] twice in each ch-3 sp around, join in beg sc. (20 ch-3 sps)

Rnd 5: Sl st in first ch-3 sp, ch 1, sc in same sp, *ch 1, [2 sc, ch 2, 2 sc] in next sp, ch 1 **, sc in next sp, rep from * around, ending last rep at **, join in beg sc, fasten off.

Finishing

Turn cuff to RS. Sew 1 jingle bell at top of each point on Rnd 3. ✥

Holiday Vest

Continued from page 134

right front measures 15(15½)(16)(16½)", ending with a WS row.

Armhole & neck shaping

Rep left front armhole and neck shaping.

Shoulder shaping

Rep left front shoulder shaping.

Finishing

Beg in first ch-1 sp at bottom of first column of ch-1 sps at front opening edge on left front, work surface ch in D to top of column, fasten off. Following Chart A for color sequence, work surface ch on each rem column across. Following Chart B, work surface ch on all columns on right front.

Sew shoulder and side seams.

Armhole edging

With RS facing, attach A with a sl st at bottom of either armhole, ch 1, sc evenly sp around armhole, join in beg sc, fasten off. Rep on 2nd armhole.

Front opening & neck edging

With RS facing, attach A with a sl st at bottom corner of right front, ch 1, sc in same st, sc evenly sp across front edge, around neck, and down left front to first sc dec for left neck shaping, place marker approxi-mately 1½" from bottom of left front for first button, place 4 more mark-ers evenly sp up left front, ending at first sc dec for left neck shaping, ch 2, *sk approximately ½" **, sc evenly sp to next marker, ch 2, rep from * across to bottom, ending last rep at **, sc evenly sp to bottom corner, fasten off.

Sew buttons to right front. ✥

Winter Berry Cardigan

Continued from page 129

Tassel

Lay a 10" length of CC across 5" edge of cardboard. Wrap CC approximately 40 times around 2½" width of cardboard, over 10" length at top. Tie ends of 10" length tog tightly; slip tassel off cardboard. Wrap another 10" length of CC around tassel, approximately ½" down from top and tie. Cut open lps at bottom. Trim bottom of tassel evenly. Attach tassel to zipper pull.

Following chart, embroider design on both front bands with tapestry needle. ✥

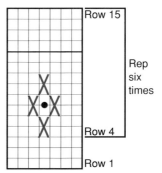

Chart A

	Row 15
	Rep six times
	Row 4
	Row 1

COLOR AND STITCH KEY
x MC Cross-stitch
● French knot with B

Festive Barrettes

Designs by Sandy Abbate

Perfect for women and girls, this trio of merry barrettes will add a splash of Christmas cheer to any outfit you wear!

Holly Barrette

Experience Level: Beginner

Finished Measurements: 4½" long x 3" wide

Materials

❋ Red Heart Sport sport weight yarn (2½ oz per skein): small amounts each jockey red #904 and paddy green #687

❋ Size E/4 crochet hook or size needed to obtain gauge

❋ 2¼"-long barrette back

❋ 23" ⅛"-wide gold ribbon

❋ Tapestry needle

❋ Craft glue

Gauge: Leaf = 2½" long

To save time, take time to check gauge.

Angel Barrette

Experience Level: Beginner

Finished Measurements: 3¼" wide x 3¼" high

Materials

❋ Red Heart Baby Sport pompadour sport weight yarn (1¾ oz per skein): small amount white #1

❋ Size E/4 crochet hook or size needed to obtain gauge

❋ 2¼"-long barrette back

❋ Small amount polyester fiberfill or cotton ball

❋ 3" length gold pipe cleaner

❋ 15" ⅛"-wide gold ribbon

❋ Small amount cosmetic blusher

❋ Craft glue

Gauge: Shell = ⅞"

To save time, take time to check gauge.

Holly Barrette

Pattern Stitch

Cl: Holding back on hook last lp of each st, dc in each of next 2 sts, yo, draw through all 3 lps on hook, ch 1 to secure.

Holly Leaf *(make 3)*

Row 1: Beg at bottom, with paddy green, ch 4, 6 dc in 4th ch from hook, turn. (7 dc, counting last 3 chs of beg ch-4 as first dc)

Rows 2 & 3: Sl st in each of first 4 sts, ch 3 (counts as first dc throughout), 6 dc in same st, turn.

Row 4: Sl st in each of first 3 sts, ch 3, cl over next 2 sts, fasten off.

Berry *(make 3)*

Rnd 1: With jockey red, leaving a 6" end, ch 4, 11 dc in 4th ch from hook, join with a sl st in top of beg ch-4, fasten off, leaving 8" end.

With tapestry needle, weave 8" end through tops of sts of Rnd 1, pull tightly to form berry, secure with small st, fasten off.

Finishing

With tapestry needle and paddy green, using photo as a guide, tack bottoms of leaves tog. Tack berries at center of leaves. Wrap ribbon around berries, knot tightly at bottom and tie into bow. Glue leaves to barrette.

Angel Barrette

Pattern Note

Join rnds with a sl st unless otherwise stated.

Pattern Stitches

Shell: [2 dc, ch 2, 2 dc] in indicated st or sp.

Beg shell: [Ch 3, dc, ch 2, 2 dc] in indicated st or sp.

Head

Rnd 1: Ch 1 (for center ch), ch 3 more (counts as first dc), 11 dc in center ch, join in 3rd ch of beg ch-3. (12 dc)

Rnd 2: Ch 1, beg in same st, [sc dec] 6 times, join in beg st. (6 sts) Stuff head lightly.

Bodice & Wings

Rnd 3: Ch 1, sc in each st around, join in beg sc. (6 sc)

Rnd 4: Ch 5 (counts as first dc, ch 2), dc in same st, [dc, ch 2, dc] in each rem st around, join in 3rd ch of beg ch-5, turn. (6 ch-2 sps)

First wing

Row 1 (WS): Sl st in last dc made and in next ch-2 sp, beg shell in same sp, ch 1, shell in next ch-2 sp, turn.

Row 2: Ch 3 (counts as first dc), shell in next ch-2 sp, shell in next ch-1 sp, shell in next ch-2 sp, sk next dc, dc in 3rd ch of turning ch-3, fasten off.

Second wing

Row 1: With WS facing, attach yarn with a sl st in next unworked ch-2 sp of Rnd 4, beg shell in same sp, ch 1, shell in next ch-2 sp, turn.

Row 2: Rep Row 2 of first wing, fasten off.

Skirt

Row 1: With WS facing, attach yarn with a sl st in next unworked dc of Rnd 4, ch 4 (counts as first dc, ch 1), [shell in next ch-2 sp, ch 1] twice, sk next dc, dc in next st, turn.

Rnd 2: Sl st in dc and ch-1 sp, beg shell in same sp, shell in next ch-2 sp, shell in next ch-1 sp, shell in next ch-2 sp, shell in 4th ch of turning ch-4, join in 3rd ch of beg ch-3.

Rnd 3: Ch 1, sc in same sp as joining, ch 3, [sc, ch 3] in each dc and ch-2 sp around, join in beg sc, fasten off.

Rose Barrette

Experience Level: Beginner

Finished Measurements: 4" long x 2" high

Materials

❊ Red Heart Sport sport weight yarn (2½ oz per skein): small amounts each jockey red #904 and paddy green #687

❊ Red Heart Baby Sport sport weight pompadour yarn (1¾ oz per skein): small amount white #1

❊ Size E/4 crochet hook or size needed to obtain gauge

❊ 2¼"-long barrette back

❊ 25" ¹⁄₁₆"-wide gold ribbon

❊ 25" ¹⁄₁₆"-wide red ribbon

❊ Tapestry needle

❊ Craft glue

Gauge

4 dc = ⅞"

To save time, take time to check gauge.

Continued on page 151

Winter Sparkle

Designs by Sandy Abbate

Joy to the world! And joy to you as you make this matching ensemble. This bright, cheery hat and mitten set will add to the happiness of any holiday occasion.

Experience Level: Intermediate

Size: 3–6 months

Finished Measurements: Chest: 19", Length: 10"

Materials

❋ Red Heart Sport sport weight yarn (2½ oz per skein): 1 skein each vermilion #918 and paddy green #687

❋ Red Heart Baby Sport pompadour sport weight yarn (6 oz per skein): 1 skein white pompadour #1001

❋ Size E/4 crochet hook or size needed to obtain gauge

❋ Size D/3 crochet hook

❋ 5 (⅝") gold buttons

❋ Tapestry needle

❋ 3" piece of cardboard

Gauge: 5 3-cl groups = 1" with larger hook in pattern st

Rows 2–5 of body = 1½" with larger hook

To save time, take time to check gauge.

Pattern Notes

Join rnds with a sl st unless otherwise stated.

Sweater is worked in 1 piece from bottom to armholes.

To change color in joining, insert hook in indicated st, drop working color to WS, yo with next color, complete sl st.

Pattern Stitches

Cl: Holding back on hook last lp of each st, work 2 dc in indicated st or sp, yo, draw through all 3 lps on hook.

Beg cl: [Ch 2, dc] in indicated st or sp.

Sweater

Body Ribbing

Row 1: With white and smaller hook, ch 9, sc in 2nd ch from hook and in each rem ch across, ch 1, turn. (8 sc)

Rows 2–88: Working in back lps only, sc in each st across, ch 1, turn; at end of Row 88, ch 1, do not turn. (8 sc)

Body

Row 1 (RS): With larger hook, working over ends of rows, 2 sc over end of last row, sc over end of each rem row across, fasten off, do not turn. (89 sc)

Row 2: With RS facing, using larger hook, attach paddy green with a sl st in first sc, ch 3 (counts as first dc throughout), *sk 3 sc, [cl, ch 3, cl] in next st, rep across to last 4 sts, sk 3 sts, dc in last st, fasten off paddy green, turn. (42 cls)

Row 3: With WS facing, using larger hook, attach vermilion with a sl st in first dc, ch 3, [{cl, ch 1} 3 times in next ch-3 sp] rep across to last ch-3 sp, [cl, ch 1] twice in last sp, cl in same sp, dc in 3rd ch of turning ch-3, fasten off vermilion, turn.

Row 4: With RS facing, using larger hook, attach white with a sl st in first dc, ch 1, sc in same st, [ch 1, sc in next ch-1 sp] rep across, ending with ch 1, sc in top of turning ch-3, turn. (63 ch-1 sps)

Row 5: Ch 3, dc in next ch-1 sp, [ch 1, dc in next ch-1 sp] rep across, ending with dc in last sc, fasten off white, turn. (65 dc)

Row 6: With RS facing, using larger hook, attach paddy green with a sl st in first dc, ch 3, sk next dc, [cl, ch 3, cl] in next dc, [sk 2 dc, {cl, ch 3, cl} in next dc] rep across to last 2 dc, sk next dc, dc in 3rd ch of turning ch-3, fasten off paddy green, turn. (42 cls)

Rows 7–11: Rep Rows 3–6, then rep Row 3; at end of Row 11, turn.

Right Front

Row 12: With RS facing, using larger hook, attach white with a sl st in first dc, ch 1, sc in same st, [ch 1, sc in next sp] 15 times, turn. (15 ch-1 sps)

Rows 13 & 14: Rep Rows 5 and 6. (17 dc on Row 13; 10 cls on Row 14)

Rows 15–20: Rep Rows 3–6, then rep Rows 3 and 4.

Right front shoulder

Row 21: Ch 3, dc in next ch-1

sp, [ch 1, dc in next ch-1 sp] 8 times, dc in next sc, fasten off, turn. (11 dc)

Row 22: Rep Row 6. (6 cls)

Rows 23 & 24: Rep Rows 3 and 4; at end of Row 24, fasten off. (9 cls on Row 23; 9 ch-1 sps on Row 24)

Back

Row 12: With RS facing, using larger hook, attach white with a sl st in same ch-1 sp on Row 11 of body as last sc of Row 12 of right front, ch 1, sc in same sp, [ch 1, sc in next sp] 33 times, turn. (33 ch-1 sps)

Rows 13 & 14: Rep Rows 5 and 6. (35 dc on Row 13; 22 cls on Row 14)

Rows 15–24: Rep Rows 3–6 alternately, ending with a Row 4.

Left back shoulder

Row 25: Ch 3, dc in next ch-1 sp, [ch 1, dc in next ch-1 sp] 8 times, dc in next sc, fasten off. (11 dc)

Right back shoulder

Row 25: With WS facing, using larger hook, sk next 15 ch-1 sps on Row 24 of back, attach white with a sl st in next sc, ch 3, dc in next ch-1 sp, [ch 1, dc in next ch-1 sp] 8 times, dc in last sc, fasten off. (11 dc)

Left Front

Row 12: With RS facing, using larger hook, attach white with a sl st in same ch-1 sp on Row 11 of body as last sc of Row 12 of back, ch 1, sc in same sp, [ch 1, sc in next sp] rep across to last sp, ch 1, sc in 3rd ch of beg ch-3, turn. (15 ch-1 sps)

Rows 13–20: Rep Rows 13–20 of right front; at end of Row 20, fasten off, turn.

Left front shoulder

Row 21: With WS facing, using larger hook, sk first 6 sc of last row, attach white with a sl st in next sc, ch 3, dc in next ch-1 sp, [ch 1, dc in next ch-1 sp] 8 times, dc in next sc, fasten off, turn. (11 dc)

Rows 22–24: Rep Rows 22–24 of right front shoulder.

With tapestry needle and white, sew shoulder seams.

Sleeve (make 2)

Sleeve ribbing

Rows 1–30: Rep Rows 1–30 of body ribbing; at end of Row 30, don't fasten off; ch 1, don't turn.

Sleeve body

Row 1 (RS): With larger hook, working over ends of rows, work 45 sc evenly sp across, fasten off white.

Rows 2–6: Rep Rows 2–6 of body.

Rows 7–17: Rep Rows 3–6 of body alternately, ending with a Row 5; fasten off at end of Row 17.

With tapestry needle and white, sew sleeve seam.

Armhole Edging

With RS facing, using larger hook, attach white with a sl st at underarm, ch 1, beg in same st and working over ends of rows, work 54 sc evenly sp around, join in beg sc, fasten off.

Rep on 2nd armhole.

With tapestry needle and white, holding RS tog, sew sleeve into armhole from WS, matching top center of sleeve with top center of shoulder.

Buttonhole Placket

Row 1: With RS facing, working across right front opening (left front opening for boy's sweater), using smaller hook, attach white with a sl st at right corner, ch 1, sc in same st, work 42 more sc evenly sp across front opening, ch 1, turn. (43 sc)

Row 2: Sc in first st, ch 2, sk 1 st, [sc in each of next 9 sc, ch 2, sk 1 st] 4 times, sc in last st, ch 1, turn.

Row 3: Sc in each sc and in each sp across, ch 1, don't turn. (43 sc)

Row 4: Work in reverse sc across, fasten off.

Button Placket

Row 1: With RS facing, working across rem front opening, using smaller hook, attach white with a sl st at right corner, ch 1, sc in same st, work 42 more sc evenly sp across front opening, ch 1, turn.

Rows 2 & 3: Sc in each sc across, ch 1, turn; at end of Row 3, ch 1, do not turn. (43 sc)

Row 4: Rep Row 4 of buttonhole placket.

Neck Edging

With RS facing, using smaller hook, attach white with a sl st over end st of Row 4 of buttonhole placket (button placket for boys), work 3 sc over row ends of placket, work 15 more sc evenly sp to right shoulder seam, work 14 sc evenly sp across back neck to left shoulder seam, 15 sc evenly sp to beg of next placket, sc over each row end of next 3 rows of placket, sl st in last row of placket, fasten off. (50 sc)

Collar

Rows 1–60: Rep Rows 1–60 of body ribbing; at end of Row 60, do not fasten off; ch 1, don't turn.

With larger hook, working over ends of rows, work 46 sc evenly sp across, fasten off, leaving 18" end for sewing.

With tapestry needle, sew collar to neck edge, leaving ends of plackets free.

Sew on buttons.

Cap
Ribbing

Rows 1–65: Rep Rows 1–65 of body ribbing; at end of Row 65, do not fasten off; ch 1, turn.

Join ribbing to form ring

Row 66: Working through both thicknesses of rem lps of foundation ch and back lps only of last row, sc in each st across, ch 1, do not turn.

Crown

Rnd 1 (RS): With larger hook, working over ends of rows, ch 1, beg in same st, work 64 sc evenly sp around, join in beg sc, changing to paddy green; do not fasten off white. (64 sc)

Rnd 2: [Beg cl, ch 3, cl] in same st as joining, [sk 3 sc, {cl, ch 3, cl} in next sc] rep around, join in top of beg cl, changing to vermilion in joining, do not fasten off paddy green; turn. (32 cls)

Rnd 3: Sl st in ch-3 sp, [beg cl, ch 1, cl, ch 1, cl, ch 1] in same sp, [{cl, ch 1} 3 times in next sp] rep around, join in top of beg cl, changing to white, do not fasten off vermilion; turn. (48 cls)

Rnd 4: Sl st in first ch-1 sp, ch 1, sc in same sp, ch 1, [sc in next sp, ch 1] rep around, join in beg sc. (48 ch-1 sps)

Rnd 5: Sl st in first ch-1 sp, ch 4 (counts as first dc, ch-1), [dc in next sp, ch 1] rep around, join in 3rd ch of beg ch-4, changing to paddy green, do not fasten off white. (48 dc)

Rnd 6: [Beg cl, ch 3, cl] in same st as joining, sk 2 dc, [{cl, ch 3, cl} in next dc, sk 2 dc] rep around, join in top of beg cl, changing to vermilion, do not fasten off paddy green; turn.

Rnds 7–13: Rep Rnds 3–6, then rep Rnds 3–5; at end of Rnd 13, do not change to paddy green.

Rnd 14: Sl st in first ch-1 sp, ch 1, beg in same sp, sc in each ch-1 sp around, join in beg sc.

Rnd 15: Beg in same st as joining, [sc dec] around, join in beg sc dec, fasten off white, leaving a 12" end; fasten off rem colors.

With tapestry needle, weave 12" end through rem sts of last rnd, pull tightly to close, fasten off.

Pompom

Wrap white 100 times around cardboard. Slip yarn off cardboard; tie 18" length white tightly around center. Cut ends open; trim evenly. Attach pompom to top of cap. ❧

Cherries Sweater & Cap

Designs by Sandy Abbate

Wouldn't you just love to dress up your little girl in this bright sweater and cap? The cheery cherries would help to brighten her on a winter day!

Experience Level: Intermediate

Size: Toddler's size 1(2)(3) Instructions are given for smallest size, with larger sizes in parentheses. When only 1 number is given, it applies to all sizes.

Finished Measurements

Chest: 21¾(23¾)(25¾)"

Length: 11(12)(13)"

Materials

❊ Red Heart Sport sport weight yarn (2½ oz per skein): 2 skeins white #1 and 1 skein each paddy green #687 and cherry red #912

❊ Size G/6 crochet hook or size needed to obtain gauge

❊ Size F/5 crochet hook

❊ 5 (½") white buttons

❊ Tapestry needle

Gauge: 12 sts and 7 rows = 3" in dc with larger hook

To save time, take time to check gauge.

Pattern Notes

Join rnds with a sl st unless otherwise stated.

To change color in sc, work last sc before color change as follows: insert hook in indicated st, yo with working color, draw up a lp, drop working color to WS, yo with next color, complete sc.

To change color in dc, work last dc before color change until last 2 lps before final yo rem on hook, drop working color to WS, yo with next color, complete dc.

Carry color not in use loosely across WS of work, working over it with color in use until it is needed again.

Body is worked in 1 piece until underarms.

Sweater

Body Ribbing

Row 1: With cherry red and smaller hook, ch 12, hdc in 3rd ch from hook and in each rem ch across, turn. (11 hdc, counting last 2 chs of foundation ch as first hdc)

Rows 2–58(64)(68): Ch 2 (counts as first hdc throughout), working in back lps only, hdc in each rem st across, turn; at end of Row 58(64)(68), do not fasten off; ch 1, do not turn. (11 hdc)

Body

Row 1 (RS): With larger hook, working over ends of rows, work 87(95)(103) sc evenly sp across, changing to paddy green in last sc, fasten off cherry red, turn. (87, 95, 103 sc)

Row 2: With paddy green, ch 3, dc in each of next 2 sts, [dc in next st with white, dc in each of next 3 sts with paddy green] rep across, changing to white in last paddy green st, turn. (66, 72, 78 paddy green dc; 21, 23, 25 white dc)

Row 3: With white, ch 3 (counts as first dc throughout), dc in next dc, [work 1 paddy green dc, 3 white dc] rep across to last st, dc in last st with white, turn. (21, 23, 25 paddy green dc; 66, 72, 78 white dc)

Row 4: With white, ch 3, dc in next dc, [work 3 paddy green dc, 1 white dc] rep across to last st, dc in last st with white, turn. (63, 69, 75 paddy green dc; 24, 26, 28 white dc)

Row 5: With white, ch 3, dc in each of next 3 dc, [work 1 paddy green dc, 3 white dc] rep across to last 3 sts, work 1 paddy green dc, 2 white dc, changing to paddy green in last dc, turn. (21, 23, 25 paddy green dc; 66, 72, 78 white dc)

Rows 6–11(13)(15): Rep Rows 2–5 alternately, ending with a Row 3(5)(3); for size 2, do not change to paddy green at end of Row 13; at end of Row 11(13)(15), fasten off paddy green.

Left Front

Row 12(14)(16): With white, ch 3, dc in each of next 20(22)(24) sts, turn. (21, 23, 25 dc)

Rows 13(15)(17)–19(21)(23):
Ch 3, dc in each rem st across,
turn. (21, 23, 25 dc)

Shape left front neck

Row 20(22)(24): Sl st in each
of first 8(10)(12) sts, ch 3, dc in
each rem st across, turn. (14 dc)

Row 21(23)(25): Ch 3, dc in
each rem st across to last 2 sts,
dc dec, turn. (13 sts)

Row 22(24)(26): Ch 3, dc dec, dc
in each rem st across, turn. (12 sts)

Row 23(25)(27): Ch 3, dc in each
rem st across, fasten off. (12 sts)

Back

Row 12(14)(16): With WS
facing, using larger hook, attach
white with a sl st in next
unworked dc on Row 11(13)
(15) of body, ch 3, dc in each of
next 44(48)(52) sts, turn. (45,
49, 53 sts)

Rows 13(15)(17)–22(24)(26):
Ch 3, dc in each rem st across,
turn; at end of Row 22(24)(26),
fasten off.

Right Front

Row 12(14)(16): With WS
facing, using larger hook, attach
white with a sl st in next
unworked dc on Row 11(13)
(15) of body, ch 3, dc in each
rem st across, turn. (21, 23, 25 sts)

Rows 13(15)(17)–19(21)(23):
Ch 3, dc in each rem st across,
turn. (21, 23, 25 sts)

Shape right front neck

Row 20(22)(24): Ch 3, dc in
each of next 12 sts, dc dec, turn.
(14 sts)

Row 21(23)(25): Ch 3, dc dec,
dc in each rem st across, turn.
(13 sts)

Row 22(24)(26): Ch 3, dc in
each rem st across to last 2 sts,
dc dec, turn. (12 sts)

Row 23(25)(27): Ch 3, dc in each
rem st across, fasten off. (12 sts)

With tapestry needle and white,
sew shoulder seams.

For sizes 1 and 2 only, beg at
underarm, sew side seam for
2(1) rows.

Sleeve (*make 2*)

Rnd 1: With larger hook and RS
facing, attach white with a sl st
at underarm, ch 3, work 39(41)
(45) more dc evenly sp around,
join in 3rd ch of beg ch-3. (40,
42, 46 dc)

Rnds 2–8(12)(16): Ch 3, dc in
each rem st around, join in 3rd
ch of beg ch-3. (40, 42, 46 dc)

Rnd 9(13)(17): Ch 3, dc in
each rem st around, working
10(11)(12) dc dec evenly sp
around, join in 3rd ch of beg ch-
3, fasten off. (30, 31, 34 sts)

Sleeve ribbing (*make 2*)

Rows 1–18(18)(20): Rep Rows
1–18(18)(20) of body ribbing; at
end of Row 18(18)(20), fasten off,
leaving a 20" length for sewing.

With tapestry needle, sew back
lps only of last row to rem lps of
foundation ch across. Sew
ribbing to bottom of sleeve,
easing fullness.

Buttonhole Placket

Row 1: With RS facing, using
smaller hook, attach cherry red
with a sl st at bottom corner of
right front, ch 1, beg in same st,
work 48(52)(56) sc evenly sp
across right front to beg of right
front neck, ch 1, turn.

Row 2: Sc in each sc across, ch
1, turn.

Row 3: Sc in each of first 2 sc,
[ch 2, sk 1 sc, sc in each of next
10(11)(12) sc] 4 times, ch 2, sk
1 sc, sc in last sc, ch 1, turn.

Row 4: Sc in each sc and in each
ch-2 sp across, ch 1, turn. (48,
52, 56 sc)

Row 5: Sc in each sc across,
fasten off.

Button Placket

Row 1: With RS facing, using
smaller hook, attach cherry red
with a sl st at beg of neck
shaping at top of left front, ch 1,
beg in same st, work 48(52)(56)
sc evenly sp to bottom of left
front, ch 1, turn.

Rows 2–5: Sc in each sc across,
ch 1, turn; at end of Row 5, do
not ch 1; fasten off. (48, 52, 56 sc)

Neck Band

Row 1: With RS facing, using
smaller hook, attach cherry red
with a sl st at right front neck
over end st of last row of
buttonhole placket, ch 1, beg in
same st, work 62(68)(74) sc
evenly sp across to left front
neck, ch 1, turn.

Row 2: Sc in each sc across, ch
1, turn.

Row 3: Sc across, working 10 sc
dec evenly sp across, ch 1, turn.
(52, 58, 64 sts)

Rows 4 & 5: Sc in each st across,
ch 1, turn; at end of Row 5, do
not ch 1; fasten off. (52, 58, 64 sc)

Sew buttons to button placket.

Leaf (*make 10*)

With smaller hook and paddy
green, ch 7, 6 dc in 4th ch from
hook, dc in each of next 2 ch, 3
dc in last ch; working in rem lps
along opposite side of foundation
ch, dc in each of next 2 sts, join
in last ch of beg ch-7, fasten off.

Cherry (*make 15*)

With cherry red, ch 4, holding
back on hook last lp of each st,
5 dc in 4th ch from hook, yo,
draw through all lps on hook, ch
1 to secure, fasten off.

Using photo as a guide, sew 2
leaves to each side of sweater
front. Sew 3 cherries underneath
each pair of leaves. With tapestry
needle and paddy green,
embroider stem in ch st from base

of leaves to top center of each cherry. Rep across upper back, placing 1 set of leaves with 3 cherries at center and 1 set of leaves with 3 cherries on each side.

Hat

Ribbing

Rows 1–42(44)(46): Rep Rows 1–42(44)(46) of body ribbing; at end of Row 42(44)(46), do not fasten off; ch 1, turn.

Row 43(45)(47): Working through both thicknesses, sc rem lps of foundation ch and back lps only of last row tog across, ch 1, do not turn.

Body

Rnd 1 (RS): With larger hook, working over ends of rows, work 65(69)(73) sc evenly sp around,

join in beg sc, fasten off.

Rnd 2: With RS facing, attach white with a sl st in any sc, ch 3, dc in each rem st around, join in 3rd ch of beg ch-3. (65, 69, 73 dc)

Rnds 3–13(14)(15): Ch 3, dc in each rem dc around, join in 3rd ch of beg ch-3. (65, 69, 73 dc)

Rnd 14(15)(16): Ch 2, [dc dec] rep around, join in beg dc dec.

Rnd 15(16)(17): Ch 2, dc in next st, [dc dec] rep around, join in beg dc.

Rnd 16(17)(18): Ch 2, dc in next 1(0)(1) sts, [dc dec] rep around, join in beg dc(dc dec) (dc), fasten off, leaving a 12" end for sewing.

With tapestry needle, weave 12" end through sts of last rnd, pull

tightly to close, fasten off. Fold ribbing to RS.

Leaf (make 2)

Follow leaf instructions for Sweater.

Using photo as a guide, sew leaves to top of hat.

Stems

[With paddy green and smaller hook, sl st between 2 leaves on hat, ch 12, fasten off] 3 times.

Cherry (make 3)

With cherry red and larger hook, sl st in end of any stem, ch 3, holding back on hook last lp of each st, 5 dc in sl st, yo, draw through all lps on hook, ch 3, holding back on hook last lp of each st, 5 dc in 3rd ch from hook, sl st in end of stem, fasten off.

Rep on 2 rem stems. ❧

Holiday Booties

Keep your little one's feet cozy and cute in either pair of these festive holiday booties!

Elf Booties

Design by Sandy Abbate

Experience Level: Beginner

Size: Newborn–3 months

Materials

❋ Worsted weight yarn: small amounts red and green

❋ Size G/6 crochet hook or size needed to obtain gauge

❋ Tapestry needle

❋ 1½" x 5" piece of cardboard

Gauge: 7 sts and 4 rows = 2" in dc

To save time, take time to check gauge.

Santa's Little Helper Booties

Design by Colleen Sullivan

Experience Level: Intermediate

Finished Measurements: Sole: 3½" long x 2" wide

Materials

❋ Sport weight yarn: 1 oz each red and white

❋ Size E/4 crochet hook or size needed to obtain gauge

❋ Tapestry needle

❋ 1" x 5" piece of cardboard

❋ Safety pin or other small marker

Gauge: 4 sts and 4 rows = 1" in sc

To save time, take time to check gauge.

Elf Booties

Pattern Note

Join rnds with a sl st unless otherwise stated.

Bootie *(make 2)*

Rnd 1: Beg at tip of toe, with red, leaving a 6" end, ch 4, 5 dc in 4th ch from hook, join with sl st in 4th ch of beg ch-4. (6 dc, counting last 3 chs of beg ch-4 as first dc)

Rnds 2 & 3: Ch 3 (counts as first dc throughout), dc in each rem dc around, join in 3rd ch of beg ch-3. (6 dc)

Rnd 4: Ch 3, dc in same st as joining, 2 dc in each rem dc around, join in 3rd ch of beg ch-3. (12 dc)

Rnds 5 & 6: Rep Rnds 2 and 3. (12 dc)

Rnd 7: Ch 3, 2 dc in next dc, [dc in next dc, 2 dc in next dc] rep around, join in 3rd ch of beg ch-3. (18 dc)

Rows 8–11: Ch 3, dc in each of next 17 dc, do not join; turn. (18 dc)

Row 12 (RS): Ch 3, dc in each of next 4 dc, [dc dec] 4 times, dc in each of next 5 dc, fasten off, leaving end for sewing.

RS tog, fold last row in half. With tapestry needle, sew tops of sts of last row tog for back seam. Turn RS out.

Cuff

Rnd 1: With RS facing, attach green with a sl st over end st of first row to the left of back seam, ch 1, 2 sc over same st, [2 sc over end st of next row] rep around, join in beg sc. (20 sc)

Rnd 2: Ch 4 (counts as first dc, ch -1), [sk next sc, dc in next sc, ch 1] rep around, join in 3rd ch of beg ch-4. (10 ch-1 sps)

Rnd 3: Sl st in first ch-1 sp, ch 1, beg in same sp, [sc, hdc, dc, hdc, sc] in each ch-1 sp around, join in beg sc, fasten off.

Tie *(make 2)*

With red, ch 75, fasten off. Weave tie through ch-1 sps on Rnd 2 of cuff.

Pompom *(make 2)*

Wrap green yarn 50 times around cardboard. Slip yarn off cardboard, tie piece of green yarn around center and knot tightly. Cut open lps at each end. Trim and shape to form pompom.

Finishing

With tapestry needle and 6" end at beg of Rnd 1, bring tip of toe up

Sides

Rnd 3 (RS): Ch 1, working in back lps only this rnd, sc in same st as joining, sc in each dc around, join in beg sc. (36 sc)

Rnds 4–6: Ch 1, sc in same st as joining and in each rem sc around, join in beg sc, fasten off at end of Rnd 6.

Instep

Row 1: With RS facing, attach red with a sl st in 10th sc after joining st, ch 1, sc in same sc and in each of next 4 sc, [sc dec, sc in next sc] twice, sc dec, sc in each of next 5 sts, ch 1, turn. (15 sts)

Row 2: Sc in each sc across, ch 1, turn. (15 sc)

Row 3: Sc in each of first 3 sc, sc dec, sc in next sc, 2-sc dec, sc in next sc, sc dec, sc in each of last 3 sc, fasten off, leaving end for sewing. (11 sts)

Turn bootie WS out. With RS tog, sew instep seam. Turn bootie RS out.

Upper bootie

Note: Do not join rnds unless otherwise stated. Mark first st of each rnd with safety pin or other small marker.

Rnd 1: With RS facing, attach red with a sl st in first sc after joining st on Rnd 6 of sides, ch 1, sc in same st and in each of next 8 sc, work 6 sc evenly sp over row ends across instep, sc in each of next 9 sts of Rnd 6. (24 sc)

Rnds 2–5: Sc in each sc around; at end of Rnd 5, join in beg sc. (24 sc)

Rnd 6: Ch 3 (counts as first hdc, ch-1), [sk next sc, hdc in next sc, ch 1] rep around, join in 2nd ch of beg ch-3, fasten off. (12 ch-1 sps)

and tack in place over center of Rnd 7. Sew pompom at tip of toe.

Santa's Little Helper Booties

Pattern Note

Join rnds with a sl st unless otherwise stated.

Pattern Stitch

2-sc dec: [Insert hook in next st, yo, draw up a lp] 3 times, yo, draw through all 4 lps on hook.

Bootie *(make 2)*

Sole

Rnd 1: Beg at heel, with red, ch 12, 2 dc in 4th ch from hook, dc in each of next 7 chs, 5 dc in last ch; working in rem lps across opposite side of foundation ch, dc in each of next 7 sts, 2 dc in last st, join in last ch of foundation ch. (24 dc, counting last 3 chs of foundation ch as first dc)

Rnd 2: Ch 3 (counts as first dc throughout), 2 dc in same st as joining, 2 dc in each of next 2 dc, dc in each of next 7 dc, 2 dc in each of next 2 dc, 3 dc in next dc, 2 dc in each of next 2 dc, dc in each of next 7 dc, 2 dc in each of next 2 dc, join in 3rd ch of beg ch-3. (36 dc)

Trim Around Sole

With sole of bootie facing up, attach red with a sl st in rem lp of Rnd 2 of sole at back seam, working in rem lps, sl st in each st around, join in beg sl st, fasten off.

Cuff

Rnd 1: With RS facing, attach white with a sl st in ch-1 sp at back seam, ch 1, beg in same sp, 2 sc in each sp around, join in back lp only of beg sc. (24 sc)

Rnd 2: Working in back lps only this rnd, ch 1, sc in same st as joining and in each rem sc around, join in back lp only of beg sc.

Rnd 3: Rep Rnd 2, ending with join in front lp only of beg sc.

Rnd 4: Working in front lps only this rnd, ch 3, [sl st in next st, ch 3] rep around, join in beg sl st, ch 3, sl st in rem lp of Rnd 2 directly below.

Rnd 5: Working in rem lps of Rnd 2, ch 3, [sl st in next st, ch 3] rep around, join in same st as beg ch-3, ch 3, sl st in rem lp of Rnd 1 directly below.

Rnd 6: Working in rem lps of Rnd 1, rep Rnd 5, join in same st as beg ch-3, fasten off.

Tie *(make 2)*

With 2 strands white held tog, ch 50, fasten off. Beg at center front, weave tie through ch-1 sps on Rnd 6 of upper bootie. Tie ch 50 in bow.

Pompom *(make 4)*

Wrap white yarn 50 times around cardboard. Slip yarn off cardboard, tie piece of white yarn around center and knot tightly. Cut open lps at each end. Trim and shape to form pompom. Fasten 1 pompom to each end of each tie. ✤

Blackberry Angel Pin

Design by Short Hill Studio

Add a sparkling, festive touch to any holiday outfit with this darling, contemporary-style angel!

Experience Level: Intermediate

Finished Measurements: Approximately 3" high x 3" wide

Materials

✳ Kreinik Tapestry #12 Braid: 1 spool each blackberry #080HL and pink #007

✳ Size B/1 crochet hook or size needed to obtain gauge

✳ Assorted scraps of metallic thread and small beads

✳ 8mm heart cabochon or bead

✳ 3" x 9" piece of black netting or lace

✳ 1"-long pin back

✳ Tacky craft glue

✳ Sewing needle and dark thread

Gauge: Work evenly and consistently throughout

Pattern Note

Join rnds with a sl st unless otherwise stated.

First Leg

Rnd 1: With blackberry, ch 4, 4 dc in 4th ch from hook, join in 4th ch of beg ch-4. (5 dc, counting last 3 chs of beg ch-4 as first dc)

Rnds 2–4: Ch 3 (counts as first dc throughout), dc in each rem st around, join in 3rd ch of beg ch-3; fasten off at end of Rnd 4. (5 dc)

Second Leg

Rnds 1–4: Rep Rnds 1–4 of first leg; at end of Rnd 4, do not fasten off.

Body

Rnd 5: Ch 3, dc in each of next 4 dc, dc in each of 5 dc on first leg, join in 3rd ch of beg ch-3. (10 dc)

Rnds 6–8: Rep Rnds 2–4 of first leg; fasten off at end of Rnd 8.

Arm *(make 2)*

Rnds 1–4: Rep Rnds 1–4 of first leg.

Head

Rnd 1: Beg at top of head, with pink, ch 3, 7 hdc in 3rd ch from hook, join in 3rd ch of beg ch-3. (8 hdc, counting last 2 chs of beg ch-3 as first hdc)

Rnd 2: Ch 2 (counts as first hdc throughout), hdc in next st, [2 hdc in next st, hdc in next st] rep around, join in 2nd ch of beg ch-2. (11 hdc)

Rnd 3: Ch 2, hdc in each rem st around, join in 2nd ch of beg ch-2. (11 hdc)

Rnd 4: Ch 2, [hdc dec] rep around, join in 2nd ch of beg ch-2, fasten off, leaving a 6" end. Push end inside head for stuffing.

Skirt

Rnd 1: With pink, ch 15, join to form a ring, ch 1, sc in same st as joining and in each rem ch around, join in beg sc. (15 sc)

Rnd 2: Ch 2 (counts as first hdc throughout), hdc in next st, 2 hdc in next st, [hdc in each of next 2 sts, 2 hdc in next st] rep around, join in 2nd ch of beg ch-2. (20 hdc)

Rnds 3 & 4: Ch 2, hdc in each rem st around, join in 2nd ch of beg ch-2; at end of Rnd 4, fasten off.

Assembly

With needle and thread, gather up top of body, attach head and sew on arms. Sew skirt to waist. Sew pin back at center back of angel.

Wings

Fold netting or lace accordion style at center, insert between base and top of pin and sew to angel on each side of pin. Spread tips of wings open.

Finishing

Glue cabochon or bead to center front of angel. Make approximately 5 chs with scraps of metallic thread ranging from approximately 2"–3½" long; attach small beads to chs. Tie ends of all chs tog in an overhand knot and attach to top of head like ponytail. ❧

Festive Barrettes

Continued from page 141

Finishing

Tie gold ribbon in bow around angel's neck. Bend pipe cleaner into circle for halo and glue to top of angel's head. Apply blusher lightly to each cheek. Glue bottom of angel's wings to barrette.

Rose Barrette

Rose

Row 1 (RS): With jockey red, ch 30 (foundation ch), ch 3 more (counts as first dc), 2 dc in 4th ch from hook, 3 dc in each rem ch across, fasten off. (90 dc)

Row 2: With RS facing, attach white with a sl st in 3rd ch of beg ch-3, sc in next st and in each rem ch across to last st, sl st in last st, fasten off.

With RS on the inside, roll piece tog along foundation ch to form rose; tack in place with tapestry needle and jockey red.

Leaf *(make 2)*

Row 1: With paddy green, ch 4, 5 dc in 4th ch from hook, turn. (6 dc, counting last 3 chs of ch-4 as first dc)

Row 2: Ch 3 (counts as first dc throughout), dc in each rem st across, turn. (6 dc)

Row 3: Ch 3, [dc dec] twice, dc in last st, turn. (4 sts)

Row 4: Ch 1, [insert hook in next st, yo, draw up a lp] 4 times, yo, draw through all 5 lps on hook, ch 1 to secure, fasten off.

Finishing

Tack 1 leaf on each side of rose at back of rose. Holding both pieces of ribbon tog, pull through 1 st at center back of rose; tie in bow. Glue rose and leaves to barrette with bow at bottom. ❧

Bright, Shining Faces

Watch the faces of your littlest loved ones light up when they open this year's Christmas gift from you! Cuddly bears, beautiful dolls and many more toys for preteen kids are waiting to be crocheted and loved!

Candy, the Christmas Doll

Design by Carol Alexander

Add a touch of grace to your mantel or table with this lovely doll. She's sure to enhance your Christmas atmosphere.

Experience Level: Intermediate

Finished Measurements: Fits 13" Music Box Doll by Fibre-Craft

Materials

❋ Caron Dawn Sayelle acrylic worsted weight yarn (3.5 oz per skein): 1 skein each Christmas red #0406 and Christmas green #0410

❋ Size G/6 crochet hook or size needed to obtain gauge

❋ 13" Music Box Doll by Fibre-Craft

❋ Christmas music button

❋ 4 (⅜") white buttons

❋ 3 size 4/0 snap fasteners

❋ 1 yd ⅜"-wide green satin ribbon

❋ 3½ yds 1"-wide white eyelet ruffle

❋ 2 map pins

❋ Yarn needle

❋ Sewing needle and white sewing thread

Gauge: 4 sts and 4 rows = 1" in sc

To save time, take time to check gauge.

Pattern Notes

Join rnds with a sl st unless otherwise stated.

To change color in dc, work last dc before color change until last 2 lps before final yo rem on hook, drop working color to WS, yo with next color, complete dc.

Carry color not in use loosely across WS, working over it with color currently in use until it is needed again.

Dress Bodice

Row 1 (WS): Beg at neck with Christmas red, ch 17, sc in 2nd ch from hook, [2 sc in next ch, sc in next ch] 3 times, 2 sc in next ch, [2 sc in next ch, sc in next ch] 4 times, ch 1, turn. (24 sc)

Row 2: Sc in each st across, ch 1, turn.

Row 3: Sc in each of first 2 sts, 2 sc in next st, [sc in each of next 2 sts, 2 sc in next st] 3 times, [2 sc in next st, sc in each of next 2 sts] 4 times, ch 1, turn. (32 sc)

Row 4: Sc in each of first 5 sts, ch 6, sk next 5 sts for first armhole, sc in each of next 5 sts, sc dec, sc in each of next 5 sts, ch 6, sk next 5 sts for next armhole, sc in each of last 5 sts, turn. (21 sc, 2 ch-6 sps)

Row 5: Ch 2 (counts as first hdc throughout), hdc in each of next 2 sts, hdc dec, sc in each of next 6 chs, [sc in next st, 2 sc in next st] 5 times, sc in next st, sc in each of next 6 chs, hdc dec, hdc in each of next 3 sts, turn. (36 sts)

Row 6: Ch 2, hdc in each of next 4 sts, sc in next st, [sc in each of next 3 sts, sc dec] 4 times, sc in each of next 5 sts, hdc in each of last 5 sts, turn. (32 sts)

Row 7: Ch 2, hdc in each of next 4 sts, sc in each of next 22 sts, hdc in each of last 5 sts, ch 1, turn. (32 sts)

Row 8: Sc in each of first 7 sts, sc dec, sc in each of next 14 sts, sc dec, sc in each of last 7 sts, ch 1, turn. (30 sts)

Row 9: Rep Row 2.

Rnd 10: Sc in each st around, join in back lp only of first sc to beg working in rnds. (30 sc)

Skirt

Rnd 11 (RS): Working in back lps only this rnd, ch 3 (counts as first dc throughout), dc in same st as joining, changing to Christmas green; 4 dc in next st, changing to Christmas red in last st, [2 dc in next st, changing to Christmas green in last st; 4 dc in next st, changing to Christmas red in last st] rep around, join in 3rd ch of beg ch-3. (90 dc)

Rnd 12: Ch 3, dc in each rem dc around, working Christmas red dcs over Christmas red dcs and Christmas green dcs over Christmas green dcs, join with Christmas red in 3rd ch of beg ch-3. (90 dc)

Rnds 13–17: Rep Rnd 12. (90 dc)

Rnd 18: Ch 3, dc in next dc, changing to Christmas green; *dc in next dc, 2 dc in next dc, dc in each of next 2 dc, changing to Christmas red in last dc **; dc in each of next 2 dc, changing to

Christmas green in last dc; rep from * around, ending last rep at **, join in 3rd ch of beg ch-3. (105 dc)

Rnds 19–23: Rep Rnd 12, at end of Rnd 23, fasten off. (105 dc)

Sleeves

Note: *Do not join Rnds 1–11; mark first st of each rnd with safety pin or other small marker.*

Rnd 1: With RS facing, attach Christmas red with a sl st in center sk sc on Row 3 of bodice at either armhole opening, ch 1, 2 sc in same st as joining, sc in each of next 2 sc, 2 sc over side of next Row 4 sc, hdc in rem lps of each of next 6 chs, 2 sc over side of next Row 4 sc, sc in each of next 2 sk sc on Row 3. (16 sts)

Rnds 2 & 3: Sc in each st around. (16 sc)

Rnd 4: [Sc in each of next 2 sts, sc dec] rep around. (12 sts)

Rnds 5–11: Sc in each st around. (12 sc)

Rnd 12: [Sc in each of next 4 sc, sc dec] twice, join in beg sc, fasten off. (10 sts)

Rep on 2nd armhole.

Waist Ruffle

Rnd 1: With RS facing, attach Christmas red with a sl st in first rem lp of Rnd 10 of bodice at back opening, ch 3, working in rem lps around, 2 dc in same st, 3 dc in each rem st around, join in 3rd ch of beg ch-3. (90 dc)

Rnd 2: Ch 3, dc in each of next 7 sts, 2 dc in next st, [dc in each of next 8 sts, 2 dc in next st] rep around, join in 3rd ch of beg ch-3. (100 dc)

Rnd 3: Ch 3, dc in each of next 7 sts, dc dec, [dc in each of next 8 sts, dc dec] rep around, join in 3rd ch of beg ch-3. (90 sts)

Rnd 4: Ch 3, dc in each of next 6 sts, dc dec, [dc in each of next 7 sts, dc dec] rep around, join in 3rd ch of beg ch-3, fasten off. (80 sts)

Cape

Row 1: With Christmas red, ch 25, hdc in 3rd ch from hook, [2 hdc in next st, hdc in next st] 5 times, 2 hdc in each of next 2 sts, [hdc in next st, 2 hdc in next st] 5 times, turn. (36 hdc, counting last 2 chs of foundation ch as first hdc)

Row 2: Ch 2 (counts as first hdc throughout), [hdc dec] twice, [hdc in each of next 12 sts, 2 hdc in next st] twice, [hdc dec] twice, hdc in last st, turn. (34 sts)

Row 3: Ch 2, hdc dec, hdc in each of next 5 sts, 2 hdc in next st, [hdc in each of next 4 sts, 2 hdc in next st, hdc in each of next 5 sts, 2 hdc in next st] twice, hdc dec, hdc in last st, turn. (37 sts)

Row 4: Ch 2, hdc dec, hdc in each st across to last 3 sts, hdc dec, hdc in last st, fasten off. (35 sts)

Hat

Note: Do not join Rnds 1–4; mark first st of each rnd with safety pin or other small marker.

Rnd 1: Beg at crown with Christmas red, ch 2, 6 sc in 2nd ch from hook. (6 sc)

Rnd 2: 2 sc in each sc around. (12 sc)

Rnd 3: [Sc in next sc, 2 sc in next sc] rep around. (18 sc)

Rnd 4: [Sc in each of next 2 sts, 2 sc in next st] rep around. (24 sc)

Rnd 5: [Sc in each of next 3 sts, 2 sc in next st] rep around, join in back lp only of beg sc. (30 sc)

Rnd 6: Ch 3, working in back lps only this rnd, dc in next st, changing to Christmas green, *dc in each of next 4 sts, changing to Christmas red in last st **; dc in each of next 2 sts, changing to Christmas green in last st; rep from * around, ending last rep at **, join in 3rd ch of beg ch-3. (30 dc)

Rnd 7: Rep Rnd 12 of skirt.

Rnd 8: Rep Rnd 7, join in front lp only of 3rd ch of beg ch-3 with Christmas red; fasten off Christmas green.

Rnd 9: Ch 3, working in front lps

only, 2 dc in same st as joining, 3 dc in each rem dc around, join in 3rd ch of beg ch-3, fasten off. (90 dc)

Finishing

With sewing needle and white thread, sew a length of eyelet ruffle around bottom of skirt and bottom of waist ruffle. Using photo as a guide throughout, sew a length of eyelet ruffle around bottom of each sleeve, with bottom of eyelet ruffle pointing toward neck. Sew a length of eyelet ruffle around neckline, with bottom of eyelet ruffle pointing up, then fold down for collar.

Sew 3 snap fasteners evenly sp down back bodice opening. Sew 4 buttons evenly sp down center front bodice. Insert music button in doll's back. Place dress on doll and arrange skirt and waist ruffles evenly around.

With sewing needle and white thread, sew a length of eyelet ruffle around bottom edge of cape, beg and ending over end sts of Row 1 and easing around corners. Cut green ribbon into 2 (18") lengths. Cut 1 (18") length into 2 (9") lengths. Lp each 9" length through 1 end st of foundation ch on each edge of cape and tack in place on WS. Place cape around doll's shoulders and tie ribbon ends into bow.

With sewing needle and white thread, sew a length of eyelet ruffle around bottom of last rnd of hat. Tie rem length of green ribbon into a bow and tack to back center of hat on Rnd 6; trim ends to desired length.

Place hat on doll's head and secure with map pins pushed through top center of doll's head. ***Note:*** *If this toy will be played with by a small child, eliminate map pins.* ❧

Topsy-Turvy Doll & Bear

Design by Sandy Abbate

To be a doll or a bear? That is the question. Use this pattern and you can have both! Flip the skirt one way or the other and you have two toys in one. What fun for a little girl's imagination!

Experience Level: Intermediate

Finished Measurements: Approximately 13" tall

Materials

❋ Red Heart Super Saver worsted weight yarn: 1 (8-oz) skein each hot red #390 and jade #369, 1 (3 oz) skein each warm brown #336, pink #371, white #311 and pale yellow #322, and small amounts each brown #328 and light blue #381 for embroidery

❋ Size G/6 crochet hook or size needed to obtain gauge

❋ 2½ yds ⅜"-wide red satin ribbon

❋ 2½ yds ⅜"-wide white satin ribbon

❋ 1 yd ⅛"-wide gold satin ribbon

❋ ½ yd ¼"-wide red satin ribbon

❋ ½ yd ¼"-wide green satin ribbon

❋ Black permanent marker

❋ Small amount cosmetic blusher

❋ Polyester fiberfill

❋ Yarn needle

❋ Safety pin or other small marker

Gauge: 4 sts and 4 rnds = 1" in sc

To save time, take time to check gauge.

Pattern Note

Join rnds with a sl st unless otherwise stated.

Pattern Stitches

V-st: [Dc, ch 2, dc] in indicated st or sp.

Beg V-st: [Ch 5, dc] in indicated st or sp.

Cl: Holding back on hook last lp of each st, 2 dc in indicated st or sp, yo, draw through all 3 lps on hook.

Beg cl: [Ch 2, dc] in indicated st or sp.

Cl shell: [Cl, ch 2, cl] in indicated st or sp.

Beg cl shell: [Beg cl, ch 2, cl] in indicated st or sp.

Bear

Head

Note: Do not join rnds unless otherwise stated; mark first st of each rnd with safety pin or other small marker.

Rnd 1: With warm brown, ch 2, 6 sc in 2nd ch from hook. (6 sc)

Rnd 2: 2 sc in each st around. (12 sc)

Rnd 3: [Sc in next st, 2 sc in next st] rep around. (18 sc)

Rnd 4: [Sc in each of next 2 sts, 2 sc in next st] rep around. (24 sc)

Rnd 5: [Sc in each of next 3 sts, 2 sc in next st] rep around. (30 sc)

Rnd 6: [Sc in each of next 4 sts, 2 sc in next st] rep around. (36 sc)

Rnds 7–14: Sc in each st around.

Rnd 15: [Sc in each of next 4 sts, sc dec] rep around. (30 sts)

Rnd 16: [Sc in each of next 3 sts, sc dec] rep around. (24 sts)

Rnd 17: [Sc in each of next 2 sts, sc dec] rep around. (18 sts)

Rnd 18: Sc in each st around, join in beg sc, fasten off. (18 sc) Stuff head firmly.

Body

Note: Do not join rnds unless otherwise stated; mark first st of each rnd with safety pin or other small marker.

Rnd 1: Attach jade with a sl st in first sc of Rnd 18 of head, ch 1, sc in same st and in each rem st around. (18 sc)

Rnds 2–4: Rep Rnds 4–6 of head. (36 sc at end of Rnd 4)

Rnd 5: [Sc in each of next 5 sts, 2 sc in next st] rep around. (42 sc)

Rnds 6–10: Sc in each st around; at end of Rnd 10, join in front lp only of beg sc; do not fasten off.

Skirt

Rnd 1: Working in front lps only this rnd, beg V-st in same st as joining, sk next 2 sts, V-st in next st, [sk next st, V-st in next st] rep around to last 2 sts, sk last 2 sts, join in 3rd ch of beg ch-5. (20 V-sts)

Rnds 2–4: Sl st in beg V-st sp, beg V-st in same sp, V-st in each rem V-st sp around, join in 3rd ch of beg ch-5. (20 V-sts)

Rnd 5: Sl st in beg V-st sp, ch 4 (counts as first dc, ch-1), *dc between same V-st sind next V-st,

ch 1 **, dc in next V-st sp, ch 1, rep from * around, ending last rep at **, join in 3rd ch of beg ch-4. (40 ch-1 sps)

Rnd 6: Sl st in first ch-1 sp, beg V-st in same sp, V-st in each rem ch-1 sp around, join in 3rd ch of beg ch-5. (40 V-sts)

Rnds 7–12: Rep Rnd 2; at end of Rnd 12, fasten off. (40 V-sts)

Arm (make 2)
Note: *Do not join rnds unless otherwise stated; mark first st of each rnd with safety pin or other small marker.*

Rnds 1–6: With jade, rep Rnds

1–6 of head. (36 sc at end of Rnd 6)

Rnds 7 & 8: Sc in each st around. (36 sc)

Rnd 9: [Sc dec] rep around. (18 sts)

Rnd 10: Rep Rnd 7. (18 sc)

Rnd 11: Ch 4 (counts as first dc, ch-1), [sk next st, dc in next st, ch 1] rep around, ending with sk last st, join in 3rd ch of beg ch-4. (9 ch-1 sps)

Rnd 12: Ch 1, sc in same st as joining, sc in each rem sp and dc around. (18 sc)

Rnds 13–16: Rep Rnd 7; at end of Rnd 16, join in beg sc, fasten off. (18 sc)

Rnd 17: Attach warm brown with a sl st in back lp only of first sc of last rnd, ch 1, working in back lps only this rnd, sc in same st and in each rem st around. (18 sc)

Rnds 18 & 19: Rep Rnd 7. (18 sc)

Rnd 20: [Sc in next st, sc dec] rep around; do not fasten off. (12 sts)

Weave a length of ⅜"-wide red satin ribbon through ch-1 sps of Rnd 11. Stuff arm lightly.

Rnd 21: [Sc dec] rep around. (6 sts)

Rnd 22: Rep Rnd 21, join in beg sc dec, fasten off, leaving a 12" end. (3 sts)

Finish stuffing arm. With yarn needle, weave 12" end through tops of sts of last rnd; pull tightly to close; knot securely.

Sleeve edging

With bottom of arm facing away, attach hot red with a sl st in any rem lp of Rnd 16 of arm, ch 1, working in rem lps of Rnd 16, sc in same st and in each rem st around, join in beg sc, fasten off.

Ear (make 2)

Row 1 (RS): With warm brown, ch 7, sc in 2nd ch from hook and in each rem ch across, ch 1, turn. (6 sc)

Row 2: 2 sc in first st, sc in each st across to last st, 2 sc in last st, ch 1, turn. (8 sc)

Rows 3 & 4: Sc dec, sc across to last 2 sts, sc dec, ch 1, turn; at end of Row 4, do not ch 1; fasten off. (4 sts at end of Row 4)

Row 5: With RS facing, attach warm brown with a sl st over side of first st of Row 1, ch 1, sc over side of same st, sc over end st of each of next 3 rows, sc in each st across Row 4, sc over end st of each of next 4 rows, fasten off, leaving 12" end for sewing.

Snout

Note: *Do not join rnds unless otherwise stated; mark first st of each rnd with safety pin or other small marker.*

Rnds 1–3: With warm brown, rep Rnds 1–3 of head. (18 sts at end of Rnd 3)

Rnd 4: Sc in each st around, join in beg sc, fasten off.

Collar

Row 1: With hot red, ch 22, sc in 2nd ch from hook and in each rem ch across, ch 1, turn. (21 sc)

Row 2: Sc in first st, [ch 3, sk next st, sc in next st] rep across, fasten off.

Doll

Head

Rnds 1–18: With pink, rep Rnds 1–18 of head for bear. Stuff head firmly.

Body

Rnds 1–10: With hot red, rep Rnds 1–10 of body for bear.

Skirt

Rnd 1: Working in front lps

only this rnd, beg cl shell in same st as joining, sk 2 sts, cl shell in next st, [sk next st, cl shell in next st] rep across to last 2 sts, sk last 2 sts, join in top of beg cl. (20 cl shells)

Rnds 2–4: Sl st in beg cl shell sp, beg cl shell in same sp, cl shell in each rem cl shell sp around, join in top of beg cl. (20 cl shells)

Rnd 5: Sl st in beg cl shell sp, ch 4 (counts as first dc, ch-1), *dc between same cl shell and next cl shell, ch 1 **, dc in next cl shell sp, ch 1, rep from * around, ending last rep at **, join in top of beg cl. (40 ch-1 sps)

Rnd 6: Sl st in first ch-1 sp, beg cl shell in same sp, cl shell in each rem ch-1 sp around, join in top of beg cl. (40 cl shells)

Rnds 7–11: Sl st in beg cl shell sp, beg cl shell in same sp, cl shell in each rem cl shell sp around, join in top of beg cl; at end of Rnd 11, fasten off. (40 cl shells)

Arm (make 2)

Note: *Do not join rnds unless otherwise stated; mark first st of each rnd with safety pin or other small marker.*

Rnds 1–3: With hot red, rep Rnds 1–3 of head for bear. (18 sc at end of Rnd 3)

Rnds 4–9: Sc in each st around; at end of Rnd 9, join in beg sc, fasten off. (18 sc)

Rnd 10: Attach pink with a sl st in back lp only of first sc of last rnd, ch 1, sc in same st, working in back lps only this rnd, [sc dec] 3 times, sc in each rem st around. (15 sts)

Rnds 11–16: Sc in each st around. (15 sc)

Rnd 17: [Sc in next sc, sc dec] rep around. (10 sts)

Rnd 18: [Sc in next st, 2 sc in next st] rep around. (15 sc)

Rnd 19: Rep Rnd 11.

Rnd 20: [Sl st, ch 3, dc, ch 3, sl st] in next st for thumb, sc in each rem st around.

Rnd 21: Sk thumb, sc in each rem st around. (14 sc)

Rnd 22: Sc in each sc around. (14 sc)

Stuff arm lightly.

Rnd 23: [Sc dec] rep around. (7 sts)

Rnd 24: Sc in first st, [sc dec] 3 times, join in beg sc, fasten off, leaving a 12" end.

Stuff arm lightly. With yarn needle, weave 12" end through tops of sts of last rnd, pull tightly to close, knot securely.

Sleeve edging

Rnd 1: With bottom of arm facing away, attach white with a sl st in any rem lp of Rnd 9 of arm, ch 1, working in rem lps of Rnd 9, sc in same st and in each rem st around, join in beg sc. (18 sc)

Rnd 2: Ch 1, sc in same st as joining, ch 3, [sc, ch 3] in each rem sc around, join in beg sc, fasten off.

Collar

Row 1: With white, ch 21, sc in 2nd ch from hook and in each rem ch across, ch 1, turn. (20 sc)

Row 2: [Sc, ch 3] in each st across to last st, sc in last st, fasten off.

Nose

Rnd 1: With pink, rep Rnd 1 of head for bear.

Rnd 2: Sc in each sc around, join in beg sc, fasten off.

Bonnet

Rnd 1: With hot red, ch 4, 11 dc in 4th ch from hook, join in 4th ch of beg ch-4. (12 dc, counting last 3 chs of beg ch-4 as first dc)

Rnd 2: Ch 3, dc in same st as joining, 2 dc in each rem st around, join in 3rd ch of beg ch-3. (24 dc)

Rnd 3: Ch 3, 2 dc in next st, [dc in next st, 2 dc in next st] rep around, join in 3rd ch of beg ch-3; do not fasten off. (36 dc)

Brim

Row 1 (RS): Ch 3, working in back lps only this row, dc in each of next 27 sts, turn. (28 dc)

Row 2: Ch 3, dc in each rem st across, turn. (28 dc)

Row 3: Ch 4 (counts as first dc, ch-1), sk next st, dc in next st, [ch 1, sk next st, dc in next st] rep across to last st, leave last st unworked, ch 1, do not turn. (13 ch-1 sps)

Rnd 4: Sc evenly sp over row ends of last 3 rows of brim, across bottom back of bonnet, across row ends of brim on opposite side, and across Row 3 of brim, join in beg sc, turn.

Ruffle

Row 1: Ch 3, working in back lps only, dc in same st, 2 dc in each rem sc across front of brim, fasten off, do not turn.

Row 2: Attach white with a sl st in 3rd ch of first ch-3 at beg of last row, ch 1, sc in same st and in each rem st across, fasten off.

Hair

With ruffle of brim pointing away from you, working in rem lps of Rnd 4 across front of brim beneath ruffle, attach pale yellow with a sl st in first rem lp at right edge, ch 1, beg in same st, [sc, ch 5, sc] in each st across front of brim, [sc, ch 5, sc] in back lps only of each st of Rnd 4 around rem of bonnet, join in beg sc, fasten off.

Assembly

Stuff doll and bear bodies firmly. With yarn needle, sew bodies tog through rem lps of Rnd 10 of bodies.

Finishing

Using photo as a guide, sew ears to bear's head over Rnds 5–10. Sew snout to front of bear's face, stuffing lightly as you sew. Fold doll's nose flat and sew to face. Sew arms on doll and bear. Place collars around necks and tack in place. Using photo as a guide, embroider faces, using 1 ply only of brown for doll's eyelashes. With black permanent marker, make pupils on doll's eyes. Apply blusher lightly to doll's cheeks.

Weave length of ⅜"-wide white ribbon through ch-1 sps on Row 3 of brim on doll's bonnet. Place bonnet on doll's head and tie a bow under chin.

Cut 1 (12)" length each of green and gold ribbon. Thread yarn needle with both lengths; take a st in top right side of doll's head through Row 3 of brim on bonnet and tie ribbon ends into bow. Rep with 1½" length each of red and gold ribbon at top right side of bear's head.

Beg at center front, weave a length of ⅜"-wide white ribbon through ch-1 sps on Rnd 5 of doll's skirt. Tie in bow. Rep with ⅜"-wide red ribbon through ch-1 sps on Rnd 5 of bear's skirt. Wrap a length of ⅜"-wide ribbon around doll's waist and tie in bow at back. Rep for bear with ⅜"-wide red ribbon.

Skirt trim

With bear's skirt facing, working through both thicknesses of back lps only of bear's and doll's skirts tog, attach white with a sl st in any st of last rnd of skirt, ch 1, [sc, ch 3, sc] in same st and in each rem st around, join in beg sc, fasten off. ❧

Snowbear

Design by Barbara Roy

Invite the snow to fall and the wind to blow with this bear who wishes he could be out in those winter elements. This pattern can easily be stitched while you watch from the inside as the snowflakes fall outside.

Experience Level: Intermediate

Finished Measurements: Approximately 15" tall

Materials

❋ Worsted weight yarn: 5 oz white, 1½ oz green and small amount black

❋ Size F/5 crochet hook or size needed to obtain gauge

❋ 18mm jingle bell

❋ 2 (½") black shank buttons for eyes

❋ 6"-diameter circle of cardboard

❋ Polyester fiberfill stuffing

❋ Tapestry needle

❋ Safety pin or other small marker

Gauge: Rnds 1–5 of body = 2¾" in diameter

To save time, take time to check gauge.

Pattern Note

Do not join rnds unless otherwise stated; mark first st of each rnd with safety pin or other marker.

Head

Rnd 1: With white, ch 2, 6 sc in 2nd ch from hook. (6 sc)

Rnd 2: 2 sc in each st around. (12 sc)

Rnd 3: [Sc in each of next 2 sts, 2 sc in next st] rep around. (16 sc)

Rnd 4: Sc in each of next 7 sts, 2 sc in each of next 2 sts, sc in each of next 7 sts. (18 sc)

Rnd 5: Sc in each of next 4 sts, 2 sc in next st, sc in each of next 8 sts, 2 sc in next st, sc in each of last 4 sts. (20 sc)

Rnd 6: Sc in each of next 9 sts, 2 sc in each of next 2 sts, sc in each of last 9 sts. (22 sc)

Rnd 7: [Sc in each of next 4 sts, 2 sc in each of next 2 sts] 3 times, sc in each of last 4 sts. (28 sc)

Rnd 8: Sc in each of next 8 sts, 2 sc in next st, sc in each of next 4 sts, 2 sc in each of next 2 sts, sc in each of next 4 sts, 2 sc in next st, sc in each of last 8 sts. (32 sc)

Rnd 9: Sc in each of next 6 sts, 2 sc in each of next 2 sts, sc in each of next 5 sts, 2 sc in next st, sc in each of next 4 sts, 2 sc in next st, sc in each of next 5 sts, 2 sc in each of next 2 sts, sc in each of last 6 sts. (38 sc)

Rnd 10: [Sc in each of next 5 sts, 2 sc in next st] 3 times, sc in each of next 2 sts, 2 sc in next st, [sc in each of next 5 sts, 2 sc in next st] twice, sc in each of last 5 sts. (44 sc)

Rnd 11: Sc in each of next 21 sts, 2 sc in each of next 2 sts, sc in each of last 21 sts. (46 sc)

Rnd 12: [Sc in each of next 9 sts, 2 sc in next st] twice, sc in each of next 6 sts, 2 sc in next st, sc in each of next 9 sts, 2 sc in next st, sc in each of last 9 sts. (50 sc)

Rnd 13: Sc in each st around.

Rnd 14: Sc in each of next 22 sts, 2 sc in next st, sc in each of next 4 sts, 2 sc in next st, sc in each of last 22 sts. (52 sc)

Rnd 15: Sc in each of next 9 sts, sc dec, sc in each of next 5 sts, sc dec, sc in each of next 16 sts, sc dec, sc in each of next 5 sts, sc dec, sc in each of last 9 sts. (48 sts)

Rnd 16: [Sc in each of next 5 sts, sc dec] 3 times, sc in each of next 8 sts, sc dec, [sc in each of next 5 sts, sc dec] twice, sc in each of last 3 sts. (42 sts)

With tapestry needle, sew eyes between Rnds 9 and 10, 7 sts apart.

Rnd 17: [Sc in each of next 5 sts, sc dec] rep around. (36 sts)

Stuff head lightly, and continue to stuff as work progresses.

Rnd 18: [Sc in each of next 2 sts, sc dec] rep around. (27 sts)

Rnd 19: [Sc in each of next 7 sts, sc dec] rep around. (24 sts)

Rnd 20: [Sc in each of next 4 sts, sc dec] rep around. (20 sts)

Rnd 21: [Sc in each of next 3 sts, sc dec] rep around. (16 sts)

Rnd 22: [Sc in each of next 2 sts, sc dec] rep around. (12 sts)

Rnd 23: [Sc dec] rep around, join in beg sc dec, fasten off, leaving 6" end. (6 sts)

Finish stuffing head. Weave 6" end through sts of last rnd, pull tightly to close, fasten off.

Ear (make 4)

Rnds 1 & 2: Rep Rnds 1 and 2 of head. (12 sc at end of Rnd 2)

Rnd 3: [Sc in next st, 2 sc in next st] rep around, join in beg sc, fasten off. (18 sc)

Sew 2 pieces tog to form 1 ear. Sew ears to Rnds 15 and 16 of head, leaving 12 sts between ears.

Body

Rnds 1–3: Rep Rnds 1–3 of ear. (18 sc at end of Rnd 3)

Rnds 4–12: Sc in each sc around, inc 6 sc evenly sp around on each rnd. (72 sc at end of Rnd 12)

Rnd 13: Working in back lps only this rnd, sc in each sc around. (72 sc)

Rnds 14–18: Sc in each st around. (72 sc)

Rnd 19: Sc around, working 6 sc dec evenly sp around. (66 sts)

Rnds 20–24: Rep Rnds 14–18. (66 sc)

Rnd 25–30: Rep Rnds 19–24. (60 sts)

Insert cardboard at bottom of body and stuff as work progresses.

Rnd 31: Rep Rnd 19. (54 sts)

Rnds 32–34: Rep Rnd 14. (54 sc)

Rnds 35–42: Rep Rnds 31-34 alternately. (42 sts on each of last 4 rnds)

Rnds 43–45: Rep Rnd 19. (24 sts on Rnd 45)

Rnds 46–48: Rep Rnds 32–34, at end of Rnd 48, join in beg sc, fasten off. (24 sc)

Sew head to top of body.

Arm (make 2)

Rnds 1 & 2: Beg at bottom of arm, rep Rnds 1 and 2 of head. (12 sc at end of Rnd 2)

Rnd 3: [Sc in each of next 3 sts, 2 sc in next st] rep around. (15 sc)

Rnds 4–20: Sc in each st around;

at end of Rnd 20, ch 1, turn. (15 sc)
Stuff arm.

Row 21: Sc in each of first 6 sc, ch 1, turn.

Row 22: Sc in each sc across, ch 1, turn. (6 sc)

Row 23: Sc dec, sc in each of next 2 sts, sc dec, fasten off. (4 sts)

Sew arms to side of body, 5 rnds below head. Tack bottoms of arms to sides of body.

Scarf

Row 1: With green, ch 85, sc in 2nd ch from hook and in each rem ch across, ch 1, turn. (84 sc)

Rows 2–5: Sc in each sc across, ch 1, turn; at end of Row 5, do not ch 1, do not turn.

Rnd 6: Sl st around scarf, join in

beg sl st, fasten off.

Tie scarf around bear's neck.

Hat

Rnd 1: With green, ch 2, 8 sc in 2nd ch from hook. (8 sc)

Rnds 2–23: Sc in each sc around to last st, 2 sc in last st; at end of Rnd 23, join in beg sc, fasten off, leaving end for sewing. (30 sc at end of Rnd 23)

Place hat over left ear and sew in place. Fold tip of hat over and tack in place. Sew jingle bell to tip of hat.

Finishing

With tapestry needle and black yarn, using photo as a guide, embroider nose and mouth on bear. ✦

Frog Prince

Design by Michele Wilcox

Kiss this royal frog and you may increase your chances of falling in love with a prince—the frog prince, that is! This quick and easy project will make a great visual to a well-loved fairy tale.

Experience Level: Intermediate

Finished Measurements: Approximately 15½" tall

Materials

✳ Worsted weight yarn: 3 oz green and small amounts each gold, black and white

✳ Size F/5 crochet hook or size needed to obtain gauge

✳ Polyester fiberfill

✳ Tapestry needle

✳ Safety pin or other small marker

Gauge: 4 sc = 1"

To save time, take time to check gauge.

Head

Note: *Do not join rnds unless otherwise stated; mark first st of each rnd with safety pin or other small marker.*

Rnd 1: Beg at top of head with green, ch 2, 6 sc in 2nd ch from hook. (6 sc)

Rnd 2: 2 sc in each sc around. (12 sc)

Rnd 3: [Sc in next sc, 2 sc in next sc] rep around. (18 sc)

Rnd 4: [Sc in each of next 2 sc, 2 sc in next sc] rep around. (24 sc)

Rnd 5: [Sc in each of next 3 sc, 2 sc in next sc] rep around. (30 sc)

Rnd 6: Sc in each sc around.

Rnd 7: [Sc in each of next 4 sc, 2 sc in next sc] rep around. (36 sc)

Rnd 8: [Sc in each of next 5 sc, 2 sc in next sc] rep around. (42 sc)

Rnds 9–15: Rep Rnd 6.

Rnd 16: [Sc in each of next 5 sc, sc dec] rep around. (36 sts)

Rnd 17: [Sc dec] rep around. (18 sts)

Stuff head lightly.

Rnds 18 & 19: Rep Rnd 6. (18 sts)

Body

Rnds 20 & 21: Rep Rnds 4 and 5. (30 sc at end of Rnd 21)

Rnds 22 & 23: Rep Rnds 7 and 8. (42 sc at end of Rnd 23)

Rnds 24–34: Rep Rnd 6. (42 sc)

Rnd 35: Rep Rnd 16. (36 sts)

Rnd 36: [Sc in each of next 4 sts, sc dec] rep around. (30 sts)

Rnd 37: [Sc in each of next 3 sts, sc dec] rep around. (24 sts)

Rnd 38: [Sc in each of next 2 sts, sc dec] rep around. (18 sts)

Stuff body lightly.

Rnd 39: [Sc in next st, sc dec] rep around. (12 sts)

Rnd 40: [Sc dec] rep around, fasten off, leaving 8" end. (6 sts)

Add stuffing if necessary. Weave 8" end through sts of last rnd, pull tightly to close, fasten off.

Leg (*make 2*)

Note: *Do not join rnds unless otherwise stated; mark first st of each rnd with safety pin or other small marker.*

Rnds 1 & 2: Rep Rnds 1 and 2 of head. (12 sc at end of Rnd 2)

Rnd 3: Rep Rnd 6 of head. (12 sc)

Rnds 4 & 5: Rep Rnds 3 and 4 of head. (24 sc at end of Rnd 5)

Rnds 6–15: Rep Rnd 6 of head. (24 sc)

Rnd 16: [Sc dec] rep around. (12 sts)

Rnds 17 & 18: Rep Rnd 6 of head. (12 sc)

Rnd 19: Rep Rnd 3 of head. (18 sc)

Rnds 20–31: Rep Rnd 6 of head. (18 sc)

Rnd 32: Rep Rnd 39 of body. (12 sts)

Stuff leg lightly.

Rnd 33: Rep Rnd 16 of leg. (6 sts)

Foot

Row 34: Flatten last row; working through both thicknesses, work 3 sc across, ch 1, turn. (3 sc)

Row 35: 2 sc in each sc across, ch 1, turn. (6 sc)

First toe

Row 36: Sc in each of first 2 sc, ch 1, turn. (2 sc)

Rows 37–40: Sc in each of 2 sc, ch 1, turn; at end of Row 40, ch 1, do not turn.

Second toe

Row 36: Sl st over ends of each of next 4 rows, sc in each of next 2 unworked sc on Row 35, ch 1, turn.

Rows 37–40: Rep Rows 37–40 of first toe.

Third toe

Rows 36–40: Rep Rows 36–40 of 2nd toe; at end of Row 40, do not ch 1; fasten off.

Arm (make 2)

Note: *Do not join rnds unless otherwise stated; mark first st of each rnd with safety pin or other small marker.*

Rnds 1 & 2: Rep Rnds 1 and 2 of head. (12 sc at end of Rnd 2)

Rnds 3–12: Rep Rnd 6 of head. (12 sc)

Rnd 13: Rep Rnd 16 of leg. (6 sts)

Rnd 14: Rep Rnd 6 of head. (6 sc)

Rnd 15: Rep Rnd 2 of head. (12 sc)

Rnds 16–23: Rep Rnd 6 of head. (12 sc)

Stuff arm lightly.

Rnd 24: Rep Rnd 16 of leg. (6 sts)

Hand

Rows 25 & 26: Rep Rows 34 and 35 of foot.

First finger

Rows 36–40: Rep Rows 36–40 of first toe.

Second finger

Rows 36–40: Rep Rows 36–40 of 2nd toe.

Third Finger

Rep Rows 36–40 of 3rd toe.

Crown

Row 1: With 2 strands gold held tog, ch 16, sc in 2nd ch from hook and in each rem ch across, ch 1, turn. (15 sc)

Rows 2 & 3: Sc in each sc across, ch 1, turn. (15 sc)

Row 4: Sc in first st, *ch 1, dc in next st, ch 2, sl st in top of dc just made, ch 1, hdc in next st **, sc in next st, rep from * across, ending last rep at **, fasten off, leaving end for sewing.

Sew seam over ends of rows at back of crown.

Eye (make 2)

Note: *Do not join rnds unless otherwise stated; mark first st of each rnd with safety pin or other small marker.*

Rnds 1 & 2: Rep Rnds 1 and 2 of head. (12 sc at end of Rnd 2)

Rnds 3–5: Rep Rnd 6 of head; at end of Rnd 5, join with sl st in first sc, fasten off.

Stuff lightly.

White of Eye (make 2)

Rnds 1 & 2: With white, rep Rnds 1 and 2 of eye; at end of Rnd 2, join with sl st in first sc, fasten off. (12 sc at end of Rnd 2)

With tapestry needle and black, embroider pupil on white of eye in satin st. Sew white of eye over opening on eye.

Assembly

Using photo as a guide, sew eyes to top of head over Rnds 4–7, approximately 1" apart. Sew crown to top of head. With tapestry needle and black, embroider mouth below eyes. Sew arms and legs to body.

Festive Fashion Doll

Design by Judy L. Nelson

Adorned in this striking winter ensemble, you can make your daughter's doll the queen of a Christmas gala!

Experience Level: Intermediate

Finished Measurements: To fit 11½" fashion doll

Materials:

❊ Crochet cotton size 10: 350 yds gold metallic and 250 yds red

❊ Size 7 steel crochet hook or size needed to obtain gauge

❊ 11½" fashion doll

❊ ⅛ yd white faux fur

❊ 5 size 4/0 snap fasteners

❊ 4 (7mm) half-pearls

❊ Sewing needle and red, gold and white sewing thread

❊ Hot-glue gun

❊ Compass

❊ Tracing paper

❊ Pencil

Gauge: 20 sts and 9 rows = 2" in dc

To save time, take time to check gauge.

Pattern Note

Join rnds with a sl st unless otherwise stated.

Skirt

Row 1 (RS): Beg at waist with gold metallic, ch 28, sc in 2nd ch from hook and in each rem ch across, ch 1, turn. (27 sc)

Row 2: Sc in first st, 2 sc in each st across to last st, sc in last st, turn. (52 sc)

Row 3: Ch 3 (counts as first dc throughout), 2 dc in next st, [dc in next st, 2 dc in next st] rep across, ch 1, turn. (78 dc)

Row 4: Sc in each st across, turn.

Row 5: Ch 3, dc in next st, 2 dc in next st, [dc in each of next 2 sts, 2 dc in next st] rep across, ch 1, turn. (104 dc)

Row 6: Rep Row 4.

Row 7: Ch 3, dc in each of next 2 sts, 2 dc in next st, [dc in each of next 3 sts, 2 dc in next st] rep across, ch 1, turn. (130 dc)

Row 8: Rep Row 4.

Rnd 9: Ch 3, dc in each of next 3 sts, 2 dc in next st, [dc in each of next 4 sts, 2 dc in next st] rep around, join in 3rd ch of beg ch-3. (156 dc)

Rnd 10: Ch 1, beg in same st as joining, sc in each st around, join in beg sc. (156 sc)

Rnd 11: Ch 3, dc in each of next 4 sts, 2 dc in next st, [dc in each of next 5 sts, 2 dc in next st] rep around, join in 3rd ch of beg ch-3. (182 dc)

Rnd 12: Rep Rnd 10. (182 sc)

Rnd 13: Ch 3, dc in each rem dc around, join in 3rd ch of beg ch-3. (182 dc)

Rnd 14: Rep Rnd 12.

Rnds 15–48: Rep Rnds 13 and 14 alternately; at end of Rnd 48, fasten off.

Waistband

With RS facing, attach gold metallic with a sl st in first rem lp of foundation ch of skirt, ch 3, dc in each of next 2 rem lps, [dc dec, dc in each of next 2 rem lps] rep across, fasten off. (21 sts)

Jacket Top

Row 1 (RS): Beg at waist with red, ch 31, dc in 4th ch from hook, dc in each of next 12 chs, 2 dc in next ch, dc in each of next 13 chs, 2 dc in last ch, turn. (31 dc, counting last 3 chs of foundation ch as first dc)

Row 2: Ch 3, dc in first st, dc in each of next 10 sts, 2 dc in next st, dc in each of next 7 sts, 2 dc in next st, dc in each of next 10 sts, 2 dc in last st, turn. (35 dc)

Row 3: Ch 3, dc in each of next 8 sts, 2 dc in next st, dc in each of next 15 sts, 2 dc in next st, dc in each of last 9 sts, turn. (37 dc)

Row 4: Ch 3, dc in first st, dc in each of next 8 sts, 2 dc in next st, dc in each of next 17 sts, 2 dc in next st, dc in each of next 8 sts, 2 dc in last st, turn. (41 dc)

Row 5: Ch 3, 2 dc in next st, [dc in next st, 2 dc in next st] 3 times, dc in each of next 25 sts, [2 dc in next st, dc in next st] 4 times, turn. (49 dc)

Row 6: Ch 3, dc in each of next 3 sts, 2 dc in next st, dc in each of next 4 sts, 2 dc in next st, dc

chs, dc dec, dc in each of next 3 chs, dc in each of next 9 sts, dc dec, dc in each of next 10 sts, dc in each of next 3 chs, dc dec, dc in each of next 3 chs, dc in each of last 10 sts, turn. (54 sts)

Row 11: Ch 3, dc in next st, [dc dec, dc in each of next 2 sts] rep across, turn. (41 sts)

Row 12: Ch 3, dc in each of next 2 sts, dc dec, [dc in each of next 3 sts, dc dec] rep across to last st, dc in last st ch 1, turn. (33 sts)

Row 13: Sc in each st across, turn. (33 sc)

Collar

Row 14: Ch 3, working in back lps only this row, dc in first st, dc in each of next 7 sts, 2 dc in next st, [dc in each of next 2 sts, 2 dc in next st] 5 times, dc in each of next 7 sts, 2 dc in next st, leave last st unworked, turn. (40 dc)

Row 15: Ch 3, dc in first st, dc in each of next 8 sts, 2 dc in next st, [dc in each of next 2 sts, 2 dc in next st] 7 times, dc in each of next 8 sts, 2 dc in last st, ch 1, turn. (50 dc)

Row 16: Sc in each st across, fasten off.

Sleeves

Rnd 1: With RS facing, attach red with a sl st in 2nd sk sc on Row 8 from the right edge of either armhole, ch 1, sc in same st, 2 sc in next sc, sc in next sc, sc in each of next 8 rem lps of ch-8, sc in next sk st on Row 8, join in beg sc. (13 sc)

Rnds 2–14: Ch 3, dc in each rem st around, join in 3rd ch of beg ch-3. (13 dc)

Rnd 15: Ch 1, sc in same st as joining and in each rem st around, join in beg sc, fasten off.

Rep on other armhole.

Jacket Bottom

Row 1: With RS facing, attach red with a sl st in 3rd rem lp of

in each of next 28 sts, [2 dc in next st, dc in each of next 4 sts] twice, 2 dc in last st, turn. (54 dc)

Row 7: Ch 3, dc in each rem st across, turn. (54 dc)

Row 8: Ch 3, dc in each of next 3 sts, dc dec, dc in each of next 4 sts, dc dec, dc in each of next 28 sts, [dc dec, dc in each of

next 4 sts] twice, dc dec, ch 1, turn. (49 sts)

Row 9: Sc in each of first 10 sts, ch 8, sk 4 sts for first armhole, sc in each of next 21 sts, ch 8, sk 4 sts for next armhole, sc in each of last 10 sts, turn. (41 sc; 2 ch-8 sps)

Row 10: Ch 3, dc in each of next 9 sts, dc in each of next 3 foundation ch of jacket top, ch 3, working in rem lps across, dc in same st, 2 dc in each of next 23 sts, leave rem sts unworked, turn. (48 dc)

Row 2: Ch 3, dc in each rem dc across, turn. (48 dc)

Row 3: Ch 3, dc in each of next 2 sts, 2 dc in next st, [dc in each of next 3 sts, 2 dc in next st] rep across, turn. (60 dc)

Row 4: Ch 3, dc in each of next 3 sts, 2 dc in next st, [dc in each of next 4 sts, 2 dc in next st] rep across, turn. (72 dc)

Row 5: Ch 3, dc in each of next 4 sts, 2 dc in next st, [dc in each of next 5 sts, 2 dc in next st] rep across, turn. (84 dc)

Row 6: Rep Row 2. (84 dc)

Row 7: Ch 3, dc in each of next 5 sts, 2 dc in next st, [dc in each of next 6 sts, 2 dc in next st] rep across, turn. (96 dc)

Rows 8 & 9: Rep Row 2. (96 dc)

Row 10: Ch 3, dc in each of

next 6 sts, 2 dc in next st, [dc in each of next 7 sts, 2 dc in next st] rep across, turn. (108 dc)

Rows 11 & 12: Rep Row 2; at end of Row 12, ch 1, turn. (108 dc)

Row 13: Sc in each st across, fasten off.

Right Front Jacket Top Edging

Row 1: With RS facing, attach red with a sl st in rem lp of foundation ch at base of first sk dc on Row 1 of jacket top at bottom of right front jacket opening, ch 1, sc in same st and in each rem lp to corner, [ch 1, sc] in corner st, sc evenly sp over row ends up right front to top corner, ch 1, sl st in top of last sk st of Row 13 of jacket top, fasten off.

Left Front Jacket Top Edging

Row 1: With RS facing, attach red with a sl st over end st of Row 13 at top of left front jacket top opening, ch 1, beg in same st, sc evenly sp down left front jacket to

bottom corner of jacket top, ch 1, sc in rem lp of ch at base of next sk st on Row 1 of jacket top, sl st in rem lp of next ch, fasten off.

Finishing

With sewing needle and red thread, sew 1 snap fastener at top and 1 snap fastener at bottom of jacket top opening. Sew 2 snaps evenly sp between. Glue half-pearls over snap fasteners on RS of right front jacket. With sewing needle and gold thread, sew 1 snap fastener at back waist opening of skirt. Using paper patterns, cut out collar, sleeves, and bottom of jacket trim from faux fur. Glue or sew onto jacket.

Hat

Using compass, cut a 4½"-diameter circle of faux fur. With white sewing thread doubled, baste closely around edge of circle. Place hat on doll's head. Draw basting sts tightly until hat fits on doll's head; fasten off thread securely. ❧

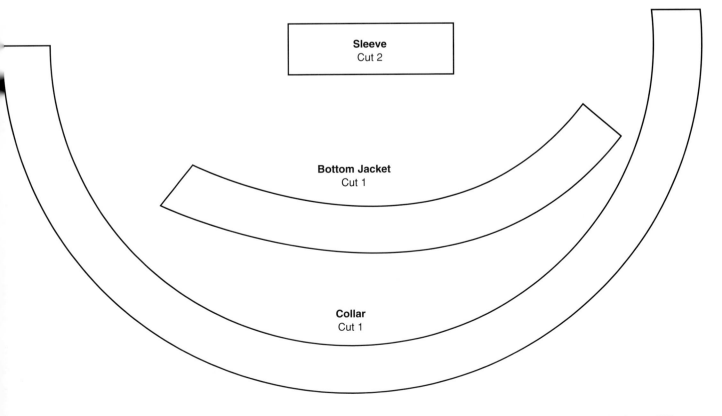

Sleeve
Cut 2

Bottom Jacket
Cut 1

Collar
Cut 1

Thomasina Bear

Design by Sandy Abbate

Here'a bear that's "pretty as a picture" with her adorable outfit. Have fun dressing her with the bodysuit, jumper and matching bag that are accented with cute buttons and motifs.

Experience Level: Intermediate

Finished measurement: Approximately 19" tall

Materials

❊ Red Heart Super Saver worsted weight yarn (8 oz per skein): 1 skein brown #328 and small amount buff #334 for embroidery

❊ Red Heart Sport sport weight yarn (2.5 oz per skein): 1 skein each skipper blue #846, and berry #744, and small amount paddy green #687

❊ Red Heart Baby Sport sport weight yarn (6 oz per skein): 1 skein white pompadour #1001

❊ Size G/6 crochet hook or size needed to obtain gauge

❊ Size F/5 crochet hook

❊ 1½ yds ³⁄₁₆"-wide white picot ribbon

❊ 30" ⅜"-wide light blue ribbon

❊ 1 yd 1⅜"-wide floral ribbon

❊ 3 (⅜") white buttons

❊ 4 (½") alphabet buttons

❊ Polyester fiberfill

❊ Black permanent marker

❊ Tapestry needle

❊ Safety pin or other small marker

Gauge: 7 sts and 7 rnds = 2" with larger hook and worsted weight yarn in sc

4 sts and 2 rows = 1" with larger hook and sport weight yarn in dc

To save time, take time to check gauge.

Pattern Note

Join rnds with a sl st unless otherwise stated.

Bear

Head and Body

Note: *Don't join rnds unless otherwise stated; mark first st of each rnd with safety pin or other small marker.*

Rnd 1: With brown and larger hook, ch 2, 6 sc in 2nd ch from hook. (6 sc)

Rnd 2: 2 sc in each st around. (12 sc)

Rnd 3: [Sc in next st, 2 sc in next st] rep around. (18 sc)

Rnd 4: [Sc in each of next 2 sts, 2 sc in next st] rep around. (24 sc)

Rnd 5: [Sc in each of next 3 sts, 2 sc in next st] rep around. (30 sc)

Rnd 6: [Sc in each of next 4 sts, 2 sc in next st] rep around. (36 sc)

Rnd 7: [Sc in each of next 5 sts, 2 sc in next st] rep around. (42 sc)

Rnds 8–13: Sc in each st around. (42 sc)

Rnd 14: 2 sc in each of next 9 sts, sc in each rem sc around. (51 sc)

Rnds 15–17: Sc in each st around. (51 sc)

Rnd 18: [Sc dec] 9 times, sc in each rem sc around. (42 sts)

Rnd 19: Sc in each st around. (42 sc)

Rnd 20: [Sc in each of next 5 sts, sc dec] rep around. (36 sts)

Rnd 21: [Sc in each of next 4 sts, sc dec] rep around. (30 sts)

Rnd 22: [Sc in each of next 3 sts, sc dec] rep around. (24 sts)

Rnds 23–25: Rep Rnds 15–17. (24 sc)

Rnds 26–28: Rep Rnds 5–7. (42 sc at end of Rnd 28)

Rnd 29: [Sc in each of next 6 sts, 2 sc in next st] rep around. (48 sc)

Rnds 30–48: Rep Rnd 19. (48 sc)

Rnd 49: [Sc in each of next 6 sts, sc dec] rep around; do not fasten off. (42 sts)

Stuff body.

Row 50: Flatten last row in half; working through both thicknesses, sc across to close opening. (21 sc)

Ear *(make 2)*

Note: *Don't join rnds unless otherwise stated; mark first st of each rnd with safety pin or other small marker.*

Rnds 1–5: Rep Rnds 1–5 of head and body; do not fasten off at end of Rnd 5. (30 sc at end of Rnd 5)

Fold ear in half. Ch 1, working

through both thicknesses, sc in each of next 15 sts, fasten off, leaving 12" end for sewing. With tapestry needle, bending ear slightly, sew bottom of ear over Rnds 2–10 of head.

Arm *(make 2)*

Note: *Do not join rnds unless otherwise stated; mark first st of each rnd with safety pin or other small marker.*

Rnds 1 & 2: Beg at paw, rep Rnds 1 and 2 of head and body. (12 sc at end of Rnd 2)

Rnd 3: Sc in each st around. (12 sc)

Rnd 4: Rep Rnd 3 of head. (18 sc)

Rnds 5–7: Sc in each st around. (18 sc)

Rnd 8: [Sc in next st, sc dec] rep around. (12 sts)

Rnd 9: [Sc in next st, 2 sc in next st] rep around. (18 sc)

Rnds 10–24: Rep Rnd 3. (18 sc)

Rnd 25: Rep Rnd 8. (12 sts) Stuff arm lightly.

Rnd 26: Rep Rnd 3. (12 sc)

Rnd 27: [Sc dec] rep around, join in beg sc dec, fasten off, leaving a 12" end for sewing.

With tapestry needle, weave 12" end through tops of sts of last rnd; pull tightly to close. Sew arm to side of body.

Leg *(make 2)*

Note: *Do not join rnds unless otherwise stated; mark first st of each rnd with safety pin or other small marker.*

Rnds 1–5: Rep Rnds 1–5 of head and body. (30 sc at end of Rnd 5)

Rnd 6: Working in back lps only this rnd, sc in each st around. (30 sc)

Rnds 7–10: Sc in each st around. (30 sc)

Rnd 11: [Sc dec] 6 times, sc in each rem sc around. (24 sts)

Rnds 12–30: Sc in each st around. (24 sc)

Rnd 31: [Sc in each of next 2 sts, sc dec] rep around. (18 sts)

Row 32: Sc in each of next 2 sts to end at side of leg, fasten off, leaving 12" end for sewing.

Stuff leg lightly. Flatten last row in half. With tapestry needle, beg at outer edge on Row 50 of head and body, sew front half of leg to front lps only of first 9 sts of Row 50 and back half of leg to back lps only of same sts.

With needle and buff, using photo as a guide, embroider face on bear. With permanent marker, make dot in center of each eye for pupil. Wrap floral ribbon around bear's head beneath ears; tie in bow at front.

Bodysuit

Pants

Rnd 1: With white pompadour and larger hook, beg at front waist, ch 50, taking care not to twist ch, join to form a ring, ch 3 (counts as first dc throughout), dc in each rem ch around, join in 3rd ch of beg ch-3. (50 dc)

Rnds 2–7: Ch 3, dc in each rem st around, join in 3rd ch of beg ch-3. (50 dc)

First leg

Rnd 1: Ch 3, dc in each of next 24 sts, join in 3rd ch of beg ch-3. (25 dc)

Rnd 2: Ch 1, sc in same st as joining, ch 3, [sc in next st, ch 3] rep around, join in beg sc, fasten off.

Second leg

Rnd 1: With larger hook, attach white pompadour with a sl st in next unworked dc on Rnd 7 of pants at center back, ch 3, dc in each rem dc around, join in 3rd ch of beg ch-3. (25 dc)

Rnd 2: Rep Rnd 2 of first leg.

Top

Row 1: Working in rem lps of foundation ch of pants, sk first rem lp at center front, with larger hook, attach white pompadour with a sl st in next st, ch 3, dc in each of next 47 sts, turn. (48 dc)

Rows 2 & 3: Ch 3, dc in each rem dc across, turn.

Left front

Row 1: Ch 3, dc in each of next 8 sts, turn. (9 dc)

Rows 2–4: Ch 3, dc in each st across, turn. (9 dc)

Left front shoulder

Row 5: Sl st in each of first 7 sts, ch 3, dc in each of next 2 sts, fasten off. (3 dc)

Back

Row 1: Sk next 5 sts on Row 3 of top for underarm, with larger hook, attach white pompadour with a sl st in next st, ch 3, dc in each of next 19 sts, turn. (20 dc)

Rows 2–4: Ch 3, dc in each rem dc across, turn. (20 dc)

Left back shoulder

Row 5: Ch 3, dc in each of next 2 sts, fasten off. (3 dc)

Right back shoulder

Row 5: Sk next 14 unworked sts of last row, with larger hook attach white pompadour with a sl st in next st, ch 3, dc in each of next 2 sts, fasten off. (3 dc)

Right front

Row 1: Sk next 5 unworked sts on Row 3 of top for 2nd underarm, with larger hook attach white pompadour with a sl st in next st, ch 3, dc in each of next 8 sts, turn. (9 dc)

Rows 2–4: Rep Rows 2–4 of left front. (9 dc)

Right front shoulder

Row 5: Ch 3, dc in each of next 2 sts, fasten off. (3 dc)

With tapestry needle and white pompadour, sew shoulder seams and crotch.

Buttonhole placket

Row 1: With RS facing, using smaller hook, attach white pompadour with a sl st over side of first st of Row 1 of top at bottom of right front opening, ch 1, beg in same st, work 15 sc evenly sp across right front opening to beg of neck, ch 1, turn. (15 sc)

Row 2: Sc in first st, [ch 1, sk next st, sc in each of next 5 sts] twice, ch 1, sk next st, sc in last st, ch 1, turn.

Row 3: Sc in each sc and ch-1 sp across, fasten off. (15 sc)

Button placket

Row 1: With RS facing, using smaller hook, attach white pompadour with a sl st over side of end st of Row 4 of left front, ch 1, beg in same st, work 15 sc evenly sp across left front opening to bottom, ch 1, turn. (15 sc)

Rows 2 & 3: Sc in each sc across, ch 1, turn; at end of Row 3, do not ch 1; fasten off.

With bottom of buttonhole placket overlapping bottom of button placket, sew bottoms of plackets to unworked sts at bottom of front opening.

Neck edging

Row 1: With RS facing, using smaller hook, attach white pompadour with a sl st over side of buttonhole placket at right front neck edge, ch 1, beg in same st, work 42 sc evenly sp across neck to outer edge of button placket, fasten off.

Collar

Row 1: With smaller hook and white pompadour, ch 38, 2 dc in 4th ch from hook, [dc in next ch, 2 dc in next ch] rep across, turn. (54 dc, counting last 3 chs of foundation ch as first dc)

Row 2: Ch 3, dc in each rem st across, ch 1, turn. (54 dc)

Row 3: Sc in first st, [ch 3, sc in next st] rep across, fasten off.

With tapestry needle, sew collar to neck edging, beg and ending at inner edges of front plackets.

Sleeves

Rnd 1: With RS facing, using larger hook, attach white pompadour with a sl st in center

sk sc on Row 3 of top at bottom of either armhole opening, ch 1, beg in same st, work 25 sc evenly sp around armhole, join in beg sc. (25 sc)

Rnd 2: Ch 1, sc in same st as joining and in each of next 4 sts, hdc in each of next 2 sts, dc in each of next 2 sts, 2 tr in each of next 8 sts, dc in each of next 2 sts, hdc in each of next 2 sts, sc in each of last 4 sts, join in beg sc. (33 sts)

Rnds 3–6: Ch 3, dc in each rem st around, join in 3rd ch of beg ch-3. (33 dc)

Rnd 7: Ch 1, sc in same st as joining, [sc in each of next 2 sts, sc dec] rep around, join in beg sc. (25 sts)

Rnd 8: Ch 3 (counts as first hdc, ch-1), sk 2 sts, hdc in next st, ch 1, [sk next st, hdc in next st, ch 1] rep around, join in 2nd ch of beg ch-3. (12 ch-1 sps)

Rnd 9: Sl st in first sp, ch 1, beg in same sp, [sc, ch 3, sc] in each sp around, join in beg sc, fasten off.

Rep on 2nd underarm.

Sew white buttons to button placket to correspond with buttonholes. Cut white picot ribbon into 3 (18") lengths. Beg at top of sleeve, weave 1 length through ch-1 sps on Rnd 8 of each sleeve. Cut rem length in half. Tie each length into a bow around st at center front on Rnd 1 of each leg. Place bodysuit on bear. Wrap light blue ribbon around neck under collar and tie in bow at front.

Jumper
Waistband

Row 1 (RS): Beg at top of waistband, with larger hook and skipper blue, ch 53, sc in 2nd ch from hook and in each rem ch across, ch 1, turn. (52 sc)

Row 2: Sc in first st, ch 1, sk next st for buttonhole, sc in each rem st across, ch 1, turn.

Row 3: Sc in each sc and ch-1 sp across, turn. (52 sc)

Skirt

Row 1: Ch 3, working in front lps only this row, 2 dc in first st, [dc in next st, 2 dc in next st] rep across to last st, 2 dc in last st, turn. (80 dc)

Rnd 2: Ch 3, dc in each rem st around, join in 3rd ch of beg ch-3. (80 dc)

Rnds 3–9: Rep Rnd 2; at end of Rnd 9, fasten off. (80 dc)

Rnd 10: With RS facing, using larger hook, attach berry with a sl st in first sc of last rnd, ch 1, sc in same st as joining and in each rem st around, join in beg sc, fasten off.

Waistband Trim

Row 1: With RS facing, using larger hook, attach skipper blue with a sl st in first rem lp of foundation ch of waistband at right edge, ch 1, sc in same st and in each rem lp across, fasten off, do not turn. (52 sc)

Rnd 2: With RS facing, using larger hook, attach berry with a sl st in first sc of last row, ch 1, sc in same st and in each rem st across, 4 sc evenly sp over row ends down side of waistband, sc in each rem lp of Row 3 across bottom of waistband, 4 sc evenly sp over row ends up side of waistband, join in beg sc, fasten off.

Bib

Row 1: With RS facing, using larger hook, sk first 18 sts on Rnd 2 of waistband trim, attach skipper blue with a sl st in back lp only of next st, ch 3, working in back lps only this row, dc in each of next 15 sts, turn. (16 dc)

Rows 2 & 3: Ch 3, dc in each

rem dc across, turn; at end of Row 3, fasten off.

Bib trim

With RS facing, using larger hook, attach berry with a sl st in back lp only of first unworked sc on Rnd 2 of waistband trim to the right of first st on Row 1 of bib, ch 1, sc evenly sp over row ends up first side of bib, across last row of bib and over row ends down 2nd side of bib, sl st in back lp only of next unworked sc on Rnd 2 of waistband trim, fasten off.

First Strap

Row 1: With RS facing, sk first 4 sts on Rnd 2 of waistband trim at left back opening, using larger hook, attach skipper blue with a sl st in back lp only of next st, ch 1, working in back lps only this row, sc in same st and in each of next 3 sts, ch 1, turn. (4 sc)

Rows 2–18: Sc in each st across, ch 1, turn. (4 sc)

Row 19: Sc dec, ch 2 for buttonhole, sc dec over next 2 sc, ch 1, turn.

Row 20: Sc in first st, 2 sc in sp, sc in last st, fasten off.

Second Strap

Row 1: With RS facing, using larger hook, attach skipper blue with a sl st in back lp only of 8th st from corner on Rnd 2 of waistband trim at right back opening, ch 1, working in back lps only this row, sc in same st and in each of next 3 sts, ch 1, turn. (4 sc)

Rows 2–20: Rep Rows 2–20 of first strap.

Strap Trim

With RS facing, using larger hook, attach berry with a sl st in back lp only of first unworked sc on Rnd 2 of waistband trim to the right of right-hand edge of either strap, ch 1, sc evenly sp around strap to bottom of opposite side, sl st in back lp only of next unworked sc on Rnd 2 of waistband trim, fasten off.

Rep on 2nd strap.

Pocket (make 2)

Row 1: With smaller hook and berry, beg at bottom of pocket, ch 7, sc in 2nd ch from hook and in each rem ch across, ch 1, turn. (6 sc)

Row 2: 2 sc in first st, sc in each st across to last st, 2 sc in last st, ch 1, turn. (8 sc)

Row 3: Sc in each st across, ch 1, turn. (8 sc)

Row 4: Rep Row 2. (10 sc)

Rows 5 & 6: Rep Row 3. (10 sc)

Row 7: Sc dec, sc in each of next 6 sts, sc dec, ch 1, turn. (8 sts)

Row 8: Rep Row 3. (8 sc)

Row 9: Sc in each of first 3 sts, sl st in each of next 2 sts, sc in each of last 3 sts, ch 1, turn. (8 sts)

Rnd 10: Sc in each of first 3 sts, sl st in each of next 2 sts, sc in each of next 3 sts, sc evenly sp over row ends to bottom, working in rem lps of foundation ch, sc in each of first 2 sts, sl st in each of next 2 sts, sc in each of next 2 sts, sc evenly sp over row ends to top, join in beg sc, fasten off.

Sew 1 alphabet button at each side of Row 3 of bib. Sew 1 alphabet button at back waistband on opposite side from buttonhole. With tapestry needle and paddy green, make a st at top center of each apple, knot, and cut end approximately ⅜" long for stem. Using photo as a guide, sew pockets to front of skirt.

Bag

Back

Row 1 (RS): With skipper blue and smaller hook, ch 21, sc in 2nd ch from hook and in each rem ch across, ch 1, turn. (20 sc)

Rows 2–16: Sc in each sc across, ch 1, turn; do not fasten off at end of Row 16; ch 1, turn. (20 sc)

Flap

Rows 17–20: Sc dec, sc in each rem st across to last 2 sts, sc dec, ch 1, turn. (12 sts at end of Row 20)

Row 21: Sc in each of first 5 sts, ch 1, sk 2 sts for buttonhole, sc in each of last 5 sts, ch 1, turn.

Row 22: Sc dec, sc in each of next 3 sts, 2 sc in ch-2 sp, sc in each of next 3 sts, sc dec, fasten off. (10 sts)

Front

Rows 1–16: Rep Rows 1–16 of back, at end of Row 16, fasten off.

Join Front & Back

With WS of front and back tog and front of bag facing, using smaller hook and working through both thicknesses, attach berry with a sl st in first rem lp of foundation ch, ch 1, sc in each rem lp across bottom of bag to corner, 3 sc in corner st, sc evenly sp over row ends to top corner, sc evenly sp around edge of flap, sc evenly sp over row ends down opposite side of bag, 2 sc in same st as beg sc, join in beg sc, fasten off.

Strap

With RS facing, using smaller hook, attach skipper blue with a sl st at upper right corner on front of bag, ch 40, sl st at upper left corner on front of bag, ch 1, turn, sc in each ch across, sl st at upper right corner on front of bag, fasten off.

Sew 1 alphabet button to top center on front of bag to correspond to buttonhole. ❦

General Instructions

Please review the following information before working the projects in this book. Important details about the abbreviations and symbols used and finishing instructions are included.

Hooks

Crochet hooks are sized for different weights of yarn and thread. For thread crochet, you will usually use a steel crochet hook. Steel crochet hook sizes range from size 00 to 14. The higher the number of hook, the smaller your stitches will be. For example, a size 1 steel crochet hook will give you much larger stitches than a size 9 steel crochet hook. Keep in mind that the sizes given with the pattern instructions were obtained by working with the size thread or yarn and hook given in the materials list. If you work with a smaller hook, depending on your gauge, your project size will be smaller; if you work with a larger hook, your finished project's size will be larger.

Gauge

Gauge is determined by the tightness or looseness of your stitches, and affects the finished size of your project. If you are concerned about the finished size of the project matching the size given, take time to crochet a small section of the pattern and then check your gauge. For example, if the gauge called for is 10 dc = 1 inch, and your gauge is 12 dc to the inch, you should switch to a larger hook. On the other hand, if your gauge is only 8 dc to the inch, you should switch to a smaller hook.

If the gauge given in the pattern is for an entire motif, work one motif and then check your gauge.

Understanding Symbols

As you work through a pattern, you'll quickly notice several symbols in the instructions. These symbols are used to clarify the pattern for you: Brackets [], curlicue brackets {}, asterisks *.

Brackets [] are used to set off a group of instructions worked a number of times. For example, "[ch 3, sc in ch-3 sp] 7 times" means to work the instructions inside the [] seven times. Brackets [] also set off a group of stitches to be worked in one stitch, space or loop. For example, the brackets [] in this set of instructions, "Sk 3 sc, [3 dc, ch 1, 3 dc] in next st" indicate that after skipping 3 sc, you will work 3 dc, ch 1 and 3 more dc all in the next stitch.

Occasionally, a set of instructions inside a set of brackets needs to be repeated too. In this case, the text within the brackets to be repeated will be set off with curlicue brackets {}. For example, "[Ch 9, yo twice, insert hook in 7th ch from hook and pull up a loop, sk next dc, yo, insert hook in next dc and pull up a loop, {yo and draw through 2 lps on hook} 5 times, ch 3] 8 times." In this case, in each of the eight times you work the instructions included in brackets, you will work the section included in curlicue brackets five times.

Asterisks * are also used when a group of instructions is repeated. They may either be used alone or with brackets. For example, "*Sc in each of the next 5 sc, 2 sc in next sc, rep from * around, join with a sl st in beg sc" simply means you will work the instructions from the first * around the entire round.

"*Sk 3 sc, [3 dc, ch 1, 3 dc] in next st, rep from * around" is an example of asterisks working with brackets. In this set of instructions, you will repeat the instructions from the asterisk around, working the instructions inside the brackets together. ❧

Buyer's Guide

To find materials listed, first check your local yarn, craft and fabric stores. If you are unable to locate a product locally, contact the following manufacturers for purchasing information.

❋ Caron, International, P.O. Box 222, Washington, NC 27889; (800) 444-2284

❋ Coats & Clark, 30 Patewood Dr., Suite 351, Greenville, SC 29615; (864) 234–0331

❋ Coats Patons, 1001 Roselawn Ave., Toronto, ON M6B 1B8; (800) 268–3620

❋ DMC Corp., 10 Port Kearny, South Kearny, NJ 07032; (201) 589-0606

❋ Kreinik Manufacturing, 3106 Timanus Ln., Suite 101, Baltimore, MD 21244; (800) 539–2166

❋ Lion Brand Yarn Co., 34 W. 15th St., New York, NY 10011; (212) 243–8995

❋ Spinrite, Box 40, Listowel, Ontario N4W 3H3, Canada; (519) 291–3780

STITCH GUIDE

Front Loop (a)
Back Loop (b)

Chain (ch)

Yo, draw lp through hook.

Slip Stitch Joining

Insert hook in beg ch, yo, draw lp through.

Front Post/Back Post Dc

Fpdc (a): Yo, insert hook from front to back and to front again around the vertical post (upright part) of next st, yo and draw yarn through, yo and complete dc.
Bpdc (b): Yo, reaching over top of piece and working on opposite side (right side) of work, insert hook from right to left around vertical post of next st, yo and draw yarn through, yo and complete dc.

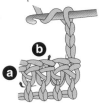

Single Crochet (sc)

Insert hook in st (a), yo, draw lp through (b), yo, draw through both lps on hook (c).

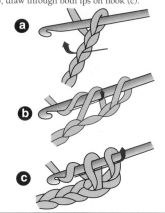

Half-Double Crochet (hdc)

Yo, insert hook in st (a), yo, draw lp through (b), yo, draw through all 3 lps on hook (c).

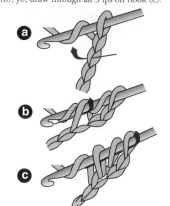

Decreasing

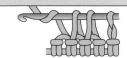

Single Crochet Decrease

Dec 1 sc over next 2 sts as follows: Draw up a lp in each of next 2 sts, yo, draw through all 3 lps on hook.

Double Crochet Decrease

Dec 1 dc over next 2 sts as follows: [Yo, insert hook in next st, yo, draw up lp on hook, yo, draw through 2 lps] twice, yo, draw through all 3 lps on hook.

Double Crochet (dc)

Yo, insert hook in st (a), yo, draw lp through (b), [yo, draw through 2 lps] twice (c, d).

Treble Crochet (tr)

Yo hook twice, insert hook in st (a), yo, draw lp through (b), [yo, draw through 2 lps on hook] 3 times (c, d, e).

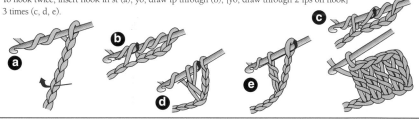

Special Stitches

Chain Color Change (ch color change)

Yo with new color, draw through last lp on hook.

Double Crochet Color Change (dc color change)

Drop first color, yo with new color, draw through last 2 lps of st.

Reverse Single Crochet (reverse sc)

Working from left to right, insert hook in next st to the right (a), yo, draw up lp on hook, complete as for sc (b).

STITCH ABBREVIATIONS

The following stitch abbreviations are used throughout this book.

beg	begin(ning)
bl(s)	block(s)
bpdc	back post dc
ch(s)	chain(s)
cl(s)	cluster(s)
CC	contrasting color
dc	double crochet
dec	decrease
dtr	double treble crochet
fpdc	front post dc
hdc	half-double crochet
inc	increase
lp(s)	loop(s)
MC	main color
p	picot
rem	remain(ing)
rep	repeat
rnd(s)	round(s)
RS	right side facing you
sc	single crochet
sk	skip
sl st	slip stitch
sp(s)	space(s)
st(s)	stitch(es)
tog	together
tr	treble crochet
trtr	triple treble crochet
WS	wrong side facing you
yo	yarn over

CROCHET HOOKS

Metric	US
.60mm	14 steel
.75mm	12 steel
1.00mm	10 steel
1.25mm	8 steel
1.50mm	7 steel
1.75mm	5 steel
2.00mm	B/1
2.50mm	C/2
3.00mm	D/3
3.50mm	E/4
4.00mm	F/5
4.50mm	G/6
5.00mm	H/8
5.50mm	I/9
6.00mm	J/10

YARN CONVERSION

Ounces to Grams

1	28.4
2	56.7
3	85.0
4	113.4

Grams to Ounces

25	⅞
40	1⅔
50	1¾
100	3½

Crochet Abbreviations

US	UK
sc–single crochet	dc–double crochet
dc–double crochet	tr–treble crochet
hdc–half double crochet	htr–half treble crochet
tr–triple crochet	dtr–double treble crochet
dtr–double triple crochet	trip–triple treble crochet
sk–skip	miss

Yarns

Bedspread weight	No. 10 Cotton or Virtuoso
Sport weight	4-ply or thin DK
Worsted weight	Thick DK or Aran

Check tension or gauge to save time.

Instructions for Filet Crochet

Filet crochet is a method of forming designs with solid and openwork squares called blocks (bl) and spaces (sp).

A bl will appear to have 4 dc; the first dc of the bl is the dc that defines the sp preceding the bl. A group of 3 bls will have 9 dc plus 1 dc of sp preceding bl.

A foundation chain is 3 times the number of sps in the first row plus 5 if the row begins with a sp (dc in 8th ch from hook) or plus 3 if row begins with a bl (dc in 4th ch from hook and next 2 chs). On following rows ch 5 if next row begins with a sp or ch 3 if row begins with bl.

Bl: Dc in each of next 3 sts.

Beg bl: Ch 3, dc in each of next 3 sts.

Sp: Ch 2, sk 2 sts, dc in indicated st.

Beg sp: Ch 5, sk 2 sts, dc in next st/dc.

Bl over a bl: Dc in each of next 3 dc.

Bl over a sp: 2 dc in sp, dc in next dc.

Sp over a bl: Ch 2, sk 2 dc, dc in next dc.

Sp over a sp: Ch 2, dc in next dc.

Sp inc at the beginning of a row: Ch 7, dc in first dc of previous row; to add several sps, ch 3 times the number of sps plus 4, dc in 8th ch from hook for first sp, *ch 2, sk 2 chs, dc in next ch, rep from *, dc of last sp inc will be in first dc of previous row.

Sp inc at the end of a row: Ch 2, yo 3 times, draw up lp in turning ch where last dc was worked, [yo and draw through 2 lps] 4 times (dtr made for 1 sp). *For additional sps,* *ch 2, yo 3 times, draw up lp in middle of

last dtr, [yo and draw through 2 lps] 4 times, rep from * as many times as needed.

Bl inc at the beginning of a row: Ch 5, ch 3 more for each additional bl inc, dc in 4th ch from hook, dc in next ch (1 bl inc), dc in each of next 3 chs for each additional bl inc.

Bl inc at the end of a row: Yo, draw up lp in top of turning ch where last dc was worked, yo and draw through 1 lp on hook (base st), [yo and draw through 2 lps on hook] twice (dc), *yo, draw up lp in base st, yo and draw through 1 lp on hook for

next base st, [yo and draw through 2 lps on hook] twice, rep from * once for 1 bl inc, rep from * 3 times for each additional bl inc.

Sp or bl dec at the beginning of a row: Ch 1, sl st in each of next 3 sts across for each sp or bl dec, sl st in next dc, ch 5, sk next 2 sts, dc in next dc if row starts with a sp or ch 3, dc in next 2 sts if row starts with a bl.

Sp or bl dec at the end of a row: Leave 3 sts of each sp or bl unworked.

Special Thanks

Special thanks to Bryan, Tiffany, Alexis, Colby and Jack Johnston for modeling many of the projects in this book and to Craig and Jan Jaynes for use of their log cabin home for on-location photography.

Pattern Index

Designer Index